The Packers, My Dad, and Me

A Family Legacy That Fed a National Obsession

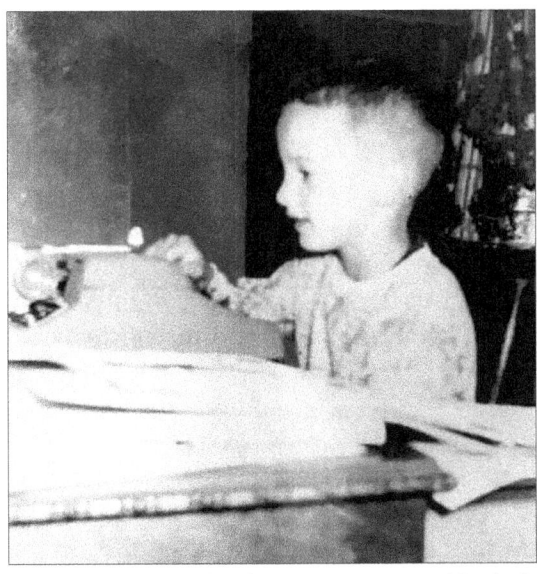

A young Tony Walter learns to type on his dad's manual typewriter. (Walter family collection)

Tony Walter

M&B Global Solutions, Inc.
Green Bay, Wisconsin (USA)

The Packers, My Dad, and Me
A Family Legacy That Fed a National Obsession

© 2020 Tony Walter

First Edition
All Rights Reserved. The author grants no assignable permission to reproduce for resale or redistribution. This license is limited to the individual purchaser and does not extend to others. Permission to reproduce these materials for any other purpose must be obtained in writing from the publisher except for the use of brief quotations within book chapters.

Disclaimer
The views expressed in this work are solely those of the author and do not necessarily reflect the views of the publisher, and the publisher hereby disclaims any responsibility for them. In the event you use any of the information in this book for yourself, which is your constitutional right, the author and the publisher assume no responsibility for your actions.

Front cover photos:
Top - Don Hutson, Hank Lebevre photo courtesy of the *Green Bay Press-Gazette* collection.
Bottom - John Walter and a young Tony Walter from the Walter family collection.

Back cover photos: Mike Dauplaise

ISBN: 978-0-9960488-3-5

Published by M&B Global Solutions Inc.
Green Bay, Wisconsin (USA)

Dedication

My dad, John Walter (left), with his cousin, John Messenger, c. 1938-39. (Walter family collection)

This book is dedicated to the man who, more than anyone, made it possible. He also helped make me possible. Assist to Mom.

Since too many of my memories involve Dad's health issues, this dedication includes an episode in his life that demonstrated his health, strength, common sense, and poise under pressure. It is also an example of his gift for storytelling.

With his brother-in-law, Vic Minahan, and seventeen-year-old Chuck McFarland, Dad planned to take his in-laws' thirty-one-foot cruiser fifty miles up the bay from Green Bay to Egg Harbor prior to the July Fourth holiday weekend in 1941. They ran into problems about fifteen miles into their journey, eventually drifting several miles south before reaching safety. His diary details what happened that night:

July 1, 1941

At 4:40 p.m., aboard the Minahan cruiser, *Inishkea*, with Vic Jr. and Chuck McFarland, started for Egg Harbor ... refueled first at Yacht club.

Started with southwest wind behind us, but it soon shifted to north and kicked up a heavy sea.

About two miles past the Harbor entrance light, crossing Dyckesville harbor, we sprung a leak and attempted to bail...Chuck very seasick, could help little...started the boat eastward for Dyckesville but after running 10 minutes the engine was swamped and stopped.

This happened at 6 o'clock ... we bailed for hours, tried to signal both shore and nearby ships, without effect ... waves higher ... stood on cabin floor up to my waist in water and handed up buckets to Victor for hours.

At 11:50 p.m. the bow went under, the boat keeled over and we took to the water, each with two life preservers.

Although temperature of air was very bitter and cold, water was warm as soup ...despite high waves, it was not hard to keep together ... Chuck in state of collapse, but Vic and I both felt strong.

We headed for lights of Acropolis tavern, on bluff above Red Banks ... at 12:45 light went out and we guided ourselves by North Star ... generally clear night, with high wind and heavy sea continuing.

At daylight we found we had been carried considerable distance south by waves, and almost back into channel ... sighted three large trees on shore and worked for them, Vic pulling Chuck and I pushing him.

Despite steady kicking for hours, our legs held up well, although both of us had cramps and had to stop to work them out ... Chuck sick several times.

Around 4:00 a.m., we could see that we were making definite progress ... got inside Point Sable, which assured us we wouldn't be swept past it by the waves ... finally touched sand bottom about four miles south of Red Banks.

Crab fishermen picked up Chuck and took him ashore ... Vic and I waded in on stones ... water still warm but air very cold.

It now was July 2 ... people at Lucas cottage took us in, gave us hot coffee and milk, rolled Chuck up in a blanket, called Bellin ambulance, which took us in to hospital.

Dr. McCarey ordered all three to bed ... packed in blankets and hot water bottles ... had several bad chills and felt rotten for a time, but by noon was better ... the younger fellows snapped back quicker.

Arms and legs very sore ... had legs rubbed down several times during day ... service excellent ... innumerable visitors ... including Father McMurray and Rev. Gast, Marion Fisk, all the Minahans, and Mary, who was the best visitor of all ... accident created quite a sensation around town, as did our long swim ... sedatives put us under early in the evening.

Except for aching legs and increased nervousness, feel little worse for the experience.

***

So this book is dedicated to John Messenger Walter. You inspired me to learn how to write.

And to learn how to swim.

Foreword

Mark Murphy
President and
Chief Executive Officer
Green Bay Packers

Nobody is more aware of the special relationship that exists between the Green Bay Packers and the local community than Tony Walter.

The Packers are a community-owned team, and I've always believed that giving back to the community had to be our top priority. After all, the Packers would not be in Green Bay were it not for the support of the community over the years.

The story of Tony's family is a unique example of the role that community and family have played in the birth, growth, and sustenance of the Packers. He writes about the impact that the Packers had on Green Bay, a relationship that helped lead to the Packers' support of the local community today: the charitable outreach, the establishment of Titletown with the full football field, a sledding hill and skating rink all available for community use. Another example of this unique relationship is the support that the Packers provided the community during the COVID-19 pandemic.

Tony also writes about the special relationship that the Packers have had with journalists over the years. Heck, the Packers' offices were in the *Press-Gazette* building for years. In the early years, the Packers and the newspapers needed each other to survive and the relationship has continued to thrive over the years.

Tony was the first reporter from Green Bay that I met when I accepted my position with the Packers. The *Press-Gazette* sent him down to Evanston, Illinois, to interview me. That started a long relationship that became one of respect for our separate roles in the Green Bay Packers story.

All Packers fans are going to love this book. Tony does an excellent job in detailing the special relationship between the Packers and the community. There is nothing else like it in all of professional sports.

My dad, John Walter, looking dapper as a young teen. (Walter family collection)

Contents

1. Roots of Legacy 1
2. The Catbird Seat 7
3. Trouble at the Plant 15
4. Perched Upon the Throne 25
5. Better Eskimos 59
6. The Way of Cheese Champions 79
7. Bow to the Inevitable 99
8. Recovery Brewing 119
9. Two Cents and a Rubber Nickel 135
10. Fall and Rise 151
11. Hope and Hutson 159
12. Herber to Hutson 187
13. More Like Fiction 205
14. My Idea of Heaven 225
15. It'll Take a Better Team 247
16. Print It 269
Epilogue 1 - Canary and Cat 289
Epilogue 2 - Veil of Chance 291
Postscript - A Champion's Legacy 293
Acknowledgements 295
About the Author 297

Chapter 1

Roots of Legacy

I inherited many things from my father.

Hair wasn't one of them.

But a sense of humor was. So was a commitment to fair and honest journalism, a lifelong affection for Green Bay and Door County (Wisconsin), the importance of good parenting, a desire to mentor youth, and a faith in God.

And, without a doubt, I was bequeathed a pathway to the mind and heart for anything related to the Green Bay Packers.

We shared many things in the fourteen years we spent together on earth. They included a fascination for Civil War generals, our Eagle badges in Boy Scouts, and hiking on railroad tracks. We shared those Saturday morning poached eggs on raisin toast at the YMCA cafeteria, a fondness for sardines, smelt and whitefish, ski trips, singing patriotic songs, games of chess, log fires in the hearth, and evening Bible readings.

A 1936 Green Bay Press-Gazette photo of my dad, John Walter.

Our emotional attachment to the Packers was separate from the professional relationships we each developed with the football network at the appointed times in our careers. Participating in that football culture in that place and at that time wasn't a hobby. It was a lifestyle, and it was so ingrained that we, along with our neighbors, probably didn't have a full grasp of its uniqueness.

We never shared a Packers championship, though. Victories weren't rife for the Packers from 1945 to 1959, and by the time I was old enough to know that defensive back Bobby Dillon was no relation to Marshal

Dillon from TV's *Gunsmoke,* the franchise never came close to even sniffing a championship game.

But the written word has staying power and an ability to create memories out of a past we weren't a part of together. It is in this way you can accompany me through the Packers' first glory years (1929-36), and meet my father through his daily diary submissions and the words he put in print for the *Green Bay Press-Gazette.* The journey includes glimpses of life and voices of people who lived near the soul of Green Bay when it boldly and proudly expressed itself on and off the football field. Along the way, we can gain a better understanding of what it was like in the Packers' universe then, who Dad was, and – I suppose – who I became.

Our traveling companions will include the Packers at a time when pro football in Green Bay felt so local and personal, in great need of being nurtured, and when fandom was still in relative infancy.

There are links to three generations on this journey. Gus A. Walter Jr., my grandfather, was the key negotiator who engineered the sale of Hagemeister Park to the city of Green Bay in 1921. This transaction enabled the construction of a new Green Bay East High School and the athletic field that became City Stadium, home of the Packers from 1925-1956.

My maternal grandfather, Victor I. (V.I.) Minahan, was one of the founders of the *Green Bay Press-Gazette*, its editor for twenty-four years, one of the early financial backers of the Packers in 1922, and a key speaker at the banquet celebrating the team's first championship in 1929. He helped nurture and guide the newspaper's supportive role in the Packers' efforts to maintain its place in the pro football world.

He also gave away his daughter, Mary, at her 1939 wedding to the newspaper's sports editor, which contributed significantly – correction, vitally – to my entry into the world six years later.

One other relative deserves a seat on this family caravan through Packers history. John B. Torinus was Grandfather Vic Minahan's stepson and my uncle. A journalist also, he was a mainstay on the Packers' Executive Committee for years, and a key link in the relationship between the football team and the newspaper. One of the many books tracing the Packers' long history came from Uncle John's pen.

Context is essential in accurately describing such a journey. Words mean more when we know what prompted them, what was in the life, mind and heart of the writer and leading characters, how relationships and environments influenced their impact, and how events that ran concurrently provided an influencing and significant backdrop.

V.I. Minahan, Gus Walter, Dad, Uncle John Torinus, and the Pack-

My parents' wedding: *Here are relatives on both sides at my parents' wedding, which took place August 19, 1939, in Egg Harbor, Wisconson. From left, Vernelli Bush (my mom's grandmother), Bertha (Bush) Minahan (my mom's mother), my parents, Mary Minahan Walter and John Walter, Gus Walter (my dad's father), and Victor I. (V.I.) Minahan (my mother's father). (Walter family collection)*

---

ers didn't operate in a vacuum. Rather, they forged their places in a world straining and often stumbling toward modern times, not knowing what the future could be, but wanting to be an influencing and successful part of it.

Dad was twelve years older than the Packers, but they grew up side by side. When they became professionally connected, the collective chronicles of their journeys helped explain how and why a sports fluke like the Packers managed to not only survive when similar teams failed, but eventually become a sporting world empire with more pro football championships than any other franchise.

Their connection also helps explain how and why the lines between professional football and professional journalism were often blurred in Green Bay for so many years.

This is a story that contains many sub-stories. Let's start with my two grandfathers.

Victor Minahan's story was more out of the spotlight to many, as he practiced law for the first fifteen years of the *Press-Gazette's* existence, interrupted by his military service in France during World War I. He took over the editorship in 1930 upon the death of his predecessor,

John Kline, and guided the newspaper's newsroom – and its treatment of the Packers – until his death in 1954.

Gus Walter's story is that of a man who lived a life of personal tragedy, civic prominence, and professional success, only to be brought down by what he believed was legal shame and humiliation. A devoted bowling, baseball, and football fan, he lived the last quarter of his life trying to convert business fantasies into a reality that never existed. He died in 1940.

My uncle, John Torinus (Walter family collection)

Uncle John Torinus's ties to the Packers were borne in the 1920s when he volunteered as a ball boy for the team's home games. He often assisted in game coverage as a member of the *Press-Gazette* staff in the 1930s, then joined the Packers' Board of Directors in 1949. Eventually, he took his seat on the corporation's seven-person Executive Committee. He always managed to deftly separate his roles as a Packers official from those he held as editor of both the *Press-Gazette* and later at the *Appleton Post-Crescent,* thirty miles south of Green Bay. He died in 1985.

Dad's is also the story of a time past, of life in the Midwestern city of his birth, when radio, sports, women, the cinema, and beer were a bachelor's entertainment and companions. Uncle John had a front row seat to many of Dad's activities and relationships then, aiding and abetting.

Theirs are also part of the story of Green Bay and how a city plowed its way through such a significant time of the twentieth century when Prohibition was getting expunged, the Great Depression was the most unwelcome visitor, and a New Deal was starting to chart a way to recovery.

And it is the story of the Packers before players and coaches became street names, before stores marketed the team brand, and before technology gave every fan access to a public forum and some fans a claim to football expertise.

My story feeds off all those stories. Reared in the community shadows of something my forefathers helped defend, nurture and preserve – journalism and the Packers – I traveled along that popular road later. My days as a sports reporter and sports editor of the *Press-Gazette* brought me into contact with some names known to my relatives and many that came after they were gone. Canadeo, Rote, Vainisi, Lombardi, Starr, Hornung, Lofton, Olejniczak, Harlan, Wolf, Holmgren, White, Thompson, Favre, Murphy, Rodgers, etc.

My pen has the luxury of knowing how history would treat my relatives, the *Press-Gazette,* and the football team. Citing my family connections and my own career, I claim an author's privilege to explain, react, and even judge.

No compliment that was ever passed my way came close to that which referred to positive actions and attributes of mine that reminded people of Dad. Being told I look like him is soothing and apparent. Being told I speak and act like he did is gold.

The massive diaries that have been left in my possession portray a man – imperfect, of course – who paired his skills with his hopes, and left so much in his wake that benefited so many.

He wrote the diaries from 1925 to 1959 with the belief that they would and could be read by others, I believe, trusting his heirs to make prudent decisions and appropriate edits. And so I shall, guided by what I think he would have shared, and what I think he would want others to know about him and the human stage on which he existed and performed. There is no possible way to describe his role without listing the Green Bay Packers among the co-stars and credits.

There are many examples of cities throughout the country that have built a fan base for their professional sports teams and attached the community's identity to the fortunes or misfortunes of the performers. There are many families whose surname fits admirably and significantly into the timeline of the professional football network that began at a meat packing plant and a newspaper office, and in the brain of someone called Curly.

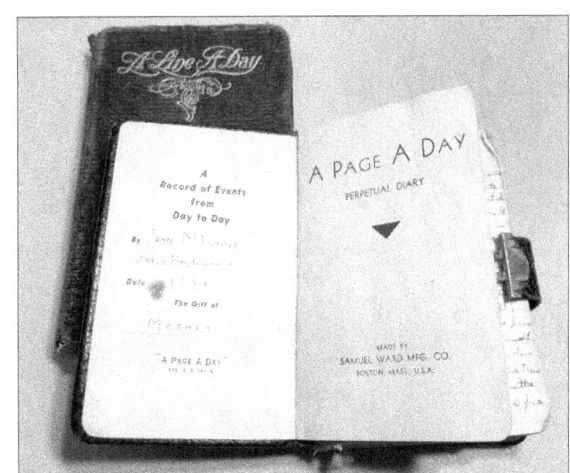

This inside page indicates my dad's 1934 diary was a gift from "Mother," which is how he referred to the grandmother who raised him.

But there is just one Green Bay, and the family that fate assigned me to has been putting its imprint on the Packers in a way unlike any other for the past century.

As the community so loyally demonstrated the force behind a citizenry committed, two grandfathers, a father, an uncle, and I became linked by choice, by profession, and by genetics to the history of this one-of-a-kind story.

It's a story of community, family, and football.

It's a story of legacy.

Chapter 2

The Catbird Seat

Romance and royalty were in the news the second Monday of December, 1936. King Edward VII had decided he would rather be husband to a twice-divorced American woman than monarch of the British Empire. It was a major story and conversation piece in many households in Green Bay just three days after the king revealed his choice.

News of a different kind was at the forefront of many thoughts and emotions for my father, John M. Walter, and the widening Green Bay Packers fan base. The football team was traveling home by train from New York, where it had defeated the Boston Redskins, 21-6, at the Polo Grounds to win the professional football title, its fourth championship in eight seasons.

The game was held in New York because Redskins owner George Preston Marshall was angry that Boston hadn't turned out enough ticket buyers during the season, and he correctly concluded that the Polo Grounds offered a better opportunity to draw a crowd. He was getting ready to move the franchise to Washington, D.C., anyway.

Dad was in the fan's catbird seat, near the end of his first full calendar year as *Green Bay Press-Gazette* sports editor, with access to the players, coaches and administrators, and a daily print forum to share his observations and opinions.

The newspaper didn't send him to New York for the title game, instead following its tradition of giving the eastern road game trips to George W. Calhoun, at the time the paper's telegraph editor and secretary of the Packers Corporation. Calhoun was better known for his role in the Packers' birth and his cheerleading in print since 1919.

Dad often clashed with Calhoun or tried to ignore him. He considered him unpleasant, a very mediocre writer, and no longer qualified to be the newspaper's leading voice about the football franchise. Cal-

Tony Walter

Green Bay Packers 1936 NFL Championship Team

Front row: Ade Schwammel, Bernie Scherer, Tiny Engebretsen, Lon Evans, Milt Gantenbein, Don Hutson, George Sauer, Ralph Miller, Champ Seibold.
Second Row: Russ Letlow, Hank Bruder, Al Rose, Frank Butler, Walt Kiesling, George Svendsen, Lou Gordon, Ernie Smith, Wayland Becker, Clarke Hinkle.
Top Row: Swede Johnston, Tony Paulekas, Paul Miller, Bob Monnett, Arnie Herber, Harry Mattos, Herm Schneidman, Dom Vairo, Cal Clemens, Joe Laws, Coach Curly Lambeau. Missing: Johnny Blood, Buckets Goldenberg. (Photo courtesy Green Bay Press-Gazette)

---

houn's cozy seat inside the Packers dominion was certainly one that Dad hoped to occupy. But Dad was well aware of the man's history and relationship with former Packers president Andrew Turnbull, who was also Dad's boss. Calhoun would have to be tolerated.

Dad's column that Monday cheered the championship with a "told you so" overtone aimed at the vanishing doubters:

> No. 1 nominee for Green Bay's forgotten man – the gent who predicted there'd be no Packer franchise here this season. Very hard to find last night. Certainly would be a pleasure to speak personally with all those people who knew the franchise was going to Milwaukee, St. Louis, Cleveland and intermediate points.
>
> Not getting away from it, that Victory banquet would have been a sad affair Wednesday night if the team had lost yesterday, despite the determination of the committee to hold it, win or lose. No getting away from it now that the Packers are champions, the banquet will be one of the greatest single testimonial events ever held in Green Bay.
>
> Fans who haven't been boosting this great team as they should have big chances this week to show they're ashamed of

John Walter

themselves. One is tonight at 10:15 when the victorious Packers roll in at Milwaukee Road station. Another is Wednesday night, the banquet date, at the Columbus Club.

But the fans who have backed the squad to the limit, who have spent their money on tickets, have traveled out of town, have listened breathlessly to radio accounts, have built the Packers to the skies as the finest football team they've ever been privileged to support – these are the folks who'll be at the station by the thousands tonight, and who'll have plates in front of them at the big affair Wednesday.

The Packers have taken their national championship the hard way, coming from nowhere to whip successively the best professional talent in the nation. And does Wisconsin know it? See you at the station tonight.

While the city residents cheered and soaked up the printed reports of the team's successes, Dad saved his personal thoughts for his diary, a daily written account he began in 1925 and would continue for the rest of his life.

December 14, 1936
"Green Bay pulsating with excitement as national championship team nears home. None more excited than I. In evening over to station at 10 o'clock. Ten thousand wildly cheering fans packed South Washington Street and split the air as the Packers' coach rolled into the station. Greeted every one of the players first, starting with Lonnie Evans. Met the Torinuses, also Clarke Hinkle and his new bride. We all went up to Karl Hagemeister's apartment and, brothers, it was a party. Finally got to bed at 2:15."

Clarke Hinkle, who was one of Dad's all-time favorite players, acquired more than a champion-

Clarke Hinkle was a Packers star who became friends with my father. (Photo courtesy of Neville Public Museum of Brown County)

Columbus Club staff prepares for the banquet celebrating the Packers' victory over the Boston Redskins to win the 1936 championship. (Photo courtesy of Neville Public Museum of Brown County)

ship on his trip to the East. While there, he married Emilie Cobden. Her welcome to Green Bay must have been memorable.

John Torinus was a friend and newspaper colleague, and later would become Dad's brother-in-law. Karl Hagemeister was Dad's first cousin, and his apartment was on the third floor of the building at 425 S. Monroe Ave. Packers head coach Curly Lambeau had an apartment just three doors down the hall. The party eventually included Lambeau and others.

Football people and newspaper people partying together – the ingredients for a classic Green Bay-style celebration. Sleep was absent. Hopefully, designated drivers weren't.

Dad lived just walking distance from Karl's apartment, so I'll assume he didn't drive home, perhaps thinking he may be needed to help produce a son someday. Perhaps not, but he provided written evidence that herb tea was not his drink of choice that night.

December 15, 1936
"You can imagine how I feel. Thank God we never have to celebrate a championship oftener than once a year. They put my homecoming story on Page One. Knocked off work after lunch and slept the rest of the afternoon. But in evening was out again, driving to Duck Creek for supper with Packer team at Bertrand's. Stewed venison. Had chats with Ade Schwammel, Ernie Smith, Bernie Scherer. Took Scherer home. He played some nice ball in his first season with the team. Didn't stay late for was ghastly tired."

***

The *Press-Gazette* headline that Tuesday blared **"10,000 FANS GREET PACKERS"** with John Walter's story topping the page:

> Ten thousand voices roared a tremendous welcome to the Green Bay Packer football team last night, as the victorious players returned from the 1936 gridiron wars in possession of the world professional championship.
>
> Green Bay's packed humanity jammed every available space in the vicinity of the Milwaukee Road freight depot as the homecoming squad's special coach rolled in from the south at 10:20, carrying the triumphant gridiron men through lanes of spitting red fire to face the thunderous greeting which the city had reserved for its champions.
>
> As far as the eye could reach from the depot platform, across Washington Street down toward the passenger station, across Adams and around Fire Station No. 1.
>
> The cheering throng waved and delivered vocal congratulations as the Packers were taken from their coach and walked along the platform to express their pleasure briefly into the battery of microphones.

Stuart Cameron, sports editor of United Press and whose game story went all over the nation, wrote: "The Green Bay Packers, the big team from the little Wisconsin town, ruled the professional football world again."

Dad rolled along with the celebrations in his sports page column the same day:

John Walter

MORALE!

That's what brought the 1936 National football championship to Green Bay. The authority – Earl L. Lambeau, who is "Curly" to thousands of Packer fans, and who has piloted a fighting brand of gridiron warriors to the world title.

It was a tired but happy Curly, who, the celebration over in the small hours of the morning, rested his head back on one of Karl Hagemeister's easy chairs and paid complete, glowing tribute to the men he has lived and worked with during the great 1936 season.

"Every man was working all the time," he said. "Can you imagine an extended professional trip during which every man was in bed every night at 11:30, and no player broke training as far as to take a glass of beer?

"We had it. These Packers, the new champions, are as fine a squad of men as ever represented any city. They have been marvelous – not only on the football field, when they came back after a crushing defeat to win the national title, but in their everyday relations toward their work, their coaches and the city they represent."

The Packers are genuinely proud of Green Bay, although no more so than the hysterical city last night demonstrated that it is proud of the Packers.

"Just too bad," shouted Lou Gordon into the microphone earlier in the evening, "that the Cardinals traded me to Green Bay."

Lou can't get over that jump from a last place to a first place team.

"Man, oh, man, is it great to be home!" fervently said Bernie Scherer, as he sucked in the night air on the station platform. That from a player who less than four months ago had his first glimpse of Green Bay.

Yes, the city has taken the team to heart. And it should, even if the sentimental side of the championship is disregarded, when the millions of dollars of advertising to Green Bay is considered.

The best story of the trip involves Lon Evans and his prize football. He lugged the championship oval all over New York getting autographs, and by barging into the National Broadcasting Company headquarters, he added such signatures as Parkyakarkas, Eddie Cantor, Kate Smith and Walter Winchell.

An autograph-a-minute pace did Lonnie follow until he collared one radio star coming out of a broadcasting room.

"What program do you sing on?" demanded Lonnie.

"Give me that football," replied the other, reaching for his fountain pen.

And he signed: "J. Edgar Hoover."

I wonder what happened to that football. In his diary, Dad covered his day's activities amidst the celebrations:

December 16, 1936
"Good night's sleep. Packers are preparing to spend Christmas at their homes. Have terrific pileup of work on desk, will clear it away during the dull holiday season. In morning met Arch Ward, sports editor of the Chicago Tribune. *This may lead to something, some day. In evening sat at speaker's table as 1,500 fans gave the Packers a magnificent testimonial banquet at Columbus Club auditorium. Had cocktails with the players first. Russ Winnie, Arch Ward principal speakers. Ward invited the Packers to play in the College All-Star game at Chicago next summer. Drank a final toast with my friend Ernie Smith. Then home."*

***

Dad was a twenty-nine-year-old bachelor living with his grandmother (he called her Mother) in Hazelwood, the historic home of Morgan L. Martin they had just purchased. It was the midst of the Great Depression, when many were short of cash and work, and when rumblings of fascism in Europe had people wondering if the world war twenty years past might not have been the war to end all wars, after all. It was three years after the repeal of Prohibition that helped accentuate and reinforce Green Bay's reputation as a "drinking" city, and was seven weeks after President Franklin Roosevelt won re-election to a second term and an endorsement of his recovery programs.

Despite the joy of the Packers' championship and his role in recording the events that created and surrounded it, despite his high-profile position in a sports-crazy community, and despite the prospect of future professional success, Dad wasn't spared the uncertainty and angst of the times.

Just three months earlier, he vented his frustration about the direction his life was going in his diary:

August 31, 1936
"My life has seemed so futile thus far... here I am, almost 29 years old, always broke between paydays and not a nickel in the bank."

Despite the happy fallout of a football championship and the holiday atmosphere of his predominantly Christian lifestyle, there was anxiety – even a hint of desperation – as he longed for what he didn't have.

December 24, 1936
"Have the Christmas Eve blues. In a black humor all day. Mother causes it. She mopes because the family is broken up and bitter toward each other. Have 31 cents to my name, good for six beers and a penny left over. Believe me, this is my last Christmas as a poor man. I mean it. Some day, maybe I'll have a family of my own and Christmas will be fun instead of a day on which I envy someone else. You never can tell."

All he could tell was that adulthood so far had seen his rise to a professional status without any financial security or a lifetime partner to share the journey.

He also carried the burden of trying to keep his father out of embarrassing financial and legal straits when pennies were scarce, and Gus had more checks to write than he had funds to cover them.

Eventually, my father would attain a status that would define him. He made his future catbird seat a pulpit for leading and serving others.

He would marry at the age of thirty-one, help raise seven children – I'm No. 4 – rise to the rank of lieutenant colonel in the U.S. Army during World War II, then plan and run a new radio station in Green Bay (WJPG), where he launched the careers of future Milwaukee Braves sportscasters Earl Gillespie and Blaine Walsh. He would become state governor of Kiwanis for a year, become an accomplished and sought-after public speaker, impact hundreds of boys and young men through his leadership of Boy Scouts programs, and withstand the fear and discomfort of a dangerously high blood pressure that eventually would kill him at the age of fifty-two.

Before all that, there was a life of education, sports, accomplishment ... searching and survival. For Dad, a relationship with the Green Bay Packers was a gift to be cherished. The football field was holy ground. The written word was therapy.

Chapter 3

Trouble at the Plant

Wisconsin Senator Robert M. LaFollette was hours away from death on June 17, 1925.

A substitute teacher named John Scopes was preparing to stand trial in Dayton, Tennessee, on a charge that he violated the state's new Butler Act that prohibited teaching about evolution in public schools. It would be a circus trial that attracted a former presidential candidate, William Jennings Bryan, for the prosecution and a famed attorney, Clarence Darrow, for the defense.

Brigadier General Billy Mitchell was drawing closer to a court-marshal for his continuous criticism of his military superiors' failure to recognize the need to strengthen the country's air force. Mitchell went so far as to suggest the country could be at risk of an air attack on Hawaii … by Japan. He would be convicted, eventually leave the military, and five years after his death in 1936, would have an airport named for him in Milwaukee, where he grew up.

There were many other noteworthy topics to choose from on that Wednesday.

Writer F. Scott Fitzgerald had just published a book about the Roaring 1920s lifestyle, but was disappointed at the initially poor sales of *The Great Gatsby*. F recovered, as the book became his recognized classic.

Benito Mussolini had declared himself dictator of Italy, and a German revolutionary named Adolf Hitler had just published his manifesto, *Mein Kampf*, which he wrote while in prison.

Historian Doane Robinson was recommending that a mountainside in South Dakota be carved with the faces of Sioux tribal leaders. However, a decision would be made to have sculptor Gutzon Borglum carve the faces of George Washington, Thomas Jefferson, Abraham Lincoln, and Theodore Roosevelt instead.

Richard Drew, working for 3M Corporation, had just invented Scotch Tape, and Walter Chrysler had just founded his own automobile corporation. The first Sears-Roebuck store opened in Chicago. And New York Yankees first baseman Wally Pipp lost his starting job a few days earlier to young Lou Gehrig, who would play in 2,130 consecutive games.

With the end of the World War only seven years past, residents of Green Bay had treated the most recent Memorial Day with reverence. More than 1,000 people attended special services at the three area cemeteries – Allouez, Woodlawn, and Fort Howard – prompting a poetic *Press-Gazette* writer to slip this past the editors:

> "While the sun shone in benediction this morning and the breeze hummed a sacred lullaby, thousands of men and women gathered at hastily erected altars and gave homage to the Most High, honoring through him the dead who gave not their lives in vain.
>
> "The soldier dead, who in the cemeteries that have passed won for those men and women who worshipped there the right to worship in peace and freedom."

Whew!

And for those holding their breaths for results of a pigeon race, Herbert Devily's bird won a special 100-mile event sponsored by the North Side Homing Pigeon Club, flying an average of 45 miles per hour from Watertown to Green Bay in two hours, eleven minutes and four seconds. The club was preparing to ship several birds to Ironton, Missouri, for a 500-mile race a week later. Results of that race are not available, and the flying athletes are most likely dead, according to sources.

Likely none of that was on seventeen-year-old John Walter's mind as he observed what was unfolding in his father's life that day.

His father, Gus, was president and general manager of the Hagemeister Food Products plant on the city's east side. Prohibition had been the law of the land for more than five years, and such facilities weren't supposed to be producing real beer and selling it. The Hagemeister plant, a former brewery, was publicly in the business of selling soft drinks, candy, and ice cream. That's all. Supposedly.

But the previous night, federal agents raided the plant, seized several barrels of alleged good beer, and arrested seven men. Five of them, according to newspaper accounts, were "Italians from Hurley (Wisconsin)."

The other two were Green Bay men, both Hagemeister employees.

I suspect the reference to the nationality of the Hurley suspects was typical of the stereotypes that were common then. Italian meant spaghetti and crime to many people, and Hurley was known for being good at both.

Gus was in Milwaukee at the time of the raid and issued a statement when he returned:

"None of the officers or directors of the Hagemeister plant were aware of the fact that beer was being sold," he told the *Press-Gazette*. "About a month ago, we put a young man in charge of our soda water department, and in his zeal to make a good showing in receipts he apparently began selling beer. We were told today that the beer was being sold to runners from the northern part of the state, when the arrests were made last night. As the employee of the soda department has disappeared, we are unable to get a statement from him as to just what actually transpired."

***

June 17, 1925
"Home most of the day alone. Up to Straubel's for awhile in the aft. Drove around awhile with Marge. Trouble out at plant. Down at Dad's in eve and for all night. Didn't sleep much."

June 18, 1925
"At Dad's all day. Not a very enjoyable one either. Trouble seems hard to clear up. Drove to Denmark with folks in aft. Down to Dad's again for all night."

June 19, 1925
"Drove to Kaukauna with Dad in a.m. Home in aft. Dad still in trouble about that damned 18th Amendment."

***

John Madden, Wisconsin's prohibition director, said three automobiles were lined up at the loading platform of the soft drink plant when federal agents arrived. One of them, a Buick coach, contained five half-barrels of what later would be confirmed as illegal beer. The back seat of the car had been removed to make room for the beer, and the license plates of all three vehicles had also been removed.

The raid came two weeks after the *Press-Gazette* used its opinion page to address the issue of illegal liquor:

"Is the 18th Amendment actually going to be enforced in Green Bay? The arrest of a considerable number of soft drink parlor proprietors here during the last 48 hours would lead one to believe so. Evidence was found that the prohibition amendment was being openly and willfully violated.

"Green Bay has long had the reputation of being one of the 'wettest' spots in the state, where illicit liquor could be purchased over the bar with little fear of being bothered by law enforcement officials."

Was the 18th Amendment actually going to be effectively enforced in Green Bay? For appearances sake, yes. In reality? Not.

The raid on his father's business would not be the only life-changing event of that summer for Dad. Almost two months after the Hagemeister raid, he wrote that he had a job.

***

August 7, 1925
"Rainy day. Offered job at Press-Gazette. Will I accept? Well, will I!"

***

Dad had an "in" at the *Press-Gazette*. One of the newspaper's founders and its first editor was John Kline, whose family once shared the Mason Street apartment building with Dad and his family. Kline saw Dad as a budding journalist and took him under his wing.

After the raid and subsequent closing of the Hagemeister plant, Gus wasn't able to keep up with Dad's freshman tuition at Lawrence College in Appleton, Wisconsin. Kline, a father figure to Dad, stepped in and made up the difference. He provided Dad with part-time work at the newspaper until graduation, and then a full-time position that launched a successful career. The impact of Kline's generosity and unselfishness was permanent and launched a pay-it-forward lifestyle for Dad.

But let's go back even further. Seventeen and a half years earlier, on October 22, 1907, the major news of the day was that Ringling Brothers Greatest Show on Earth had purchased the Barnum & Bailey circus.

John Kline (Photo courtesy Green Bay Press-Gazette)

John Messenger Walter was just hours old the same day when a different announcement appeared in the *Green Bay Gazette* (which merged with the *Green Bay Free Press* in 1915 to form the *Green Bay Press-Gazette*):

"A baby boy arrived at the home of Mr. and Mrs. G.A. Walter, East Mason Street, this morning."

He was a day old when the newspaper ran a story beneath the headline:

"Mrs. G.A. Walter Dead"

"It was reported that Jessie Messenger Walter, aged twenty-six, died at 9 o'clock the previous evening at her East Mason Street home, and that survivors included her husband of two years, Gus. A. Walter; her mother, Mrs. Warner Clisby; a sister, Elta; a brother, John Messenger; and an infant son.

"The mortality rate of women giving birth in the United States in 1907 was 8.5 deaths for every 1,000 births, according to the U.S. Department of Health. Jessie was not one of the 991.5 who survived. She gave birth in the house on East Mason Street and died there hours later."

My paternal grandparents, Gus and Jessie Walter, c. 1905. (Walter family collection)

Two days later, the paper gave more space to details of the funeral:

"Rites yesterday afternoon were held at the residence on Mason Street under the auspices of First Church of Christ Scientists. The text of the reading was beautiful in its simplicity and a fitting tribute to the memory of the deceased.

"Floral offering of unsurpassed beauty attested mutely to the esteem to which the late Mrs. Walter was held by hosts of mourning friends. At the grave in Woodlawn Cemetery where the deceased was laid to rest, a brief ceremony was also conducted. The pallbearers were Harry Joannes, Holmes Ellis, Samuel Hastings Jr., Douglas Basche, Ralph Joannes and H.R. Erikson."

Jessie Walter's mother, Flora Clisby, filled her daughter's role as the baby's chief nurturer and would forever be called "Mother" by her grandson. Dad would live with her until her death in 1938.

Gus had his career and civic duties to manage. This was chronicled in Deborah Martin's 1913 volume *History of Brown County, Wisconsin*, in which she profiled many of the community's leading citizens:

Dad and "Mother," his grandmother, Flora Clisby. (Walter family collection)

"Gus A. Walter Jr., is one of the prominent and representative young businessmen of Green Bay, Wisconsin, and has carried out the progressive policy with which he began his business career. He is secretary and treasurer of the Hagemeister Brewing Company, with which he has been connected since his arrival in Green Bay in 1901, and he has served in his present capacity since 1903. He also holds the office of secretary and treasurer in the Hagemeister Realty Company, which is affiliated with the brewing business.

"Mr. Walter was born in Wheeling, West Virginia, in 1880 and is a son of Gus. A. and Mary Hagemeister Walter. He attended the public schools of Pittsburgh, Pennsylvania, later took a high school course there, and afterward a course in a business college in Green Bay. He acquired a good education, which he considers one of the most valuable assets in his business career. It was in 1901 that he came to Green Bay and entered the office of the Hagemeister Brewing Company.

"His promotion was rapid and due to his undoubted ability. After three years service he was appointed secretary and treasurer of the Hagemeister Brewing Company with a similar office in the realty company of the same name. He is one of the energetic and alert young men who are the bulwark of municipal life and he has already become an influencing force in the commercial expansion of Green Bay. He is a member of the board of education of the city and has held the office since July, 1910. He is also a member of Lodge No. 259, B.P.O. of Green Bay.

"In 1905, Mr. Walter was united in marriage to Miss Jessie Messenger of Green Bay, who died Oct. 22, 1907, leaving a son, John, now five years of age. Mr. Walter is well versed in his business and though still a young man he has exhibited a shrewd and discriminating business sense and energy, unfaltering ambition and powerful determination, which promises well for larger success in the future."

The clubhouse at Hagemeister Park prior to its removal for the new Green Bay East High School. (Photo courtesy of Neville Public Museum of Brown County)

Gus married a second time and was widowed a second time before he was 40. He served as the Green Bay School Board president from 1914 to 1917, and gained some recognition by writing local musical stage shows.

Gus's mother, Mary, was the daughter of Henry Hagemeister, whose father had started the brewery in the nineteenth century. Gus was secretary-treasurer of the Hagemeister enterprises and properties, and was the principal contact when the Green Bay School Board was looking for a site for the new East High School.

Gus appeared before the school board in July 1920 to say the company would be willing to sell either part or all of Hagemeister Park on the city's east side adjacent to the plant. Three months later, he returned to the board and said the entire twenty-four acres could be purchased for $80,000. He also gave the city the option of buying eighteen acres for $34,000.

The board chose the entire Hagemeister Park site as its preferred location, but had to get approval from the city council, which would provide the funds. It took a while as Mayor Elmer Hall said he thought the price was a little high, but the council eventually signed off on the sale.

An aerial shot of Green Bay East High School and the accompanying City Stadium on the former Hagemeister Park property. The Green Bay Packers played here from 1925-1956. (Photo courtesy of Neville Public Museum of Brown County)

The transaction meant Gus played his initial role in the history of the Green Bay Packers just two years after the team was born.

Then there was the raid in 1925. Gus, who lived for fifteen years after the raid, told family that he wasn't aware that illegal beer was being sold from the plant. When I asked Dad about that in the 1950s, he mentioned his dad's denial, but also told me that a company president always knows what's going on in his company's basement. I always sensed it was an uncomfortable topic for Dad. I understood why when I started reading the diaries long after Dad died. My father didn't relish having to keep his father out of financial trouble when his own resources were so limited, but he never deviated from the belief that family took care of family, despite the strain and the circumstances.

Gus's plea and testimony in the 1926 trial confirmed that he knew a lot. He copped a plea. He pled guilty to conspiracy to violate the Volstead Act, and became the chief prosecution witness in similar charges against Green Bay dentist Leon J. Patterson and former department store owner Henry Herrick. Both men were on the board of directors at Hagemeister.

He said both men knew that real beer was being sold in 1925. Beer was sold to two Milwaukee men who ran a trucking business, and the sales were brokered by Dr. Richard Schneider, president of the Industrial Chemical Institute in Milwaukee. The beer was transported by automobile, truck and railroad, and billed as potatoes and furniture.

Gus said he collected $2,500 from the Milwaukee men, but a second shipment of beer was confiscated before it could be delivered.

Herrick and Patterson were convicted and sentenced to a year in the House of Corrections and fined $1,000 each.

Gus issued a statement at the Milwaukee trial in federal court.

"I appeared as a government witness and waived immunity to do so. I requested the right after I discovered an attempt was being made to accuse me of being dishonest. At the trial it was shown that I had not profited from the sale of illegal beer and that my fortune had been dissipated in the business."

He was fined $500 and sentenced to ten months in the House of Corrections, which was served at a work camp in northern Wisconsin.

***

June 10, 1926
"Dad got 10 months, $500. Damn prohibition. Otherwise dull day."

June 14, 1925
"Dad left for Milwaukee. It'll be some time before I see him again."

***

Gus Walter (left) and my dad, John Walter. (Walter family collection)

Gus never recovered from what he must have felt was public shame and lived most of the final years of his life at the Green Bay YMCA, repeatedly dreaming about promising business opportunities that never came to fruition, planning to write short stories that never went to print, and borrowing money from his son throughout his final decade. No doubt, this created tension between Gus and Dad, although Gus happily stood in the receiving line at Dad's 1939 wedding in Egg Harbor, Wisconsin.

Gus died suddenly of an embolism in 1940 at the age of sixty.

Chapter 4

Perched Upon the Throne

As the 1929 winter was beginning to serve its record-setting cold to Wisconsin, Packers head coach Curly Lambeau had to be feeling both pride and anxiety along with the chill.

His 1928 team had finished its tenth season in fourth place with a 6-4-3 record, capped by the 6-0 victory over the Chicago Bears in the final game when Red Dunn passed to Dick O'Donnell for the winning touchdown late in the fourth quarter.

There was likely some satisfaction when Lambeau read about the All-American pro team a week later and saw the names of three Packers: Lavvie Dilweg, Verne Lewellen, and Eddie Kotal.

Lambeau would also have seen the names of other top players on the list: the Bears' Paddy Driscoll, New York Giants tackle Cal Hubbard and quarterback Benny Friedman, New York Yankees guard Mike Michalske, and the Chicago Cardinals' all-everything Ernie Nevers. And he didn't have to think back too far to remem-

Verne Lewellen starred on Packers teams from 1924-32. (Photo courtesy of Neville Public Museum of Brown County)

ber the November 1928 Sunday when the Pottsville Maroons, in their last victory before becoming extinct, embarrassed the Packers 26-0 behind the running and punting of halfback Johnny (Blood) McNally.

But there also had to be some angst and frustration as Lambeau looked ahead to the 1929 season with the knowledge that many of his teams hadn't been far from challenging for the championship, but had never been able to win it.

His 1925 team, led by the sensational Lewellen – whose absence from the Pro Football Hall of Fame is unexplainable and indefensible – started out by winning seven of its first nine games before fading to an 8-5 finish. The highlight for the team was the new football field, to be called City Stadium and the site of Packers home games through 1956.

The 1926 team outscored opponents 151-61, but its 7-3-3 record fell short. It was the season in which football legend Red Grange helped organize the original American Football League, which flopped.

The 1927 Packers finished 7-2-1, its only losses coming at the hands of the Chicago Bears by scores of 7-6 and 14-6. That was the year the Packers were initially scheduled to play at the New York Giants on December 4, but the game was taken off the schedule when the Grange-led New York Yankees were granted a franchise, limiting the Giants' number of home games. The Giants finished the season 11-1-1 and ignored the Packers' requests to meet at the end of the season in a sort of playoff, this being before the league established a playoff system.

Looking ahead to the team's eleventh season in 1929, Lambeau must have known the obvious: that many communities of similar size had seen their efforts to sustain a pro football team evaporate; that a growing fan base was forming around his team; that there were still no championships for Green Bay; and some better players would be needed to get to that level.

He knew there had never been a losing season for the Packers, that a season ticket push was planned to help pay expenses, and that the corporation structure was attracting many of the more influential men of the Green Bay community.

The future of the Green Bay Packers was still undefined, unsettled, and very uncertain.

But pro football wasn't the only topic of interest in Green Bay as 1929 dawned. For Dad, there was school ... and girls as he drew closer to the end of his college days at Lawrence, but no closer to settling down with a significant other or to think about fathering a special son or two.

***

January 1, 1929
"Up at 12:30. Saw Karl who just got back from California. We may go to Europe this summer."

January 5, 1929
"Heavy snow. In eve took Trudy to 4th annual brawl at the frat house. Think she had a good time but she knows our dates are numbered."

January 17, 1929
"Conferences with Dr. MacHarg and Dr. Baker. I may not graduate this year."

January 18, 1929
"Semi-formal with Peggy tomorrow night. Letters from Mary, Katy. Have a wonderful new fur coat - Siberian wolf."

January 20, 1929
"Up to Green Bay in the a.m. - on train. This fur coat is the bennies these cold days."

January 22, 1929
"Pretty near exam time. I have 7 this year. Did considerable studying, for me, all day - in eve over to libe and took Julia home. Stayed out at her house at midnight - educational work."

February 8, 1929
"In eve took Lucille home from libe. We explored the Main Hall bell tower."

February 9, 1929
"Studied all evening, writing thesis. First Saturday evening I've stayed in for a helluva while."

February 14, 1929
"In eve took Trudy to all college valentine party at gym. Managed to have a pretty good time. Dances with Charlotte, Lucille, Marion and Trudy, of course."

February 15, 1929
"Dinner with Mr. Kline at his house."

February 23, 1929
"Twelfth Night play in eve. Peg and I did the stage work. Then we had a battle - one of the usual kind - and left each other not on speaking terms."

February 28, 1929
"Still no girl, same as last year at this time. Still hanging tight. I don't plan to make up with Peg this time. Blue Key meeting in eve. Saw Peg and didn't speak to her. Am very proud of myself."

The second-to-last page in Dad's 1929 diary includes every bowling score he had that year.

The last page in the diary contains a list of nineteen names. They are Barbara, Elsie, Margaret, Katherine, Evelyn, Eileen, Ruth, Trudy, Charlotte, Frances, Lucille, Penelope, Mary Franke, Josephine, Dorothy, Dorothy, Dorothy, Helen, and Peg.

I don't think that was the bowling team.

***

The prospect of a continuation of business prosperity infected the city, as it did the state and country. Green Bay bankers said as much when they gathered for their annual meeting two weeks into the new year.

"We can see nothing ahead for the next six months but smooth sailing in the business world," said John Rose, president of the Kellogg Citizens National Bank.

Peoples Savings and Trust president R.T. Bennie echoed the optimism.

"We have just closed a very good year and will be perfectly satisfied if the next year is as good," Bennie said. "At the same time, we have no reason whatever to believe that 1929 will not be as good or better than 1928."

But the bankers also sought a solution to the increasing number of bank robberies that were infesting the area. They tried to organize a county security guard program and even suggested that placards be placed at every bank with the wording: "$1,000 for dead bank robber, $500 for a live one."

I have no idea if anyone ever collected.

Outgoing Green Bay mayor James McGillan was looking further ahead, preparing to name a tercentennial commission for the city's 300th anniversary in 1934. He also predicted that some of the towns adjacent to the city might soon be available for annexation, namely Allouez and Preble on the east side.

There was retail business news as the year began. The Montgomery Ward company in Chicago announced plans to purchase property on Green Bay's Main Street and build a department store.

Statewide, Republican Walter Kohler was being sworn in as governor over the objections of Progressives Phillip LaFollette and William Evjue, who filed a petition claiming Kohler violated the corrupt practices act in his campaign. (Just in case anyone thought political drama in Wisconsin was a twenty-first century invention.)

The stain of Prohibition continued to boost Green Bay's wet reputation as resistance to the dry law remained evident. Five days into the year, federal agents descended upon the city and padlocked nine more soft drink parlors – mostly on Broadway and Main Street – bringing to forty-eight the total that had been shut down so far.

Meanwhile, federal prohibition agent Henry Strawn was charged with accepting bribes of more than $5,000 from thirteen Green Bay soft drink/saloon keepers.

Ten supporters of the dry law petitioned the Green Bay Police and Fire Commission to have Police Chief Thomas Hawley dismissed, claiming he "permitted and encouraged" liquor law violations. He remained on the job.

Forces against the Eighteenth Amendment managed to put a referendum on the spring ballot in Wisconsin to collect public opinion on the Severson Act, which sought to permit 2.75 percent beer. The *Press-Gazette* considered the effort a waste of time, and used its opinion page to say so:

> "The referendum is dishonest because it purports to do something that cannot be done, to legalize something that cannot be legalized. It is dishonest because it is both a direct and indirect invitation to violation of federal law and federal constitution."

Regardless, and despite a blizzard on spring election day, voters overwhelmingly sided with the "wet" forces. Green Bay voted three-to-one to support less-stringent beer laws.

Still, the editorial writer was not swayed:

> "Adoption of the proposal was a futile and senseless thing to do. The people were swayed by feelings. Nothing whatever was accomplished toward giving Wisconsin a better legalized supply of intoxicating beverages. The beer referendum is too absurd to be taken seriously."

Nationally, a group of prominent businessmen and celebrities, led by Henry Ford, Thomas Edison, and J.C. Penney, followed the lead of President-elect Herbert Hoover and released a statement urging Americans to give the Eighteenth Amendment a chance in an effort to simmer some of the heated debate over the issue.

Green Bay had other problems. Two months into the year, a severe water shortage occurred when the level of the city wells dropped drastically. Initially, it was thought to be the fault of the Hoberg Paper Company that required considerable water for its sulphate plant. Further investigation revealed the villain was a broken main that was leaking well water into the East River.

The *Press-Gazette* took the city's water department to task in an editorial:

> "It is incomprehensible that a city would permit its water department to degenerate to this extent, but it appears to be a fact. Green Bay has grown rapidly in the last 20 years and very little has been done to improve the water system."

Lake Michigan and its almost unlimited water supply beckoned. Green Bay would respond later.

Meanwhile, the city of Chicago got a favorable court ruling to permit it to divert water from Lake Michigan. The city also tried to send a message to gangsters by arresting 3,000 of them in a police roundup.

While that was going on, seven members of George "Bugs" Moran's North Side Gang in Chicago were gunned down in a North Clark Street garage, an event forever dubbed the St. Valentine's Day Massacre. While never proven, it was assumed that mobster Al Capone was behind the shootings, and some of his henchmen, including George "Nosey Joe" Lewis were eventually arrested. Chicago police said ninety-one killings in the past five years were linked directly or indirectly to Capone.

Federal agents did manage to arrest Capone three months into the year, accusing him of falsifying an affidavit when he claimed to have pneumonia in Miami so he couldn't appear for a grand jury investigating beer smuggling. The case didn't get far.

Another sign of the times took place in Mississippi when convicted murderer Charley Shepherd – an African-American – was dragged out of his cell and lynched. Governor T.G. Bilbo said he wouldn't initiate an investigation, stating, "I have neither the time nor the money to investigate two thousand people."

Press-Gazette editor John Kline wrote an editorial about the lynching of people of color:

> "It is encouraging to learn that there were only ten lynchings in the United States in 1928 as against 16 in 1927 and 30 in 1926. It is disgraceful that there are any at all. During 1928, there were 28 instances where officers prevented attempted lynchings. Some of these were in northern states. Most of them were in the South. The country cannot afford to let lynchings go on. It is bad for our own souls. It mocks and handicaps justice. It puts off indefinitely any sane solution of the race question. Mob violence is as hideous and uncivilized as any crimes it seeks to avenge."

And some newsmakers suffered from an absence of foresight. John George Bucher, of the Bureau of Commercial Economics in Washington, D.C., spoke to the Green Bay Lions Club about his interactions with German citizens during his European visits.

"Most conspicuous among the changes is the free and hearty attitude displayed by all classes of the German population," Bucher said. "Especially, Americans are made to feel that they are welcome, that Germans want others to know and understand them, that the war is over and is a thing of the past."

The recently completed Rose Bowl football game featured a bizarre result when California captain Roy Riegels picked up a Georgia Tech fumble and ran 66 yards in the wrong direction. That led to a safety and was the winning margin in an 8-7 Tech victory, forever earning Riegels the nickname "Wrong Way."

The pro football league held its annual meeting in Chicago, where Lambeau was able to confirm the signing of Bo Molenda, a husky runner who starred at the University of Michigan.

Reporters asked league president Joe F. Carr how a city the size of Green Bay could survive in a league dominated by teams from larger metropolitan areas.

"Green Bay is one of the staunchest spokes we have in our wheel," Carr said. "There is a community spirit behind the Packers that is not equaled anywhere else in the organization. This helps make the wheels go round and enables the Packers to hold their own both financially and on the gridiron with teams representing cities many times larger."

Football rules underwent a couple changes. One stated that a recovered fumble was dead at the spot of recovery, an apparent reaction to Riegels's blunder, and the extra point attempt was moved from the 3-yard-line to the 2-yard line.

Green Bay West graduate Arnie Herber earned a football letter in his freshman season at the University of Wisconsin in 1928, but prepared to transfer to Regis College. Herber struggled with the academic requirements in Madison.

He would be heard from again in Green Bay.

There was a Hollywood flavor in the Green Bay area a couple months into the year. Actor Lon Chaney, famous for his roles in silent horror films, was involved in the filming of a movie in the Green Bay area. Called *Thunder*, it was about a locomotion engineer named Grumpy. Chaney borrowed overalls from railroad man Ludie LeMay, who lived on South Chestnut Street.

Comments from area residents who met Chaney described a very friendly individual, a contrast to many of the film images that were associated with him.

Most of the film has been lost, with only half a reel still in existence. Some biographers have suggested that the Green Bay visit might have contributed to Chaney's death eighteen months later. He developed pneumonia during the filming, was later diagnosed with bronchial lung cancer, came down with a throat infection, and went steadily downhill. He died August 26, 1930, in Los Angeles.

Charles Lindbergh, less than two years removed from his historic solo flight to Paris, became engaged to Anne Morrow, the daughter of the U.S. Ambassador to Mexico, Dwight Morrow.

And the year wasn't two weeks old when famed Western lawman Wyatt Earp died at the age of eighty-one. It was the same week that Soviet General Secretary Joseph Stalin banned Leon Trotsky from the Politburo, and a Catholic missionary named Mother Teresa arrived in Calcutta to begin caring for the sick and poor.

All this took place as Herbert Hoover zeroed in on his inauguration to succeed fellow Republican Calvin Coolidge. Hoover defeated Democrat Al Smith in the 1928 election, but the result energized a future adversary, New York Gov. Franklin D. Roosevelt.

"I think it is a safe statement to make that the effect of our failure at the polls last year is encouraging members of the Democratic Party to be aroused and given the will to win," Roosevelt said.

Dad was keeping himself busy with an active social life that included the cinema and women.

***

March 24, 1929
"Went to see Lois Wilson in 'Conquest.' A talking picture. The movies sure have found their voice."

March 27, 1929
"Saw Trudy and she actually spoke to me, for a change. Wonder if I'll ever have another date with her. In eve, the most godawful blind date I've ever had."

***

In the spring, human drama was front page news when the disappearance of a four-year-old Green Bay girl made headlines and captured the attention of many outside of the state. Edith Dorschel, who was picnicking with her family near Sturgeon Bay on Memorial Day, was picking flowers near a cottage the family was visiting.

Suddenly, Edith was nowhere to be found and an immediate search by the family was unsuccessful. Several alarming possibilities faced the family. Did she fall into Sawyer Bay and drown? Was she kidnapped? One theory even suggested she could have been carried off in the claws of an eagle. The bay was dragged and 100 Boy Scouts from Green Bay went to Door County to help with the search.

Nothing was found.

Brown County Sheriff William Nicolai received permission from District Attorney Verne Lewellen to dynamite Sawyer Bay in hopes of bringing a body to the surface. (Lewellen earned his law degree while a member of the Packers and defeated teammate Lavvie Dilweg in the 1928 election.)

Then, three days and three nights later, a fourteen-year-old Sturgeon Bay boy who had joined the search party found Edith, alive. She had wandered deep into the woods, slept on the ground for three nights when temperatures dipped into the thirties, hadn't eaten or drunk anything while lost, but was otherwise sound. Asked by her mother if she had seen any of the people who had been searching for her, Edith said no, but added that she did see a bunny and a squirrel. A few days in the Sturgeon Bay hospital and Edith was back picking flowers.

Her father had offered a $1,000 reward for anyone who found his daughter alive, and the family of the fourteen-year-old boy said it was happy to accept it if the Dorschels could afford it.

Financial optimism continued as spring moved into summer, but there were warning clouds forming. H.H. Simmons, president of the New York Stock Exchange, told a Chicago audience that too many banks were living in the past.

"It seems unlikely that our prosperity can be maintained by employing obsolete or fallacious theories of banking or inexpert banking practices," he said.

There were other signs of changing times. The Green Bay Weather Bureau announced that it was doubling the size of its staff from two to four so it could begin providing forecasts and other weather data for aviators.

A treasure chest of newly published books that spring would find their way into Green Bay homes and classrooms including: Erich Remarque's *All Quiet on the Western Front*, William Faulkner's *The Sound and the Fury*, Ernest Hemingway's *A Farewell to Arms*, and Thomas Wolfe's *Look Homeward, Angel*.

There was concern, however, about an influx of some European books that many felt crossed the line of obscenity. In an editorial, the *Press-Gazette* supported censorship:

> "In junior high schools recently, in big cities, there have been found quantities of erotic poetry and prose hidden in classroom desks and between the leaves of school books. Parents have found similar stuff under pillows.
>
> "It is one thing for sophisticated grownups to read dubious classics of an older and ruder time. It is quite another thing for boys and girls to be corrupted by current filth spread on the newsstands."

Just eighteen months after the release of Al Jolson's *The Jazz Singer*, talking motion pictures were becoming the norm and hugely popular, bringing fame to such stars as Mary Pickford, Gary Cooper, the Marx Brothers, and George Arliss.

June featured the diamond jubilee in Ripon to commemorate the seventy-fifth anniversary of the founding of the Republican Party, reminding party loyalists that six years after it was formed in 1854, it succeeded in getting its presidential candidate, Abraham Lincoln, elected.

Gov. Kohler signed a bill requiring all public schools to have exercises planned every November 11, the anniversary of the signing of the armistice that ended the World War.

And, after four months of negotiations in Paris, an agreement was reached on Germany's obligation to pay reparations for its role in the war. The pact provided for Germany to pay the full $24 billion over fifty-nine years.

Hopefully, the negotiators weren't holding their breath waiting for the money.

Dad was one semester short of graduation as he traded his studies and fraternity parties for a summer of travel and work. But his impact at Lawrence was already well-documented.

He was editor of the college's newspaper, president of the men's honorary society called Mace, president of the National Collegiate Players at the school, president of the Sunset Players theater group, and president of the journalism fraternity called Pi Delta Epsilon.

The 1929 Lawrence yearbook, *The Ariel*, described him this way:

"Jack M. Walter: A fair youth who has a 'way with women,' a quick wit, and an air of self-secureness. Jack always seems to know just what he wants and how to go about getting it. He is something of a cross between a politician and a Romeo."

Maybe that trait skips a generation? Wondering for a friend.

Dad's summer job at the *Press-Gazette* was delayed while he took an automobile trip with his cousin, Karl Hagemeister. Their travels included Niagara Falls, Quebec, Atlantic City, and New York City. One of their stops included Yankee Stadium.

***

June 20, 1929
"Drove thru Central Park in a.m. and went to the Metropolitan Museum of Art. In aft out to Coney Island for some fun. In eve saw Janet Gaynor in '4 Devils' at new Roxy Theater."

June 21, 1929
"Rode on subway and elevated, thru Woolworth Tower in a.m. In aft saw Yankees and Athletics split a doubleheader – Babe Ruth hit 2 home runs."

(This was startling to me. As often as Dad and I talked baseball – he took me to the 1955 All-Star Game in Milwaukee and to several Milwaukee Braves games – and while he often mentioned his all-time favorites such as Rogers Hornsby, Honus Wagner, Walter Johnson, and Lou Gehrig, I don't remember him telling me he saw Ruth hit homers.)

June 26, 1929
"Harvard University and Bunker Hill in a.m. Then drove through Lexington and Concord to Portsmouth NH and then to Portland Maine."

June 27, 1929
"Thru White Mts. of New Hampshire then north to Newport, across into Canada to Sherbrooke, where we spent the night. Everybody here talking French. Don't think I like Canada."

June 28, 1929
"To Quebec in a.m. Stopping at Chateau Frontenac, wonderful place. In aft drove to Plains of Abraham and other points of interest in hansom cab."

June 29, 1929
"Drove down to Montreal. At Hotel Windsor. Have decided I like Canada - the dominion is saved."

August 5, 1929
"Started work for the rest of the summer at the Press-Gazette. Busy day, too. Hope for date with Penelope next Saturday. In eve saw Dad. No dates until Thursday."

August 6, 1929
"Rainy day but bought new slicker and survived. Running short of money. Drove around with Bid in eve - still breaking in that new Essex. Ran into Trudy in Kaap's - and did she look sweet!"

***

Dad's job at the newspaper that summer would include getting news from the city fire department, the hospitals, the police department, and any other place his editors would send him. He had one more semester of study, but was well on his way to a career in journalism.

The news mirrored the times, so let's jump into that first Green Bay Monday of August.

Two young adults were in trouble for embezzling money from the Brown County State Bank when they were tellers there. In all, they squirreled away about $10,000 by pocketing small amounts at a time. They paid almost all of it back, but the bank's insurance company wanted them arrested anyway.

Embezzlement also brought former Green Bay School District superintendent Ira Mcintyre into court for a preliminary hearing on charges that he kept $5,000 of the school district's money that had been collected for supplies.

The day featured a visit by Gov. Walter Kohler, who flew into the city airport with his wife and spoke at a meeting of the Loyal Order of Moose at Bay Beach. The Kohlers were then scheduled to fly over to Manitowoc, but their plane, while taxing in preparation for takeoff, collided with a tractor that was being used to pull stumps from the airport grounds near the intersection of Ashland Avenue and Highland Avenue (renamed Lombardi Avenue in 1968). The Kohlers weren't hurt, but they chose to drive to Manitowoc instead.

Needless to say, trunk-pulling tractors and machines that go up in the air stopped sharing the same runway.

There was news about the Green Bay Packers that day. A former Nebraska quarterback named Elbert (Al) Bloodgood signed a contract to play for the team and, at the least, assure the Packers of having one of the best football names on their roster.

Just a few days earlier, a signing of much greater significance occurred. The Packers purchased the contract of 280-pound tackle Cal Hubbard from the New York Giants football team. That name would be etched into both pro football and Major League Baseball history. Hubbard later became a Major League Baseball umpire and is the only man to be inducted into both the pro football and pro baseball halls of fame.

Packers lineman Cal Hubbard is the only person to have been inducted into both the Pro Football and National Baseball halls of fame. (Photo courtesy of Neville Public Museum of Brown County)

Hubbard, who also took up boxing, umpired a Sally League baseball doubleheader between Spartanburg (South Carolina) and Macon (Georgia) shortly before joining the Packers. Macon lost both games and their fans were so enraged with Hubbard that he had to be escorted from the park by local police. One irate fan then jumped on the running board of Hubbard's car and tried to put him in a headlock. The police interceded, most likely to the relief and future health of the irate fan.

Tony Walter

Dr. Webber Kelly, president of the Packers Football Corporation. (Photo courtesy of the Green Bay Press-Gazette)

In late July, the growing number of stockholders in the Packers Football Corporation met and elected Dr. Webber Kelly as its president. They also set a goal to dramatically increase the number of season ticket holders so the corporation's consistently lean resources would have some relief.

The *Press-Gazette* beat the drum for the ticket drive, pointing out in an editorial that "the Packers are Green Bay's greatest asset so far as national advertising is concerned."

Statewide, the Wisconsin Senate voted down a proposed amendment that would have permitted the state to get into the business of manufacturing and selling alcohol. Some legislators argued that the Volstead Act only applied to individuals and private corporations. But it didn't work.

The nation's economy was still enjoying some of the residuals of a decade that featured economic progress. Nevertheless, some warned that clouds were gathering over the banking and investment skies, and that the boom of the Roaring '20s was on fragile financial footing.

Residents learned that the divorce rate in Brown County was 15.9 for every 100 marriages. That was a lot better than Douglas County in the far north, which saw 77.5 of every 100 marriages fail. But it couldn't match Kewaunee County, where only 4.2 of 100 marriages broke up.

Green Bay's city council decided it was time to pave Kellogg, Elm, Jackson, Grignon and St. George streets to keep up with the expanding use of automobiles. It also approved putting traffic lights at the intersection of Walnut and Washington, the busiest place in town.

There was football news again on August 27. The Packers signed a running back and receiver named John McNally, who previously played for Pottsville. He came to Green Bay when that franchise folded. McNally didn't play under his given name. He played as Johnny Blood after the title of a Rudolph Valentino movie, *Blood and Sand*, and found work immediately in Green Bay with Schuster Construction.

Legendary status loomed for Blood.

With Hubbard and Blood both under contract, the Packers made one more major move. They signed August (Mike) Michalske, a former Penn State guard who also had labored for the New York Yankees football team. Michalske was described as the best guard in the National Football League. He was familiar to Lambeau and the Packers players

The Packers signed two future hall of famers in 1929 with the addition of the versatile Johnny (Blood) McNally (above) and guard Mike Michalske. (Photos courtesy of Neville Public Museum of Brown County)

because he helped the underdog Yankees team play the Packers to a 0-0 tie in November of 1928. He was known as the "Trafton Tamer" because of his domination of Chicago Bears talented center George Trafton, who would go into the Pro Football Hall of Fame in 1964, along with Michalske.

Late August and early September brought the signings of several veteran players. One was halfback Eddie Kotal, who played football for Lawrence College in nearby Appleton. Kotal also played third base and managed the Appleton city baseball team, and played professional basketball in the winter months.

Another veteran Packer signed to play again. LaVern (Lavvie) Dilweg agreed to a contract for a third season with the team. Dilweg, a future U.S. Congressman, is one of just two players voted in 1969 to the NFL 1920s All-Decade Team who is somehow not in the Pro Football Hall of Fame. Interestingly, the other is former Chicago Bear Hunk An-

A meeting of two legends

In the early 1980s, I experienced something that anyone absorbed in Packers history would have coveted. Told that Johnny Blood was visiting Green Bay and spending the night at the Beaumont Hotel, I called him and set up an interview.

He greeted me at his hotel room door, dressed splendidly in a smoking jacket and strikingly handsome for a man in his early eighties. He spoke kindly of his friendship with my father and told some stories about his playing days with the Packers.

Midway through the interview, there was a knock on the door and in walked Mike Michalske, the man who entered the Packers' orbit the same month in 1929 as Blood. Their respect and admiration for each other was obvious.

The dashing Johnny (Blood) McNally during his post-football days. (Photo courtesy Green Bay Press-Gazette)

For me, it was time to bask in the moment, to listen as two men who were among the very best at their craft shared memories of a time that was generally unknown to fans of my generation and generations that followed.

Blood, known for his non-football reputation in his bachelor days, talked briefly about "stewardesses in New York," but I decided to take notes about his on-the-field life instead.

Then it was time for me to leave – to let football legends have their reunion – hoping that as they neared the end of their lives, they realized the might of their contributions to Green Bay Packers history. Two years later, both men had died.

Dedicated students of pro football history know the level of skill brought to the game by John McNally and August Michalske.

derson, who played a game for the Packers in 1921 under an assumed name because he was still a member of the Notre Dame team.

Fire and politics welcomed the post-Labor Day world of Wisconsin.

The worst forest fires in twenty years raged through Oconto and Forest counties to the north, with one family managing to stay alive by covering themselves with wet blankets as their home burned around them.

Money and politics butted heads. The first hearing was held in a civil suit filed against Gov. Walter Kohler for alleged violation of the Corrupt Practices Act. His opponents claimed he benefitted from a $100,000 donation that helped him get elected.

Phillip LaFollette was one of the plaintiffs, and so was William T. Evjue, publisher of the *Capital Times* in Madison. Evjue spoke to the Federal Trades Council meeting at Bay Beach in Green Bay, saying "the government of Wisconsin was put on the auction block last fall and sold for $250,000."

He claimed that organized wealth was dictating governmental policies.

The *Press-Gazette* editorial page wasn't subtle in its reaction to Evjue's address:

> "The publisher of the *Madison Capital Times* delivered a characteristic demagogic speech in Green Bay on the observance of Labor Day. It was the kind of misrepresentation and hokum that politicians expect organized labor to applaud. This particular speaker indulged in the usual generalities about the degradation of the poorer classes in the United States, the menace and wrongs of great wealth and the claim that people are headed toward economic slavery, in fact most of them being now in that condition.
>
> Prosperity he described is a myth and delusion. It is strange how people will give credence to such tomfoolery when they are confronted on every hand by facts which disprove it."

It wasn't a safe holiday weekend on the streets and highways, with several accidents. At the same time, a proposed law to put a 45-mile-per-hour speed limit on county roads was vetoed by Kohler.

British statesman Winston Churchill was touring the western United States when he was asked about his opinion of Prohibition. He said the British are voluntarily drinking less and criminal convictions have been cut in half.

"The British have a deep-rooted prejudice against compulsion," he said. "We realize 1,000,000 pound sterling a year from our liquor taxes, which I understand you give to your bootleggers."

The Packers held their first organized practice on Sunday afternoon, September 9. More than 2,000 fans turned out at the Joannes Park field to watch the workout.

The season schedule was unusual, although common in those first couple decades of Packers history, in that the first seven games were to be played in Green Bay and the remaining six games on the road. Travel time and costs required that.

The Dayton Triangles came to Green Bay first. Hubbard still hadn't arrived three days before the game, sending a telegram to Lambeau that he was "unavoidably delayed."

The Packers won anyway, 14-0. The game drew more than 5,000 people and was highlighted by a Lewellen punt from the Packers' 20-yard line to the Triangles' end zone. It also featured sterling play from Michalske, who sports editor Arthur Bystrom wrote "broke through on nearly every play."

The next opponent was the Chicago Bears, promising to be a true test for the upgraded Packers. They weren't.

***

September 29, 1929
"In aft saw Packers slaughter Red Grange and the Chicago Bears, 23-0."

***

Bystrom's game story lead was:

"How the mighty have fallen. The Chicago Bears, once powerful and ferocious rulers of the Midwest professional football kingdom, have undergone an evolution and today are seeking shelter in the lowlands, and the Green Bay Packers are perched upon the vacated throne."

The 23-0 Packers victory was the most lopsided loss in Bears history, and was fueled by two of the new Packers – Molenda and Blood. It was a Bears team that included the great Red Grange, but was decisively overmatched.

The *Press-Gazette's* Monday editorial went for superlatives:

"The 13,000 spectators who were so fortunate as to witness yesterday's game between the Packers and Chicago Bears saw the greatest and most perfect football machine they have ever seen. They saw a brand of football played by the Packers that would have beaten any team in the world. The Bears were simply swept off their feet, outclassed and demoralized. Even the celebrated Mr. Grange did not seem to know what it was all about.

"The country wonders how a town of 40,000 people can maintain a team of such caliber and of national reputation. The answer is quite simple. It has been done by sound and clean business and professional management. This has created a civic interest and popular loyalty to the team quite analogous to college football spirit.

"Without a doubt, we have the strongest team ever assembled here and an excellent chance for the championship. The value of Packer football to Green Bay is very real. It is just such events as was staged yesterday that make Green Bay stand out as a city."

From domination one Sunday, the Packers found tension and relief the next Sunday. For Lewellen, there was redemption. Facing the Chicago Cardinals at City Stadium, the Packers trailed 2-0 at halftime. Lewellen fumbled twice near the goal line, but a Red Dunn field goal and a short touchdown run by Lewellen in the fourth quarter gave the Packers a 9-2 victory.

***

October 6, 1929
"Packers beat the Cards, 9-2 — four straight."

***

Wrote Bystrom:
"Fumble, the nemesis of every football player, camped on the trail of the Green Bay Packers here Sunday and until the final whistle, it was anybody's game. That turn of fate fumble met the Packers star halfback at every turn. But Lewellen, like Sampson of old, broke the chains of the jinx and brought in the single touchdown that was marked on the board for the afternoon's work."

Next to visit Green Bay were the Frankford Yellow Jackets, a team from the northeastern section of Philadelphia that had won the championship three years earlier.

The Yellow Jackets were two years away from the decline that would have them give up their franchise, later to be obtained by Bert Bell, who then established the Philadelphia Eagles.

The Packers prevailed 14-2 before about 10,000 fans, with Eddie Kotal and Lewellen getting the touchdowns. The only Frankford score came on a safety when the snap from center went over Blood's head and through the end zone. The game was stopped early in the first period so the Frankford backfield players could change their jerseys. The ones they were wearing were too similar to the Packers' jerseys, and players and officials were having difficulty.

Packers management passed the hat during the game and collected $302 to help pay for the Lumberjack Band to travel to Chicago for the next game there against the Bears.

A *Press-Gazette* editorial cheered on the Packers:

> "By defeating Philadelphia, the Packers prove themselves the greatest football team in America at the present moment. This is some distinction for a town of 40,000 people. For the rest of the season, two things are needed. One is morale, the will to win. The other is that indefinable something that puts star players in any contest on his game.
>
> "For the first time we have a really championship team. Go out and win it, men. The town is loyally and enthusiastically with you."

***

October 13, 1929
"In aft with Dad and Marion to see Packers beat Frankford Yellowjackets, 14-2. That's 5 in a row."

***

The final home game followed and it wasn't close. The Packers blanked the Minneapolis Red Jackets 24-0, a team led by back Herb Joesting. Molenda and Lewellen each scored twice, with Lewellen's final TD coming on a 30-yard interception return.

A columnist for the *Minneapolis Star Tribune* took a more positive view:

> "You notice that Herb's Red Jackets took a 24-0 lacing from the Green Bay Packers. Well, you needn't waste any sympathy on Herb and his heroes because they were playing the best team in the National league, and if they had won, it would have taken the pennant in the upset league.
>
> "The Packers have a mighty team with the best aerial attack anywhere and a backfield that can call upon Lewellen, Kotal, Red Dunn, Bo Molenda, Cully Lidberg and one or two other sociable souls."

October 20, 1929
"Guess Dot had a nice time at the party —-she said so, anyway. In aft she went with Dad, Marion and me to see Packers beat Minneapolis Redjackets 24-0. No date in eve."

(Dad was devoted to his fraternity at Lawrence, and he and others in Beta Sigma Phi were stunned when two fraternity brothers disappeared while fishing on Lake Winnebago.)

October 22, 1929
"My 22nd birthday. Celebrated by taking two 6-week exams. Folks down for supper. Horrible accident – believe Ted Bolton and Cast Roth are drowned in lake."

October 23, 1929
"Up at 4 o'clock – out in storm all day looking for Bolton and Roth. No luck. The boys are gone, I guess. Two wonderful fellows."

***

The Packers went on the road for the first time, traveling to Comiskey Park in Chicago for a rematch with the Cardinals. This time, the talented Ernie Nevers, who missed the Cardinals' game in Green Bay, would be on the field. He almost succeeded in giving the Packers their first defeat of the season.

Green Bay scored in the second period on Lewellen's 5-yard run and Dunn's extra-point kick that would prove critical. The Cardinals came alive in the final ten minutes of the game. Nevers threw a TD pass, but his conversion kick sailed to the right and the Packers escaped with a 7-6 victory.

The Associated Press writer covering the game sent this lead to the story that went throughout the country: "The Green Bay Packers added another scalp..."

Political correctness hadn't been invented yet in 1929.

An interesting sidelight to the Packers' trip to Chicago was a statement released by the team's administration and published in the *Press-Gazette* for the benefit of fans traveling to the Windy City.

It read: "The Packers will be staying at the Cooper-Carlton Hotel and as is customary most of the fans will want to visit them at their Chicago home. For those who are interested in saving a few dollars in taxicab fares, the team management announced the following route to the hotel. Take a taxicab or Parolee bus from either the Union Station or Northwestern terminal to the Van Buren station of the Illinois Central. Take any Express to fifty-third street which is just a block and a half from the Cooper-Carlton."

It's a customer service practice gone the way of morning milk delivery.

An unnamed fan sent a letter to the newspaper in mid-October, applauding the team's success to that point and offering a suggestion.

"Couldn't it be improved?" he wrote. "Well, I should say so. Build up for the future. Connie Mack will tell you this in baseball. He has always a yearling on hand to replace any player who is showing a downhill course. Did you know that there is no Green Bay player with the Packers? There is one youngster though that is from Green Bay but he was just in uniform. Got in one game for a few plays but would not be given the ball to carry."

Football wasn't the only news that October. The fight over Prohibition raged on with no final resolution. Belle Ady of Sparta, state director of Social Morality & Purity in Literature and Art, spoke to the Women's Christian Temperance Union and challenged her audience.

"God gave the womanhood of America the ballot to help hold Prohibition," she said. "In 1930, will you vote for beer with poverty, sickness and death, or milk with health, happiness and wealth?"

She was preaching to the choir. In time, the choir would be outvoted.

Retired Gen. Billy Mitchell continued his campaign to awaken the military to the importance of a future air corps. He used a national radio broadcast to strongly criticize the country's War and Navy departments, predicting that the next war would be controlled by submarines and airplanes, and said the U.S. has "but a paltry few airplanes."

Addressing the issue of the War and Navy departments being left to oversee the buildup of an air corps, Mitchell said, "You might as well try to develop electric lights in a candle factory."

Speaking of airplanes, a short item on an inside page of the *Press-Gazette* during the first week of October told how a local youth was commissioned a 2nd lieutenant in the air corps. Just a month later, Austin Straubel was forced to parachute from 2,000 feet when his Army plane caught on fire over Michigan. The event qualified him for the Caterpillar Club, a fraternity of Army, Navy and Air Mail pilots who made forced parachute jumps. The club included Charles Lindbergh and Henry Stimson.

Thirteen years later, Straubel became the first Green Bay aviator killed in World War II and had Green Bay's airport named after him.

October wasn't over before events occurred that would change the world forever. The collapse of the stock market led to panic among investors, with few recognizing the impact it would have over the next decade and for generations beyond.

People scurried to find optimism. Dr. Julius Klein, assistant secretary of commerce, voiced the official Washington mantra that American business need expect no adverse result from the collapse of the stock market.

Wisconsin Gov. Walter Kohler said the market mess would actually be a good thing because it would drop prices and stimulate home building.

"As one who never speculates, I look at the situation from a business viewpoint and I believe the country as a whole is sound and that the readjustment will in the end be beneficial. In fact, it will help some industries."

There was caution from the *Press-Gazette* editorial page:

> "The chaos in the stock market is something to be reckoned with. Possibly we may expect a slight slowing down of industry and commerce, but there is no reason for fearing it will be permanent or extensive. Basically, the country is in too prosperous a condition to suffer a serious reaction. It is wholly unlikely that a demoralized stock market will have any grave effects except to the losers in the great national pastime of speculation."

John Rose, president of Kellogg Citizens Bank, said similar things:

"I do not expect business to be affected in the least by what has taken place on the stock market," he said. "Business and speculation are entirely separate. There is a possibility that money will be cheaper but that is the only effect on business that I can see. It is a notable fact that only two insignificant financial institutions were forced to suspend. That indicates that there is a tremendous amount of money in the country. Twenty-five years ago everybody would have been dragged down with it."

Syndicated columnist David Lawrence predicted on November 6 that the stock market chaos would have no long-term effect:

> "The banks will have ample funds for commercial purposes and deposits of banks are likely to increase materially. In fact, reports already show substantial increases in deposits. The sincere confidence here to the continued growth and prosperity of the country is really undiminished."

How could they have known?

Tragedy struck close to home when two Lake Michigan steamers collided in the fog twenty miles offshore from Port Washington, claiming seventeen lives.

Controversy in college football included the decision by the president of New York University to support his football coach's decision to bench star halfback Dave Myers, an African-American, for the team's game at Georgia.

A New York congressman took umbrage in a letter to the president:

"For Coach Meehan to bench Myers in deference to southern racial prejudice is a slap in the face to good sportsmanship and places you, your faculty and NYU opprobrium. (censure)."

Meanwhile, the Packers took their perfect record to Minneapolis for a return game with the Red Jackets the first Sunday of November. It didn't go as easily as their first meeting in Green Bay, but the Packers won 16-6 with Red Dunn passing to Johnny Blood for one score and Verne Lewellen connecting with Lavvie Dilweg for another.

Milwaukee native LaVern (Lavvie) Dilweg was a star end for the Packers from 1927-34. (Photo courtesy of Neville Public Museum of Brown County)

A visit to Wrigley Field and Halas's Bears followed, and it was a colorful rematch. Halas set 2,000 seats aside in the bleachers for Packers fans, charging them $1.50 apiece.

The Packers won 14-0 in a drizzly rain, with Hurdis McCrary scoring both touchdowns. But Dunn suffered a dislocated shoulder, Michalske missed parts of the game after being knocked out, and Hubbard was ejected when he punched the Bears' Bill Fleckenstein. Statistics in the *Chicago Tribune* credited Lewellen with a 75-yard punt.

Grange didn't play and the late stages of the game were played in semi-darkness since Wrigley didn't have lights.

***

November 10, 1929
"Church with Dot in a.m. In aft saw Packers-Chi Bears game over grid-graph. Packers won, 14-0."

***

The *Press-Gazette* felt compelled to dash rumors that the newspaper was controlling the grid-graph that sent the play-by-play of the Packers' road games to the city, which was shared with fans at the Columbus Club. Editors also denied reports that they tried to prevent radio station WGN in Chicago from broadcasting the Bears game. They said they attempted to find out if it would be aired and were told that Bears management refused permission to WGN.

The grid-graph flashed the play-by-play on a screen minutes after a play occurred so fans at the Columbus Club in downtown Green Bay could follow the action. At the same time, vaudeville acts and the Lee Smith Orchestra provided entertainment.

A third game against the Cardinals, again at Comiskey Park in Chicago, had Lambeau concerned because injuries were piling up. In fact, for the first time in the 1929 season, Lambeau inserted himself into the game to give Verne Lewellen a breather.

It was a 12-0 victory for the Packers, with Lavvie Dilweg catching two touchdown passes, one from Johnny Blood on a fake field goal. Blood was also a defensive star, intercepting Ernie Nevers three times.

***

November 17, 1929
"Packers beat the Cardinals, 12-0. That team can't lose."

***

So the stage was set for what would be the Packers' biggest game ever. It would take place at the Polo Grounds in New York against a Giants team that had won every game except one, and that was a tie.

Prior to leaving Green Bay, the Packers' board of directors hosted the team at a private banquet at the Beaumont Hotel. The public wasn't invited to the affair that featured talks by Andrew Turnbull, Jerry Clifford, and Lambeau.

One of the conversation topics was a column written by P.R. Reddy Gallagher of the *Denver Post* that was reprinted, in part, in the *Press-Gazette:*

> "Despite the protests of the great army of collegiate authorities, professional football is here to stay. Although there is no pro team west of Chicago, interest is picking up in the game, even in our own Rocky Mountain region.
>
> "A Denver friend of mine now in the east for the football season, recently saw the Green Bay, Wis. Packers, at present tied for the leadership of league play. Never particularly enthusiastic over the professional's play, he changed after he saw Green Bay. He wrote me they could spot the best college team three touchdowns and still beat them."

The Packers departed by train three days before the game and were treated to a banquet by the Milwaukee Road at the Schroeder Hotel in Milwaukee. They then traveled to Chicago and Pittsburgh, finally arriving in New York on Saturday morning.

Dr. Webber Kelly, president of the Packers, initially didn't intend to make the trip to New York, but was persuaded to accompany the team because of the slew of injuries.

The Giants were led by Benny Friedman, the former Michigan quarterback who had established himself as the premier passer in the pro league. The team's only non-victory was a scoreless tie against the Orange Tornadoes, a team out of Newark that played just two seasons in the league.

Oddsmakers put the Giants as a 6-5 favorite, influenced, no doubt, by their 34-0 dismantling of the Bears the previous week and the fact they had outscored their opponents 204-29 up to that point. The *New York Daily News* hyped the game on its sports pages, although it incorrectly identified the Packers' premier guard as Mike Michaeleske.

The game was billed as Benny Friedman Day in New York, and some of the gate receipts were going to go to the Young Men's Philanthropic League, which he supported. About one dozen fans from Green Bay paid the $79.60 roundtrip train ticket fee to attend the game. Fans in Wisconsin would be able to get updates through WTMJ in Milwaukee. Pat Gannon of the *Milwaukee Journal* planned to be at the game and would wire play-by-play to Russ Winnie and Ollie Kuechle in Milwaukee, and they would broadcast them.

It was a drizzly day in New York and 25,242 fans turned out to watch the game. The Packers took a 7-0 lead in the first period when

Verne Lewellen threw a 4-yard scoring pass to Hurdis McCrary, who then kicked the extra point. The Giants scored in the third period when Benny Friedman passed to Tony Plansky for the touchdown, but Friedman's kick was wide when he was rushed by several Packers.

The Packers then marched 80 yards down the field, with Bo Molenda scoring on a short run and then kicking the extra point. With two minutes remaining in the game, the Packers scored again, this time Johnny Blood crossed the goal line. According to Calhoun, who covered the game for the *Press-Gazette,* Blood shouted, "Make them like it!" as he scored.

Calhoun wrote that it was "the most notable victory the Green Bay Packers have ever scored on the professional football gridiron."

New York Daily News sportswriter C.A. Lovett wrote:

> "Pro football's irresistible force met the game's reputedly immovable object at the Polo Grounds yesterday afternoon and half of the old bromide was proven. It was Benny Friedman Day, according to the advance notices, but it was Verne Lewellen Day and Bo Molenda Day and Hooks McCrary Day and Johnny Blood Day when the summaries were completed."

Harold Burr of the *Brooklyn Daily Eagle* wrote:

> "The Green Bay Packers brought a giant human can-opener of five prongs to the Polo Grounds yesterday. It punched holes and pried through the Giant line like steel cutting tin. Those husky forwards from Wisconsin were always bearing down on the hectored and harried Benny Friedman, spoiling his forward passing game before he could get it started."

Dr. Kelly sent a post-game telegram to the *Press-Gazette*: "We made them look like amateurs. We could not be stopped."

The Packers' Red Dunn, who had to sit out the game because of injury, wrote a mini-column for the *Press-Gazette* the next day:

> "Well, I sat on the bench yesterday and saw our Packers hand the Giants the finest football lesson they could have. Every now and then I would look at Eddie Kotal and wink. You know, Eddie and I are nursing some splinters due to something that happened when those nasty Bears forgot to be gentlemen.
>
> "Several times I looked at Capt. Lambeau wondering if he

was going to shoot the works. But all he did was to give me a stony stare, and not once did he say, 'Get out there and warm up.'"

***

November 24, 1929
"Church - Episcopal in a.m. Dot was there, but didn't see her to speak to. In aft saw Polygraph of Packer game - Green Bay 20, New York 6. Saw vaudeville in eve and came back to Appleton on bus."

***

One day later, an unnamed writer for the *Stevens Point (Wis.) Journal* penned a column that looked at the game and the Packers in a broader perspective:

"Professional football, after the impetus given it by Red Grange's recruiting, had a slump for a year or two. It was not strong financially last season. But it has shown a comeback this fall.

"The Bay Packers victories have brought the game to high esteem in this state. There is a place for the paid game. It will take organization and all that, but there may come a day when professional football will provide the safety valve which college amateur ball now does not have in the efforts of facilities to deflate the bubble which the gridiron sport has blown up so far as to overshadow the main purpose of having colleges and universities.

"When that day comes, college football may occupy a spot on the athletic stage comparably to that which college baseball now holds."

The victory motivated the *Press-Gazette* to establish what it called a Championship Fund, asking subscribers to help raise $5,000 to be distributed to the players.

"No event in many years has brought so much pleasured satisfaction to Green Bay as the victory of the Packers over the New York Giants, and probably winning of the Professional Football League championship. It was one of the greatest football games ever played. In distinguishing themselves, the Packers have distinguished Green Bay.

"The Press-Gazette believes this is an opportune moment to demonstrate in a substantial way the town's appreciation and loyalty to the boys of this splendid football team."

The fund would be administered by Andrew Turnbull, and the newspaper donated the first $200.

The Packers stayed in the East to prepare for their Thanksgiving Day game against the Frankford Yellow Jackets at their suburban Philadelphia stadium. The team practiced at Atlantic City before checking into the Adelphia Hotel in Philadelphia on the eve of the game. It happened to be the same place that fans of Cornell University were staying in preparation for their team's holiday game against Penn.

The pro game ended in a scoreless tie, but the Packers left the field angry.

Wrote Calhoun: "The Packer players were hot under the collar at the close of the game as they figured that they had been gypped in the time. Every one of the players was willing to bet their season's salary that there was at least four minutes to go. Lewellen just a few plays earlier had asked about the time and was informed there were seven minutes left."

But after Kotal caught a pass to put the Packers on the Frankford 9-yard-line, the whistle blew to end the game.

The *Philadelphia Inquirer* reporter wrote that the Packers had more to gain by the tie:

"It ended as it started. It was the first time any team had cut into Green Bay's slate of victories. By the tie, the Packers virtually clinched the league crown and Frankford was eliminated, unless an unexpected and normally impossible number of upsets occur in the handful of remaining games."

Interestingly, on the same day, the Chicago Cardinals defeated the Chicago Bears 40-6. Nevers scored every point for the Cardinals with six touchdowns and four extra points, a single-game record that still stands.

It was Nevers, a future shoo-in hall of famer, who praised the Packers a week later in an interview with the *New York Graphic.*

"The only team in our league I take my hat off to is Green Bay," Nevers said. "We're better than the rest of them and every time we lost to Green Bay it was close. The classiest player of the year is Michalske of Green Bay. He isn't a flashy back. He's a guard and a wonder. There's nobody like him on the college or professional field today."

There were two more games on the schedule, both on the road, and both 25-0 shutouts by the Packers over the Providence Steam Rollers and the Chicago Bears.

***

December 1, 1929
"Church in a.m. Saw Dot but not to speak to. Dinner over at Marion's and then listened to Packer game - Green Bay 25, Providence 0. Supper at home. With Mother to see Will Rogers in 'They Had to See Paris.'"

December 8, 1929
"Slept too late for church. In aft Packers won title in national football league by beating Bears 25-0. Great team, there. In eve Dot and I saw Joan Crawford in "Untamed." Dot and I are about through."

***

The championship theirs, the Packers and their fans basked in national attention as they never had before.

National columnist Frank Menke's piece was printed throughout the country:

> "Those who scatter their enthusiasm between collegiate and pro football are arising these days and proclaiming like this: 'The greatest team ever assembled together is the Packers, a professionalized group of former collegians who represent Green Bay, Wisconsin, in the pro big league.
>
> "And that comes from persons who have been squinting at gridiron activities for three decades and have seen all that Harvard, Yale, Princeton, Carlisle, Pittsburgh, Notre Dame and all the others had to offer in the way of matchless elevens.
>
> "These hurrahs for the Green Bay Packers do not hedge their statements with ands, ifs and buts. They leap constantly to the rostrum and repeat – The greatest ever. They will tell you with fevered words that when it comes to possession of brains, speed, power and football skill, there never was anything like these Packers.
>
> And what a machine the Packers became, one that is the super team of pro football history, and one which the old and the young, the expert and the near expert, point to with enthusiastic gestures and declare: The greatest football team of all time."

It was heady stuff for the Packers, who had enjoyed a welcome home parade through downtown Green Bay after returning from Chicago.

Congratulations came in from many places, including a telegram from Bears founder George Hallas, who wired: "The West is proud of the Green Bay Packers – but look out next year."

The team was given a celebration banquet at the Beaumont Hotel that was attended by 400 people. The players were each given $220 raised from the *Press-Gazette's* Championship Fund, pocket watches purchased by the Packers Corporation, and a framed team picture compliments of Otto Stiller. The Bohemian Bakery and Walnut Street Bakery provided giant cakes.

Richard Malia served as toastmaster and made reference to two other Green Bay success stories.

"A girl (Lucille Meusel) went forth from Green Bay and returned a member of the Chicago Opera Company. A boy (Jim Crowley) went out and returned one of the Four Horsemen. And now our Packers have come back from foreign fields, champions of the National football league."

My Grandpa Minahan spoke of the time the state legislature tried to outlaw football but failed, he said, because "football is truly American, representing strength, sportsmanship and vigor, and is here to stay."

The *Press-Gazette's* Andrew Turnbull recalled the early financial struggles of the team, saying there was a time he had to go into the team's locker room at halftime and ask the players to play for half their salaries because money was so tight.

Lambeau was looking ahead.

"It is going to take a lot of hard work, energy and loyal support of the fans to give Green Bay another championship next year," he said, noting that every past league champion finished in the second division the following year. "We're going to break that precedent."

One night later, the team was hosted for another banquet at Kaap's Bakery on Washington Street.

But there was one more commitment to meet. While the Packers were still in the East, Tennessee millionaire grocer Clarence Saunders negotiated an exhibition game over long distance phone. Saunders, who introduced self-serve groceries through his Piggly Wiggly chain, had formed a football team in Memphis called the Tigers who played an independent schedule of teams in the South. The Tigers hosted the Packers a week after the final victory over the Bears.

Calhoun watched the Packers practice a couple times before leaving for Memphis.

"The players managed to get in two good practice sessions Thursday and Friday afternoon at the field in the rear of East High School," he wrote. "The way they steely stepped through plays indicates that the Memphis eleven will have a real task trying to stop them."

But the unexpected happened. Saunders' Memphis Tigers won, 20-6, a game that has been mostly lost in the telling of the Packers first championship season. After all, it didn't count.

Observers said the Packers were listless.

Oliver Kuechle, a *Milwaukee Journal* sportswriter, wrote a column two days later that implied the Packers got caught up in celebrating their championship:

> "Out of Green Bay, where the shock of Sunday's defeat still has the faithful fans tearing their hair, now comes the word that the Packers did dance most of the last week. They danced, so to speak, from the time they were feted at the great civic demonstration of appreciation last week Tuesday for their victory in the National league football race. Somewhat weary, tis said, they boarded the train Saturday morning for Memphis. And even after that, some accounts have it, they danced again.
>
> "No wonder they paid. In this case, the Memphis Tigers were the fiddlers, 11 of them, one for every Packer who danced and every one of them wanted his pay, and failing to get it, took it right out of Green Bay's hide... According to all accounts of the game by those who saw the Packers in their league contests and in this exhibition, they were no more themselves than night is day. Even the great Verne Lewellen, whose punting all through the National league season was one of the high spots of the season, was out kicked most of the way by a little fellow named Moore from Rolla School of Mines in Missouri."

Lambeau said injuries and the weather were the major factors. Hurdis McCrary broke an arm, Lavvie Dilweg was knocked unconscious, Jim Bowdoin dislocated a knee, and Carl Lidberg suffered a broken nose.

"The weather was the greatest handicap," Lambeau said. "Before the players took the field they were perspiring and before the game ended they were so weakened they could barely run. The temperature was 77 and the crowd at the game sat in their shirt-sleeves. The game was the roughest we have ever played."

He said Johnny Blood wasn't scheduled to play because of an arm injury, but was pressed into action anyway.

The Packers, My Dad and Me

Green Bay Packers 1929 NFL Championship Team

Front row: Curly Lambeau, Paul Minnick, Bo Molenda, Roy Baker, Eddie Kotal, Red Dunn, Dick O'Donnell, Mike Michalske, Bill Kern, Whitey Woodin, Carl Lidberg.
Top Row: Cal Hubbard, Hurdis McCrary, Tom Nash, Bernard Darling, Claude Perry, Red Smith, Verne Lewellen, Roger Ashmore, Johnny (Blood) McNally, Jim Bowdoin, Lavvie Dilweg, Jug Earp. (Stiller photo courtesy Green Bay Press-Gazette)

A *Press-Gazette* editorial didn't take the setback too seriously:

"The fans should not take too much to heart the debacle at Memphis. It is not at all a serious problem. In the first place, the Packers were not playing this exhibition game on their hook. They did not appear under the auspices of management of the football corporation. It was their own private expedition.

"They achieved what they set out to accomplish, namely winning of the professional league championship. What happened at Memphis cannot detract from this. There is only one thing of concern and that is 1930."

When the All-Pro team was announced (then called the All-American team) Verne Lewellen, Lavvie Dilweg, and Mike Michalske were named to the first team, while Bill Kern, Jug Earpe, and Johnny Blood were placed on the second team.

As the curtain came down on the decade, many issues remained fertile. Forces for and against Prohibition remained strong and the long-term effects of the stock market crash were still unknown.

Steel company tycoon Charles Schwab, in a speech in Illinois, referred to the "Wall Street affair," but insisted that U.S. industry was in good shape and forecast wholesome expansion of business.

And the debate over a possible waterway from the Great Lakes to the Atlantic Ocean raged on. Sen. Copeland of New York said only "selfish interests" from wheat growers in the west were in favor of a St. Lawrence seaway, and said it was "out of the question."

It was a pivotal year in so many ways and would define the decade to come.

But the Packers won a championship.

Chapter 5

Better Eskimos

A new decade brought its list of unanswered questions, fears, and changes. For Dad, there only remained his last final exams at Lawrence College, then the continued pursuit of a journalism career, financial stability, beer, and female companionship.

***

January 7, 1930
"Am looking forward to the end of school. Suppose I'll have to start studying pretty soon."

January 22, 1930
"Letter from Dot Davis. In eve dated Dot Augustine. I am always making a dash after a Dot."

(For any of my acquaintances who have labeled my sense of humor as corny, I submit Exhibit #1.)

January 30,1930
"Wrote Canadian history exam, the last one I'll ever have to take. School seems to be over."

February 17, 1930
"Started working at Press-Gazette. Guess it's for good this time. They have me doing features."

April 8, 1930
"Bystrom was sick so had to handle all sports in addition to my own run. Damn near died."

April 11, 1930
"On Bystrom's sports work again, as he is sick. Wish I could hold it for awhile - suppose I'll have those damned features for Monday."

April 26, 1930
"Spent a dateless Saturday night, my first since Jan. 4."

***

The Packers weren't officially named 1929 champions until the team owners met in Dayton, Ohio, the last week of January in 1930. Team schedules were not consistent, with some playing more games than others. The Packers finished 12-0-1, the New York Giants 13-1-1, and the Frankford (Pennsylvania) Yellow Jackets 9-4-5. The vote was unanimous, however, that the Packers had earned the trophy.

Curly Lambeau and Dr. Webber Kelly attended the meeting with representatives from Orange, Providence, Boston, Buffalo, the New York Giants, Stapleton, the Chicago Bears, Chicago Cardinals, Minneapolis, Dayton, and Frankford.

Dr. Kelly was named to the league's executive committee, and the owners voted to allow teams to increase their rosters from nineteen to twenty-two players after their third game, but limiting them to twenty players in uniform.

Many of the Packers players found off-season diversions. Bernard Darling joined the Oshkosh All-Stars pro basketball team organized by his uncle. Cal Hubbard trained to enter pro prize-fighting, and fought to a draw against Ed Platten in a four-round bout at the Columbus Club. Richard "Red" Smith became baseball coach at Georgetown University. Hurdis McCrary landed a job with Schuster Construction in Green Bay.

For some players, full-time jobs signaled the end of their playing careers. Eddie Kotal was hired to be head football coach at his alma mater, Lawrence College in Appleton, Wisconsin. Tom Hearden was named football coach at Racine (Wisconsin) St. Catherine High School. And tackle Bill Kern accepted a job as assistant football coach at the University of Pittsburgh, where he played as a collegian.

***

June 9, 1930
"Probably a red letter day. In a.m. drove to Appleton with Mother and Aunt Lillian for 80th annual Lawrence commencement exercise, but only the first for me. Right home after and on the job."

(Lillian Olmstead was Dad's aunt in name only. Her father was the attending physician at Dad's birth. Lillian's closest friend in 1907 was Jessie Messenger Walter, who didn't survive the day she gave Dad to the world.)

June 20, 1930
"An awful day. Got all tied up with story on British Open golf tourney, which Bobby Jones won. And a man dropped dead at the office, one of the printers."

***

In June, the Packers Corporation held its annual meeting and elected Lee Joannes to succeed Dr. Kelly as president. Jerry Clifford was named vice-president, C.J. O'Connor treasurer, and George Whitney Calhoun again was named secretary. Andrew Turnbull and Charley Mathys were added to the executive committee, with the board of directors also including Ward Black, Ed Schweger, Marcel Lambeau, Lewis Peal, J.H. Golden, H.G. Barkhausen, and H.J. Bero.

Dr. Kelly spoke for the corporation:

"This was the most successful season in the history of the Green Bay Football Corporation," he said. "Financially, the corporation had a good year, our receipts exceeding all previous records. This was due to two factors. First, the weather conditions which prevailed at our home games, and second, to increased attendance."

It was also announced that the Packers would expand the stadium behind East High School from 11,500 to 13,000 seating capacity. The contract was awarded to board member Marcel Lambeau, father of Coach Curly Lambeau.

But all was not rosy that summer. Kelly, who also served as president of the Green Bay School Board, received an anonymous, threatening letter from someone who objected to the board's decision not to renew the contract of East High Principal O.F. Nixon.

The letter read: "Four years ago we warned you to keep out of politics. We have your past record. We still love Nixon and if you love your family, don't delay. Do as we suggest. We are watching you closer than you think. Resign or be picked off like Dist. Atty. Clinton G. Price."

It was signed "K.K.K."

Price was the Juneau County prosecutor who had been acquitted of federal charges of violating the Prohibition Act, and then was assassinated.

Kelly didn't resign and issued the following statement:

"If this kind of persecution is the price one must pay for gratuitous public service undertaken with the city's good as the sole motive, it is all right with me."

Nothing came of the incident.

Green Bay was able to take a bow when a study by Johns Hopkins University listed the city as the second best in the country for cities 30,000-50,000 population in the quality of its services. The survey included public works, protection and welfare. Interesting that Sheboygan, Wisconsin, was rated the best in that population division.

Crime continued to get headlines. In February, an efficient burglar used a glass cutter and padded hammer to cut a six-square-inch hole in the front window of the J. Vander Zanden Jewelers store on North Washington Street and made away with $620 in watches.

Two incidents in August within days of each other showed the ability of some inmates to cleverly escape jail, although none of them had mastered a skill of staying out for long.

A convicted bank robber from Onalaska named Joseph Stemac slipped out of the breakfast line at the Wisconsin State Reformatory in Allouez and managed to scale the west wall, the first such escape in thirty years from the prison.

He tried to rob a man south of the prison by pretending he had a pistol under a sheet he carried, but the ruse didn't work. He then hitched a ride to De Pere and managed to steal a car from a garage. But driving west toward Pulaski, Stemac was spotted by police, engaged in a brief physical struggle, and was promptly returned to the prison.

A couple days later, two inmates at the Green Bay jail – one awaiting trial on rape charges and the other accused of robbery – used hacksaw blades to cut their way to freedom.

Captured a day later, it was discovered that the blades had been hidden in the false soles of their shoes. Back they went as guests of the city of Green Bay.

***

July 11, 1930
"In eve went to see first night baseball game ever played in Green Bay. California Owls lost to Green Sox 4-2. Interesting spectacle."

July 15, 1930
"In eve went on picnic to Bay Beach, went on new roller coaster."

July 22, 1930
"Packers are lining up great team for next fall."

August 11, 1930
"Back on the job at the Press-Gazette, and glad to be there. Finances are in terrible shape - owe $2,000 and no money to pay. What will it be like a year from now?"

August 12, 1930
"Have officially launched economy program - no luxuries from now on - just the three necessities of life - eating, sleeping and dating."

August 13, 1930
"Second day of economy program. Haven't spent a cent. To that matter, haven't a cent to spend. No paycheck until Monday. In aft, accepted part-time job at YMCA, starting Sept. 1 - will get $4.50 per week. That'll help."

September 9, 1930
"Dot A. and I are breaking up. She doesn't know it yet, but think she's tired of me anyway. Heard Sen. Bob LaFollette talk - political speech."

***

The run-up to the 1930 season featured the normal contract signings and a couple minor surprises. Red Dunn, who announced at the 1929 celebration banquet that he was retiring from football – a statement that likely had many of his teammates rolling their eyes – reversed course in mid-summer and signed on for another season.

The team signed former Purdue tackle Elmer "Red" Sleight to take Kern's place in the line, and then added two Green Bay natives. One was halfback Dave Zuidmulder, a Green Bay East graduate. The other was Green Bay West grad Arnie Herber.

Football continued to serve as both a source of entertainment and a timely diversion for residents of Green Bay and the growing Packers fan base. Timely because the impact of a financial depression and increasing business unemployment were becoming evident, even in a community that was holding on to its share of the paper industry.

Despite the agreement the previous year on Germany's reparations for its role in the war, there were increasing signs of unrest in Europe. One of them was the rise of a fascist party in Germany.

The *Green Bay Press-Gazette* made note of it in an editorial in September:

> "Adolf Hitler is causing a commotion in Germany and throughout Europe. Head of the National Socialist Party, the fascists of Germany, he declared that he is out to remake the government of Germany.
>
> "His violent hatred for the republic is expressed in the declaration that a guillotine awaits the men who made the German revolution in 1918 if his party ever gets into power.
>
> "He says he and his companions will adhere to the constitution until they are in power and then they will draft the constitution to suit themselves.
>
> "Germany may fall prey to a bold adventurer with a program like that announced by Hitler, and Hitler may be that adventurer, though we doubt it. Time will have to determine this. There is one quality of the German people that stands in the way of this achievement. It is their inborn common sense and level-headedness.
>
> "A dictator in Germany might for a very brief period have an easy time of it were it not for the very thing Hitler proposes to escape, namely the peace treaty and reparation settlement. France nor any of her allies has anything to fear in the near future from German bad faith. What 20 or 30 years may bring forth is another thing. Hitler can conceivably get Germany into infinite trouble, but he cannot do anything to serve or improve it by the program he disclosed."

The Packers played an exhibition game against the Oshkosh All-Stars, a professional team organized by Lonnie Darling, who said his team would give the Packers the surprise of their lives.

They didn't. As about 5,000 fans looked on, the Packers won 46-0.

Press-Gazette sports editor Art Bystrom pointed out the obvious:

"The Oshkosh All-Stars may be a good football team but it has a lot to learn about the brand of football played by the Green Bay Packers. There's a world of difference between the play of National champions and independent professional squads."

The game featured some impressive play by local players Zuidmulder and Herber, both of whom were playing their first game for the Packers.

***

September 14, 1930
"Got my first taste teaching a Sunday school class. In aft went to first Packer football game - Green Bay 46, Oshkosh 0."

September 15, 1930
"In eve over to office to help with election returns. Voted for Kohler in aft, but he lost to Phil LaFollette, who will be our next governor."

***

The league season started a week later when the Chicago Cardinals came to Green Bay. The occasion included the raising of the championship flag prior to the game, with Cardinals owner Dr. D.J. Jones representing the league, Packers President Leland Joannes, Dr. Kelly, and Turnbull there for the team, and Mayor John Diener for the city.

The Packers won 14-0 on touchdowns by Verne Lewellen and Lavvie Dilweg, and 8,000 fans soaked it all up. Mike Michalske played most of the game with a broken finger, Arnie Herber had a 70-yard punt, and the Cardinals' Ernie Nevers played despite enduring an injury so severe he could barely lift his left leg.

Such was the warrior ways of pro football in that era.

***

September 21, 1930
"In aft with Dad and Marion to see the Packers raise the National league pennant. Then they beat the Chicago Cardinals 14-0."

***

Next to visit were the Chicago Bears, and it was a 7-0 Packers victory. Those in attendance would remember the massive collision during an incomplete pass between Johnny Blood and Red Grange that left the Bears legend temporarily unconscious and having to be removed from the field on a stretcher. He returned to the game, of course.

The Packers passed the hat through the bleachers to raise money to send the Legion Band to Chicago when the team would play at Wrigley Field. They collected $261.75.

***

September 28, 1930
"In aft saw Packers defeat Chicago Bears 7-0. A tough game."

The New York Giants were next, and Friedman, the talented quarterback that Bystrom wrote "throws a football like Lefty Grove of the Athletics throws a baseball."

But the Packers were a touchdown better, winning 14-7 at City Stadium when Blood ran 55 yards after catching a pass from Red Dunn in the fourth quarter. He stiff-armed one defender, and then roared past Friedman in the secondary "like a locomotive going by a tiny town," Bystrom wrote.

Speed, in those days, was identified with trains, apparently.

Portsmouth lost on the same day, so the Packers found themselves alone in first place.

***

October 5, 1930
"In aft went to see Green Bay Packers beat New York Giants 14-7. Johnny Blood made thrilling run."

***

The Frankford Yellow Jackets came to Green Bay a week later. The game was virtually decided in the first period when the Packers scored three touchdowns, one of them on an interception by Dilweg. The game ended 27-12.

***

October 12, 1930
"Ate at Kaap's & then saw Packers beat Frankford, 27-12."

(Grief cut into Dad's life unexpectedly when *Press-Gazette* editor John Kline, his mentor and benefactor, suddenly became ill with what turned out to be pneumonia.)

October 22, 1930
"My 23rd birthday - and neither married nor engaged. Mr. Kline believed dying. Felt sick all day. I never have a happy birthday."

October 23, 1930
"Mr. Kline is dead and I've lost the best friend a fellow ever had. When I go down, I hope I can leave a hole like this. Gloomy day at office."

October 24, 1930
"Sick at heart all day. It's such a loss. In eve called on Mrs. Kline with Mother."

October 26, 1930
"In aft with Billy to see Packers beat Minneapolis 19-0."

October 27, 1930
"Sort of dazed. So much has been happening lately. In a.m. Mr. Kline's funeral - saw him for last time. Out to cemetery then back on job."

***

The schedule had the Packers playing back-to-back games against the Minneapolis Red Jackets, the first one in the Twin Cities. It wasn't a cakewalk, but touchdowns by Lewellen and Bo Molenda accounted for the 13-0 win. Minneapolis failed to complete a single forward pass and finished with just four first downs. Wrote Calhoun:

> "The Green Bay Packers proved to be better Eskimos than the Minneapolis Red Jackets and the freezing temperature that was on tap at Nicolet field Sunday afternoon proved so much to the liking to the national champions that they scampered away with a 13 to 0 win."

Lambeau made only four substitutions in the game, letting most of his starters go all the way, with several playing both offense and defense. Johnny Blood wasn't available, having been hospitalized with a kidney injury sustained in the Giants game.

Minneapolis came to Green Bay a week later, and the result was a near repeat. The Packers won 19-0 and the Red Jackets again didn't complete a pass.

The game also featured breakout performances by local players, as Bystrom wrote:

> "Arnold Herber and Dave Zuidmulder who a few short years ago heard the cheers of Green Bay high school fans, heard the shouts of acclaim by pro football followers for their exploits."

It probably seemed too easy to many fans when the Packers won their seventh straight without a loss the following Sunday, hammering the Portsmouth (Ohio) Spartans 47-13 at City Stadium.

Bystrom reported:

"It would be hard to find a team that completes passes like the Packers completed them Sunday. Seven of nine passes tried were good for yardage. Not bad, when it is considered that no less an authority than Knute Rockne says that a team that completes 35 percent of its passes has a great passing attack."

Seven of nine passes.

There was a scare in the fourth quarter when Michalske had to be carried from the field with what was at first suspected to be a broken ankle. An examination revealed that he only fractured a small bone, but might have to miss a game.

***

November 2, 1930
"In aft saw the Packers trim Portsmouth in a National league game 47-13."

November 4, 1930
"Election day - voted practically straight Democratic ticket. Of course, LaFollette got in."

***

With all home games on their schedule completed, the Packers began their stretch of seven straight road games. The Bears and new running back Bronko Nagurski, recently of the University of Minnesota, were the first opponents. The Packers took an early Saturday afternoon ride on the Milwaukee Road line to Chicago, accompanied by dozens of fans who planned to go to the game and take advantage of Chicago's theater offerings.

The game at Wrigley Field remained close throughout. The Packers scored two touchdowns – one on a Lewellen pass to Blood, the other a Dunn pass to Lewellen – that gave Green Bay a 13-6 lead late in the fourth period. A 25-yard punt return set up the Bears in Packers territory, and Nagurski scored on a short run with just two minutes remaining. But the extra-point kick was wide, and the Packers escaped 13-12 for their ninth straight victory.

Lavvie Dilweg, Elmer Sleight, Cal Hubbard, and Verne Lewellen played the entire game for the Packers, never leaving the field.

***

November 8, 1930
"Took care of the football extra - Calhoun out of town."

November 9, 1930
"In aft heard the Packers play a great game with the Chicago Bears. Green Bay won 13-12. Blood and Dunn saved the game."

November 10, 1930
"Took Mother to see Nancy Carroll in 'Follow Through' also pictures of yesterday's Packer-Bear game."

***

The game was the Packers' twenty-third straight without a loss, a streak only surpassed in NFL history by the Canton Bulldogs (25) in 1921-23, and the Chicago Bears (24) in 1941-43.

But Ernie Nevers ...

He was the Cardinals' head coach and best player, was destined to be in the first Pro Football Hall of Fame class, and still holds the record for the most points in a single game (40).

He led the Cardinals to a 13-6 victory over the Packers on the third Sunday of November at Comiskey Park, scoring one touchdown, throwing for the other, and kicking an extra point.

***

November 16, 1930
"Packers lost for first time since 1928, to Chi Cardinals 13-6."

November 18, 1930
"I am going to work on Calhoun's desk while he's in east with Packers and then am going on the street again."

November 19, 1930
"In eve went over to Art Bystrom's - played bridge and lost $1.35. That will never happen again."

November 20, 1930
"Calhoun left on eastern trip - tomorrow I start the two week grind."

November 21, 1930
"On Calhoun's desk, which means up at 6 a.m. and through at 3:30. Six a.m. is the middle of the night for me."

***

There was little time to brood over the loss as the Packers had the New York Giants on their schedule next. The game was set for the Polo Grounds.

Calhoun, who would make the trip with the team, started pumping up the game right away:

> "The Green Bay Packers went to work at Joannes Park practice his morning in a way that forecasts trouble for the Giants when these clubs meet Sunday afternoon at the Polo Grounds in a game which probably will decide possession of the National league bunting for 1930," he wrote three days before the team boarded the train.

If the Packers were tense, it apparently wasn't evident, at least as far as Johnny Blood was concerned. He woke some of the late-sleeping players with a wet towel, a prank that prompted Red Dunn to chase him down the coach aisle. But Blood went into the next coach car, knowing that Dunn, still in his blue pajamas, wouldn't follow because there were women there.

The game was getting plenty of press in New York, with Mayor Jimmy Walker, ex-Gov. Al Smith, and league president Joe E. Carr all scheduled to attend. Calhoun's story the day before the game was entertaining, at least, and likely made sense to readers at the time:

> "Never before has a postgraduate gridiron fracas stirred up so much interest along Broadway, and Tim Mara, owner of the Giants, who recently had a legal skirmish involving thousand to one Gene Tunney, hopes to make up the difference here Sunday to the tune of a merry turnstile click."

Mara, who had been a bookie, sued Tunney for $410,000, claiming Tunney owed him that as his share of the fight receipts in the championship boxing match against Jack Dempsey. Tunney would eventually settle the case by paying Mara $30,000 three years later.

The Giants won the game 13-6 before 37,000 fans.

November 23, 1930
"Heard Packers get trimmed at New York 13-6."

***

Calhoun's game story was classic "we was robbed." He wrote that the Packers had fifteen first downs to the Giants' nine. But the fact that the Packers had 78 yards in penalties and the Giants just 10 set the tone for the rest of the story he telegraphed to Green Bay:

> "Referee Tommy Hughitt and his associates seemed to spend the majority of their time watching the yellow sweatered Packers. Possibly this color was a bit easier on the eyes than the dirty maroon of the Giants. Anyway, their decisions certainly seemed to be off color and one ruling on a touchdown play, which took away a glorious chance for the Packers to knot the count even drew a Bronx cheer from the spectators."

According to Calhoun, Dunn was penalized for taking a punch at Hughitt. Then, when Bo Molenda scored on a 1-yard run late in the fourth quarter with the Packers trailing 13-6, the score was nullified by head linesman John Reardon, who said both teams were offside. A do-over. Molenda again plunged into the line to what Calhoun thought was a touchdown, "but Hughitt couldn't see it that way."

As players walked off the field after the game, a Packers player yelled at Hughitt.

Calhoun wrote: "Anyway, Sir Thomas couldn't penalize the Packers again because the game was over."

Just the routine game story, 1930 Green Bay style.

The Giants jumped ahead of the Packers in the league standings with their 11-2 record compared to the Packers' 8-2 mark. But there was little time for either team to rest, as each had a Thanksgiving Day game four days later.

The Packers stayed in the East to face Frankford outside Philadelphia, while the Giants traveled over to Staten Island to play the Stapletons.

The Packers scored twice in the final period and beat Frankford 25-7, with Dunn throwing two scoring passes to Blood. Bob Haines, business manager for Frankford, told Packers coaches after the game: "If you don't win the championship again, I'll miss my guess, because I have never seen an outfit which went about touchdown making in such a businesslike way."

November 27, 1930
"Packers beat Frankford 25-7 and are now back in first."

***

The victory was expected, but what wasn't anticipated was a Giants loss to the Stapletons the same day. Staten Island, with budding star and future Hall of Fame inductee Ken Strong leading the way, beat the Giants 7-6, thereby lifting the Packers back into first place.

A third game in a week awaited the Packers as they took their turn against the Stapletons. It was a rout in the rain, with the Packers winning 37-7 and referee Tom Thorpe calling them "the greatest football team I ever laid eyes on."

The Stapletons' only highlight was a brilliant 70-yard touchdown run by Strong, but he was hit by three Packers as he crossed the goal line, broke three ribs, and didn't return.

One Packers highlight was Hubbard catching a touchdown pass from Dunn. Another was Blood catching a Dunn pass, breaking into the open, and walking the final three yards for the score.

When the Packers returned to their New York hotel, they learned that the Giants lost again, this time to the Brooklyn Dodgers 7-6.

With two games left, the Packers stood at 10-2, the Giants 11-4, and Brooklyn 7-3-1.

***

November 30, 1930
"In aft listened to the Packer-Stapleton game which the Packers won, 37-7. New York lost to Brooklyn so Green Bay is close to another pennant."

***

But another game against the Bears at Wrigley Field awaited, and this time the Bears dominated, winning 21-0 for their first victory over the Packers since 1927. Bronko Nagurski and Red Grange were at their best. The Packers went to a huddle system in the second half because they suspected the Bears were familiar with the verbal signals.

***

December 7, 1930
"In aft Packers took beating from Chi Bears 21-0, but N.Y. lost too."

***

Green Bay Packers 1930 NFL Championship Team

Front row: Jim Bowdoin, Ken Radick, Wuert Engelmann, Hurdis McCrary, Red Dunn, Dave Zuidmulder, Merle Zuver, Paul Fitzgibbon, Arnie Herber, Ken O'Donnell, Carl Lidberg
Back Row: Bernard Darling, Whitey Woodin, Bo Molenda, Claude Perry, Tom Nash, Lavvie Dilweg, Cal Hubbard, Red Sleight, Verne Lewellen, Johnny Blood, Jug Earp, Mike Michalske, Curly Lambeau. (Photo courtesy Green Bay Press-Gazette)

With the Giants' season finished and their record of 13-4 on the books, the Packers needed only to avoid a loss in their final game at Portsmouth to repeat as champions. They avoided that loss by tying Portsmouth 6-6, completing their season at 10-3-1 for a .769 percentage, ahead of the Giants' .765.

***

December 14, 1930
"In aft heard football game - Packers 6, Portsmouth 6 - giving Green Bay its second consecutive national championship."

***

Calhoun's game story captured the Packers' celebratory mood, writing "the players dashed to their bus which was to take them on the first lap back to God's country."

But the veteran scribe couldn't resist a reference to the officiating:

> "As usual, the Packers took it on the nose via the penalty route. Two fifteen-yard afflictions came in the last couple of minutes of play and the Packers were mad as hornets but it was so near the close that they just sawed wood and smeared Coach Griffen's outfit all the harder."

The story wandered into interesting diversions. Calhoun noted that Lambeau and Griffen "haven't much use for each other," and added that league president Joe E. Carr "sat in box No. 11 and smoked a brand of cigars called Ruskins."

In-depth reporting ahead of its time.

***

December 15, 1930
"Packers came home in eve and were given great reception."

***

The celebration back in Green Bay featured red flares along the train tracks from De Pere to the Chicago and North Western station, and a parade that carried the team through city streets to a welcome-home fete at the Columbus Club.

A public banquet a night later at the Beaumont Hotel was attended by 295 fans. Most of the players received $200 checks from the fund raised by the *Press-Gazette*, although Dave Zuidmulder, Bill Kern, and Ken Radick were given only $100 each, since they didn't play as much. Property manager Bud Jorgenson was given $50.

The parade of speakers that night was anything but dull. Lambeau paid tribute to Andrew Turnbull, calling him the "all-time, all-American quarterback of the Packers" for his longtime support and promotion of the team.

Mayor John Diener said the greatest need of professional football was fair and impartial officials.

"Until there are honest, impartial officials, the future of professional football is not safe," he said.

Dr. Kelly, the former team president, took issue with a variety of things.

"There is a small body of kickers (fans) who think that every time a football team loses a game, the players must have been drunk the night before or the corporation officials were bribed, but the vast body of fans are loyal in every sense of the word.

"Those people who write communications to the newspapers, and who like to talk about contributions going into the river, and the conflict with a charity, are not fans – they are just people who happen to be in town."

Blood responded to a letter-to-the-editor writer who proposed that the donations sent to the Packer fund be given to the unemployed instead of the players.

"As far as I'm concerned, this is going to the unemployed," Blood said.

He also took issue with a report in the *Press-Gazette* the night before that he told a "somewhat risqué" story at the welcome-home event at the Columbus Club.

Then Blood said he no longer wished to be referred to as the "vagabond" halfback.

He still is.

Lambeau announced that the Packers would not play any post-season games, refuting a Milwaukee newspaper report that the team would play again in Memphis, where it lost the previous year. But several players indicated they planned to join some of the Bears and Cardinals to play an all-star team in St. Louis at the end of the month.

Calhoun's style of Packers coverage was a continuation of his support for the team whose birth he attended. It was hardly unusual in an era when newspapers throughout the country picked sides and chose their coverage accordingly, whether in sports, business, or politics.

The *Press-Gazette's* cheerleading fit comfortably into the form of parochial coverage that considered loyalty to its local interest one of its prime functions.

Turnbull laid the groundwork for the newspaper's treatment that was eventually considered too benevolent in the 1970s. Then the newspaper's business manager, he rallied the financial troops to keep the team afloat in 1922. He also saw the need to promote the team so it wouldn't go the way of the great majority of similar teams that didn't survive the 1920s. Turnbull instructed his sports department to refrain from open criticism of the Packers, fearing any loss of local fan support could lead to the city's team losing its franchise. For Turnbull, it was a business strategy given the potential financial benefits for area businesses, including the *Press-Gazette*.

Turnbull kept his hand in Packers business, serving as corporation president from 1923 to 1928, and as a member of the executive committee or board of directors until 1949. He made certain there was always a *Press-Gazette* voice in the workings of the Packers Corporation.

My grandfather, Victor (V.I.) Minahan, continued the friendly coverage when he became editor in 1930, and his stepson, John Torinus, was on the Packers Board of Directors and later a member of its executive committee. Turnbull's son-in-law, Daniel Beisel, was a longtime member of the team's board of directors. Turnbull's grandson, Michael Gage, became publisher of the *Press-Gazette*, was on the Packers' board of directors, and served as president of the Packers Hall of Fame.

My father became Minahan's son-in-law in 1939, and although he brought a slightly more aggressive form of coverage involving the Packers, adhered to the basic ground rules. In 1939, when the Packers' championship game against the Giants was moved from Green Bay to Milwaukee to take advantage of a larger stadium, the *Press-Gazette* supported the decision despite an outcry from Green Bay residents. In his diary, Dad wrote that he didn't agree with the paper's decision, adding "but orders are orders."

Press-Gazette beat writers Art Daley and Lee Remmel were eventually inducted into the Packers Hall of Fame, both deservedly so. The coverage style changed in the early 1970s under the tutelage of sports editor Len Wagner, with Cliff Christl succeeding Remmel as the beat writer. Remmel became the Packers' publicity director and official team historian.

Other *Press-Gazette* employees worked as press box volunteers for home games.

V.I. Minahan died in 1954, my father in 1959, and Turnbull in 1960. The Minahan family's financial stake in the *Press-Gazette* ended in 1961 in what the family referred to as the "corporate divorce," and the Turnbull/Kline descendants gave up their interest in the *Post-Crescent* in Appleton. Torinus became editor at the *Post-Crescent* and Vic Minahan Jr. became its publisher. My older brother, Mike Walter, served as editor.

My mother, Mary, remained as an editorial writer at the *Press-Gazette* until the early 1980s despite her management role in the Post Corporation.

I preferred not to work where my family had ownership, and was hired as a part-time sports writer at the *Press-Gazette* in 1967. I was hired full-time in 1969, became sports editor in 1977, and served in that and several other positions there until my retirement in 2012.

It is understandable that the public saw the Green Bay Packers and the *Green Bay Press-Gazette* as travelers in the same boat. They were for many years.

Turnbull's contention that criticism of the team and corporation in the first decades of the Packers could have resulted in the loss of the franchise won't be challenged here. He was right, the evidence being all the other city teams couldn't survive without the benefit of promotional support from the local newspaper.

Another title for the Packers was balm for a community that was feeling its way along in the business and unemployment depression gripping the nation. Some were saying it didn't constitute a city-wide problem, but there were ominous signs. The Green Bay Apostolate announced that its 1929 list of families in need had risen to 110 in 1930. Associated Charities saw its case load grow from 84 families to 114 over the same period.

But a University of Wisconsin survey indicated the business drop in Green Bay was the smallest in the state.

***

December 30, 1930
"This year is practically shot, and a helluva year it's been for everybody. Business depression, etc."

Chapter 6

The Way of Cheese Champions

Headlines aplenty helped fill newspapers in 1931.

Notable deaths included Notre Dame football coach Knute Rockne, who died with seven others in a plane crash in Kansas the last day of March, and inventor Thomas Edison, who died in October.

The Empire State Building in New York City was dedicated, Al Capone was sentenced to prison after being convicted of income tax charges, and Pope Pius XII issued an encyclical condemning trial marriage, divorce, and birth control.

Dad continued to focus on what a bachelor did in 1931.

***

January 1, 1931
"Drove up from Oshkosh after party. Bed at 4:50 a.m. That was one wonderful evening. Slept until 1 o'clock. "

January 7, 1931
"Went to see El Brendel in 'Just Imagine,' a picture about life in 1980. I'll be 73 years old then, if I live that long."

January 21, 1931
"Cracked under the strain and lined up date for Friday with Margaret. I've been spoiling for a date with her for weeks."

January 28, 1931
"Spent a peculiar evening wandering around by myself. Saw Constance Bennett in 'Sin Takes a Holiday,' great picture. Did some hot bowling - 166, 204, 242, 231."

January 30, 1931
"Just to show I was sore at Margaret, didn't drop in to see her in the a.m. But in eve cracked under the strain, stopped in and took her home. I seem to be leading a genuine double life. Not the first time."

February 4, 1931
"Went to a fortune teller. I am to marry a widow and have a secret wedding. I will change my profession at 26, and will die at 68 in a foreign port. Will break my toe this spring. All interesting."

February 5, 1931
"Fortune teller told me Bill Meyer is to be killed in accident. Nice for Bill."

February 6, 1931
"Bill hasn't been killed yet."

(Bill Meyer was a close college friend who would serve as a groomsman at Dad's 1939 wedding. When his life ended many years later, it was not in an automobile.)

***

Many Green Bay soft drink parlor proprietors were still using soft drinks as a cover for their ongoing covert alcohol business. With the Eighteenth Amendment still the law of the land, federal agents descended upon the community on a Saturday night in mid-February. As many as fifty agents from Milwaukee and Chicago coordinated simultaneous raids of eleven area establishments, arrested sixteen people, and seized large quantities of whiskey, moonshine, and gin. Fines were paid and little changed in Green Bay's attitude toward Prohibition.

The *Press-Gazette*, in an editorial, mocked the legal process that contributed to the defiance of the liquor law:

> "Prohibition cases give the defendants a lot of mental exercise but not much worry. They seem to proceed upon the theory that all that need be done is to furnish the jury with some sort of sickly pretext for an acquittal.
>
> "There was that case but a while ago of the five men bringing a boatload of beer down through the serene waters of Green Bay. The jury promptly acquitted them after they told their story of how sadly they had been misled by some mysterious

person, unnamed and since unseen, who induced them to walk upon the boat.

"Of course they did not know it carried beer. Of course they had no idea the boat itself was stolen. Most certainly they did not expect the boat would unlawfully sail from Canadian into American waters. Sooner would they have cast themselves into the sea than partake in such an unlawful enterprise."

Local news abounded. In March, Green Bay annexed part of the town of Preble that included 1,500 residents. In May, two vehicles crashed through the barrier on the open Walnut Street Bridge, and three people drowned. The Green Bay School Board decided that its experiment of promoting some students to the next grade level at mid-year wasn't working. Dr. Webber Kelly, president of the board, told PTA groups that the practice was making it difficult for teachers because they had to split their classes into groups, and it didn't benefit high school seniors because they had to wait for the following fall to enroll in college.

The Orpheum Theater underwent a major remodeling when Dr. J. R. Minahan spent $300,000 to demolish most of the old building and construct a new theater that he hoped would attract top vaudeville acts and newly released motion pictures.

There was no longer any point in hiding from the pollution that was filling the area's waterways. In August, prompted by a State Board of Health investigation, the park board closed Bay Beach to swimmers, or at least made it clear that anyone bathing at the beach did so at their own risk.

A report from J.H. Holterby, assistant state sanitary engineer, described the water as "grossly polluted and absolutely unfit for public bathing," detailing the untreated sewage flowing down the Fox River.

"There is no obvious method capable of producing immediate results which can be applied to remedy the pollution existing in Green Bay," he said. "Probably the best solution to the entire problem lies in closing the present beach and developing an artificial pool where sanitation can be definitely controlled."

Green Bay Mayor John Diener said a solution was obvious. "There's nothing to do except build the intercepting sewers."

Meanwhile ...

***

February 9, 1931
"Margaret had date last night. She said she behaved herself. The odds are against it."

February 11, 1931
"This Margaret-Sally combination is driving me nuts. I'll weather it."

February 19, 1931
"Getting plenty fed up with the Press-Gazette. Suppose I don't know when I'm well off."

February 23, 1931
"Back on job and sick of it. The place has changed since Mr. Kline died."

February 27, 1931
"Out to cover fire in Town of Preble. Marge drove up with another fellow - and the fight is on. Sulked around all evening, then drove her home from work. Told her we were all through, but I know better. We're just getting started."

March 1, 1931
"In aft dropped in to Northland to see Marge. She wanted to make up and so did I."

March 10, 1931
"Asked Marge to party Saturday. But we won't go, for in eve I caught her two-timing; petting with Goemans in front of Adeline. She called up and denied it, but she is a liar. I saw her. Just another affair charged up to experience."

March 24, 1931
"In aft saw Marge at hotel but we didn't make up. Both too stubborn, I suppose."

March 25, 1931
"This Margaret fascinates me. Dropped in to see her in eve, hoping to make up, but instead we quarreled. Well, Saturday there's Joan McGillan."

March 27, 1941
"In eve went to see Edmund Lowe in 'Don't Bet on Women.' That's a pretty sound philosophy."

March 29, 1931
"In aft went to Neenah-Menasha where I met Joan McGillan - something new and very attractive."

March 30, 1931
"In eve went to Naval Reserve drill. Am going to re-enlist in the outfit."

March 31, 1931
"Knute Rockne, famous Notre Dame football coach, killed in airplane crash."

April 15, 1931
"My gosh, my hair is turning gray. And I'm only 23 years old. This may be a false alarm but it looks bad."

April 16, 1931
"In eve visited spiritualist medium - got my future lined up. She mentioned that secret marriage again."

April 18, 1931
"Writing some big stories these days, but still getting $25 per week."

April 27, 1931
"In eve went with Bid Gage to see Bela Lugosi in 'Dracula.' And what a thriller that turned out to be. All about vampires."

***

The reality of the country's and world's financial depression and banking crises finally hit home in late May. The McCartney Bank suddenly closed in the wake of events that became more intriguing as the year went on. Four months later, J.H. Taylor, chairman of the McCartney board of directors, was arrested and charged with misappropriating funds. Taylor was convicted fifteen months later.

The closing, which preceded similar bank closings in Sturgeon Bay, Oconto, Oconto Falls, and Pulaski, came a week after McCartney president George Richardson committed suicide in the bank's bathroom.

Kellogg-Citizens Bank President John Rose, fearing a possible panic when the McCartney Bank closed, had friends make sizable deposits in his bank to reassure the public that their money was safe. It worked, and Kellogg-Citizens didn't have a run on withdrawals.

***

June 2, 1931
"Black Friday. Runs on every bank in Green Bay. Two banks closed. Mine is still operating."

June 3, 1931
"City still hysterical. Dr. John Minahan pledges $2,000,000 to banks, halting runs. No more closed."

***

But the problem of bank robberies continued. In July, several men with pistols and machine guns entered the South Side State Bank on Taylor Street and stole $7,000. The police were called as the heist was in progress and a spectacular gunfight ensued. Police Chief Thomas Hawley and detective Gus Delloye were wounded in the battle, but both survived. The robbers were never caught. Witnesses told police "they appeared to be Italian."

***

July 20, 1931
"South Side bank robbed in a.m. Whole staff worked on story. And was it ever fun!"

***

Statistics would show there were thirty-five bank robberies in Wisconsin in the first ten months of the year, compared to twelve in Michigan over the same period.

The *Press-Gazette's* editorial writer bemoaned: "They tell a story of defeat and humiliation for Wisconsin, a mortifying record for Badgerites. From the standpoint of 'getting away with it,' it has been a brilliant success in Wisconsin."

Michigan credited the quick response by police for discouraging would-be bank robbers.

Money wasn't the only thing sought by robbers. In a mid-March weekend, bandits broke into the Hostel Company at the corner of Jackson and Main streets and made off with between 200 and 300 dresses. The police reasoned the loot was being peddled out of town, because the market in Green Bay would be limited.

Dating, for Dad, was often complicated.

***

July 30, 1931
"Joan forbidden to see me but she sneaked out and we had date for about an hour. Ended up with a fight - the church issue again. Those damn priests. What a lousy religion."

(I don't recall any issues that Dad expressed about the Catholic Church later in his life, but I suspect his 1931 bias had a lot to do with the church's restrictions on its members and their relations with non-Catholics.)

***

Prohibition continued to divide the nation as pressure increased to repeal the Eighteenth Amendment. A leading voice against repeal came from Methodist Bishop James Cannon. In an interview with H.L. Mencken, Cannon called beer "an unpalatable and sickening drink." Told that New York Gov. Franklin Roosevelt might run for president in 1932 and support repeal, Cannon said, "Let the wets have him. We don't trust him."

The drama in Europe was gaining more attention as Benito Mussolini had established a fascist dictatorship in Italy and similar unrest was being stirred by the growing National Socialist (Nazi) party in Germany under Adolf Hitler's leadership.

The *Press-Gazette* addressed it on its editorial page in October:

> "A near dictatorship exists in Germany although Hindenburg is making it as soft as possible. He doesn't want power in the sense that Mussolini wants it. He merely wants to prevent disorder.
>
> "The trouble is we have quite a number of people who do not know how to handle liberty, so they rove in mobs, throw stones, assault, kill, just to indicate their political opinion.
>
> "They are apparently without sufficient mentality to realize that if they abuse liberty to the extent of depriving others of it, they will come in time to be deprived if it themselves. The Germans who are doing this have forgotten – how soon men forget – that such manifestations under the kaiser were met with machine gun fire and the disturbers were thoroughly cowed if not killed.
>
> "Meanwhile, the German fascists with their leader Hitler can hardly withhold their impatience. Disorder made Mussolini and abolished liberty as we know it from Italy. It would do the same thing almost anywhere else.
>
> " 'What fools we mortals be.' "

By contrast, Mahatma Ghandi, through peaceful protest, was making inroads against the British in his quest to gain independence for India. Wrote V.I. Minahan in a *Press-Gazette* editorial:

"To appeal instead to instincts of fairness and justice, to talk quietly but firmly to point out the claimed wrongs, to plead for help and cooperation, these have finally won the day and against bias and prejudice."

Independence was years away, but a voice was being heard.

General Billy Mitchell, now retired, still wasn't keeping silent with his views on the country's future vulnerability to a Japanese attack. Visiting his sister in Milwaukee, Mitchell told a reporter that Japan was a menace to world peace.

"Why, I would guarantee to put that gang out of commission in two months," Mitchell said. "Do it with air forces, strike from Alaska and the string of islands that run westward from Hawaii."

And Dad took a step that would have a huge influence on his life:

***

August 23, 1931
"Sworn in yesterday as 2nd Lieutenant in U.S. Army Organized Reserves."

***

More and more, Dad was called on to work on the sports desk, which he loved, and it brought him into increased contact with the Packers.

***

August 26, 1931
"Still on sports desk. Watched Packers practice in aft."

August 27, 1931
"Mike Michalske, Packer star, will pitch for Collegians Sunday."

August 30, 1931
"Drove to Appleton with Michalske and Engelman. All-Stars gave Collegians a hell of a licking, 17-0. But it was fun playing with the Packer boys."

August 31, 1931
"Met Hank Bruder, Packer backfield man from Northwestern U. A fine fellow. Dunn, Lewellen have signed."

September 3, 1931
"Still on sports desk. Out to see Packers practice in a.m. They have wonderful team."

September 5, 1931
"Last day on sports desk. Wrote long Packer story. The squad of 32 men weighs 6,300 odd pounds."

***

The Packers were in unchartered waters entering the season after back-to-back titles. The *Press-Gazette*, in an editorial before the season opener, urged fans to show up with the headline "You Should Be There."

> "At two o'clock tomorrow afternoon the whistle is due to blow at the City Stadium in Joannes Park, the pigskin will soar up and float a treacherous zigzag course down near the goal posts, twenty-two muscled, determined men will hurtle themselves through the air, thousands of hearts will miss a beat or two or more throats will go hoarse and then raw, and the Green Bay Packers football season of 1931 will be officially on its way. It may sound porcine to pull for a third straight pennant – but let's pull."

If readers weren't catching their breaths after the interminable opening sentence in the editorial, they were going to the dictionary to look up the meaning of "porcine."

The opening game, against the Cleveland Indians, was played in mid-summer-like heat and intermittent rain that didn't stop the Packers from a relatively easy 26-0 victory.

Wrote Bystrom in the *Press-Gazette*:

> "True, the opposition was not like the Giants, Brooklyn or the Bears, but the chances are good that the team will keep up the pace. The team didn't need to go into its repertoire of new plays or overhead game."

***

September 13, 1931
"Went to football game. Packers opened season by trimming Cleveland Indians 26-0. Saunders starred."

A week later, the Brooklyn Dodgers came to town and offered similarly limited resistance to the Packers' attack. This time, newcomer Hank Bruder, who had starred at Northwestern, threw a touchdown pass to Milt Gantenbein. Bystrom wrote that the Packers "ran, they passed, they blocked and how they blocked."

In 80-degree heat, the Packers won 32-6.

***

September 20, 1931
"In aft to see Packers defeat Brooklyn Dodgers, 32-6. Day's hero was Lavvie Dilweg who caught pass and ran 55 yards for touchdown."

***

It didn't make the papers at the time, but Green Bay resident Willard Bent, sitting in the top row of bleachers on the northwest corner of the stadium, fell twelve feet to the pavement during the first quarter. The bench on which he and others were sitting became dislodged as fans stood to watch a play at the other end of the field. Bent was taken to St. Mary's Hospital on Webster Avenue with multiple injuries. The incident would have a significant impact on the Packers organization over the next three years.

But, at present, it was time for a renewal of the rivalry with the Chicago Bears, who came to Green Bay a Sunday later. The newspaper's promotion included a prediction that the game would attract the largest crowd in history for the home team, and reference to the Bears' talented center, George Trafton, noting his talent for getting Packer fans angry.

It was a tight game, and an estimated 13,500 fans showed up. It also came down to a single score, when Verne Lewellen went over left tackle from the 2-yard line in the second quarter, cutting untouched between Red Grange and Bronko Nagurski. Lavvie Dilweg and Mike Michalske each played the full sixty minutes to help the Packers record their twentieth straight home victory, 7-0.

***

September 27, 1931
"In aft took Marianne to see great Packer team defeat Chicago Bears 7-0. Lewellen making only touchdown, Dunn kicked goal."

***

Success brought a new kind of problem for the city. Hours before the Packers' game against the New York Giants the first Sunday in October, Green Bay resident Charles O'Connor walked into the team's box office at the Columbus Club to make sure the game tickets he had just purchased on the street corner outside were legitimate.

E.A. Spachmann, in charge of ticket sales, told him they were counterfeit. O'Connor returned to the ticket-seller at the corner of Jefferson and Walnut streets, and the man pretended to be surprised and went into the Columbus Club. He quickly threw his remaining fake tickets behind a radiator, but he was apprehended by Dilweg, who happened to be in the building at the time. The police were called and three other youths from Milwaukee, who were also peddling the counterfeit tickets, were rounded up. One of them tried to flee, but was tackled on the courthouse lawn by Dilweg.

A local hotel owner later told police he had been given two of the phony tickets in exchange for a night's lodging. In all, 110 unsold fake tickets were collected, and the four were guests of the city until they appeared in municipal court the following day. Fans were advised to contact Packers attorney Jerry Clifford if they were ever offered tickets on the street.

The Packers trounced the Giants 27-7, but the game story was confined to the sports pages while the top headline on the front page blasted the result of the World Series baseball game, "Cards Whip Athletics, 5-2." Bystrom wrote:

> "Twenty-seven to seven. Think of the ignominy of such a beating to the team representing the world's greatest city! And at the hands of a team representing Green Bay, not big enough to fill one of the 100 sections of New York.
>
> "Why, many Gothamites never heard of Green Bay – their football players have heard of it, however. Too much, in fact. So much that they are wishing they were among the uninformed today."

The Giants scored first on a blocked punt in the first period, but the Packers controlled the game after that, with veteran Jug Earpe grabbing two interceptions.

***

October 4, 1931
"Drove to Menasha and brought Joan up for Packer game. She looked stunning. Packers whipped New York 27-7 with Blood, Engleman starring."

The Chicago Cardinals came to town next and took a 7-0 halftime lead. But Johnny Blood scored three second-half touchdowns, one on an interception, and the 26-7 victory was the Packers' fifth straight to start the season.

***

October 11, 1931
"To Green Bay for game. Packers beat Chi Cardinals 26-7, with Johnny Blood starring."

***

Blood, at the peak of his matchless skills, scored both touchdowns a week later when the Philadelphia Yellow Jackets (formerly the Frankford team) came to Green Bay and absorbed a 15-0 defeat. At the same time, rumors circulated that the Packers might add a December 13 game to their schedule to play Portsmouth (Ohio), which was also undefeated so far.

Portsmouth, whose franchise would be purchased three years later to create the Detroit Lions, won its first eight games. But in a strange schedule setup that saw it play two games on the same weekend, the Spartans finally lost to the New York Giants and Chicago Bears. A game against the Packers at the end of the season was in the discussion stages, according to Packers President Leland Joannes.

Johnny Blood in a promotional photo taken at City Stadium. (Photo courtesy Green Bay Press-Gazette)

***

October 18, 1931
"A perfect day. Drove to Menasha, got Joan. Arrested for speeding in Kaukauna, then to Green Bay for football game. Packers 15, Phil 0. Blood starred."

October 19, 1931
"Thomas A. Edison, world famous inventor, died Sunday."

***

When the Packers posted a 48-20 romp over Providence, Bystrom penned a lead game story for the ages, centered on the Steam Rollers' star halfback, Deck Shelley, and a dead poet:

> "In the old days, Shelley was a poet of quite some repute. Today, Shelley is a football player – of equal repute.
> "Instead of saying it with odes, the modern Shelley says it with footballs. Sunday afternoon he made things mighty interesting for the Green Bay Packers.
> "However, Shelley wasn't able to do it all and before the National league game here ended, he probably wondered if the Packers weren't like the nightingales Percy Shelley wrote about as the Green Bay players flitted and fluttered all over the field, like birds on wings, to pluck footballs out of the air and romp around the field."

That's what you got when your sports editor was an English major in college.

A sidelight to the one-sided game was a kickoff by the Packers' Wuert Englemann that the *Press-Gazette* reported traveled 75 yards, through the uprights and into the bleachers at the east end of City Stadium.

***

October 25, 1931
"Game in aft. Packers 48, Providence Steam Rollers 20. Engleman starred."

***

With seven home games and seven victories under their belts, the Packers prepared to play six of their final seven games on the road as they sought a third straight title. It began in a familiar place, Wrigley Field, against the Bears.

***

November 1, 1931
"Over to house to hear football game. Packers 6, Chi Bears 2. Michalske starred."

November 5, 1931
"Have a nice selection of Packer football pictures. Plan to have them framed."

***

The game was defined by a single play following big gains by the Bears' Nagurski and Grange. Midway through the second quarter, Bears quarterback Carl Brumbaugh dropped back to pass and was rushed by Cal Hubbard. His pass was intercepted by Mike Michalske at the Packers' 20-yard line, and with blocks from Dick Stahlman, Hubbard, and Milt Gantenbein, Michalske ran 80 yards for the touchdown.

The game ended 6-2 in the Packers' favor.

"Were you one of the 30,000 fans who saw Michalske dash 80 yards for a touchdown here yesterday?" wrote Bystrom. "If you were not, gather around and we'll tell you about one of the greatest runs seen in many years that gave the Packers a 6 to 2 victory over the team they would rather beat than any other National league team. It came unexpectedly like a gift from heaven."

The final home game the next weekend produced an easy 26-0 victory over the Staten Island Stapletons, with the phenomenal Johnny Blood scoring two more touchdowns, and Dilweg and Hank Bruder each getting one.

***

November 8, 1931
"To Green Bay with Joan, saw Packers beat Stapleton 26-0 with Hank Bruder starring."

***

The unbeaten season ended there. Just like the previous year, Ernie Nevers led the Cardinals to a late-season victory over the Packers. This time the score was 21-13.

"Well, it probably had to come," wrote Bystrom. "Even the Packers can't go on forever winning football games. There are other good teams in the National league."

***

November 15, 1931
"Out to Wrigley Field to see Packers lose football classic to Cardinals 21-13."

November 18, 1931
"Calhoun goes on vacation, Bystrom goes on telegraph desk and I'll be sports editor for awhile."

***

One of the good teams was waiting a week later when the Packers returned to the Polo Grounds in New York to face the Giants. With 35,000 fans in the stadium, the Packers beat the Giants 14-10, with Blood catching a touchdown pass from Red Dunn and tossing one himself to Hank Bruder.

***

November 22, 1931
"In New York, Packers won great game from Giants, 14-10."

November 23, 1931
"Still on sports desk. The New York papers are giving Hank Bruder plenty of ink for his play Sunday."

***

When the news came that Portsmouth was beaten the same day by the Chicago Cardinals, a third straight title drew closer.

First, there was a Thanksgiving Day game at Providence three days later. The game had been scheduled after the Frankford team cancelled its home games. The Yellow Jackets' stadium had been destroyed by fire in July. The team had to split its home games between Baker Bowl, the former baseball home of the Philadelphia Phillies, and Municipal Stadium. It wasn't working out.

***

November 26, 1931
"Heard Packer-Providence game. Blood made 3 touchdowns and Green Bay won 38-7."

***

The Packers had no trouble with Providence, 38-7. Nevertheless, Calhoun, traveling with the team, couldn't resist pointing out that the Packers had 125 penalty yards while Providence had 45. And he wrote that the lone home team touchdown was set up by a pass interference call against Paul Fitzgibbons.

"Fitzgibbons made a legitimate attack to knock down a pass but the umpire couldn't see it that way and he gave the ball to the home club not far from the Packers' goal," wrote Calhoun. "The final play for the score could have been called either way."

The opposition was soft enough that Lambeau kept Earpe, Michalske, Saunders, and Dunn on the sidelines the entire game.

***

November 29, 1931
"Heard Packers win national pennant by beating Brooklyn 7-0."

***

When the Packers won 7-0 at Ebbets Field against Brooklyn three days later, giving them a two-game edge over Portsmouth with one game remaining, the third straight championship was in the bag. All that remained was a final game against the Bears at Wrigley Field.

Lambeau told the *Press-Gazette* that the commitment of his players to be in good condition for games was a key factor in the season's success.

"During the entire eastern trip, there was no dissipating in any way," he said. "And the players displayed a willingness to keep every single training rule, even to getting to bed early at night."

There is no record of Blood's reaction when he read the comment in the newspaper. But, surely, eyes rolled.

Portsmouth's season ended with a 3-0 victory over the Bears on the last Sunday of November, leaving the Spartans with an 11-3 final record. With the Packers at 12-1 with one game to play, Portsmouth renewed the discussion about a game in Ohio against the Packers a week after Green Bay played the Bears.

Lambeau considered it, with an important condition.

"We do not plan to put our title in jeopardy," he said. "But if the Packers defeat the Chicago Bears, thereby clinching the pennant, we may follow through with a game against Portsmouth."

A reporter from the *Portsmouth Times* sent a telegraph seeking confirmation that the Packers refused to play in the Ohio game as scheduled. He was reminded that the game was never scheduled.

So the Packers headed to Chicago knowing their claim to the 1931 title wouldn't be in danger. The Chicago and North Western and the Milwaukee Road offered $4 roundtrip fares to any fans wanting to make the trip.

***

November 30, 1931
"Still on sports desk. Calhoun should be home Wednesday. Love this work."

December 3, 1931
"Still on sports desk. Packers getting ready for last game - against Bears."

December 5, 1931
"Crashed through a railway barrier and just backed up in time to avoid being hit by train."

December 6, 1931
"Packers lost to Bears in Chicago 7-6 but are champions anyway."

***

The Bears won the game 7-6, and Joannes announced immediately that there would be no game at Portsmouth. The Spartans, trying to stay in shape in case the game against Green Bay happened, played a practice game against a team called the Columbus Taxicabs, and won 101-7.

But the cancellation of a Green Bay-Portsmouth game didn't go quietly away. After the Packers announced they wouldn't play, voices from Ohio were heard.

Two days after the season ended, the *Portsmouth Times* ran a team picture of the Spartans under the headline "The Spartans - the Team the Packers are Afraid to Play." The caption read "Above is shown the REAL CHAMPIONS of National Professional Football league – the Portsmouth Spartans. Green Bay, leading by a game over the Spartans, refuses to play the deciding game that would give them a clear title or the Spartans a tie. It is poor sportsmanship, to say the least."

A day later, sportswriter R.E. Hooey of the *Columbus State Journal*, took up the cause:

> "Outside of Green Bay, the championship of the Packers is a hollow one, as empty as a broken egg shell. It is a championship which was not defended against a deserving opponent."
>
> "Since the start of the season patrons of the Portsmouth eleven have been led to believe they would get opportunity to see the leading Green Bay eleven. The supposed contest had been widely advertised for the past several weeks. Result of the Packer and Spartan contests of late made a natural out of the game.
>
> "Green Bay withheld its decision until after the Chicago Bear game Sunday. The Bears won and the Packers' crown was

Green Bay Packers 1931 NFL Championship Team

Front row: Red Dunn, Nate Barrager, Jim Bowdoin, Wuert Engelmann, Lavvie Dilweg, Mike Michalske, Mule Wilson, Paul Fitzgibbon
Middle row: Roger Grove, Waldo Don Carlos, Hank Bruder, Milt Gantenbein, Bo Molenda, Rudy Comstock, Russ Saunders
Back Row: Curly Lambeau, Dick Stahlman, Johnny Blood, Red Sleight, Cal Hubbard, Tom Nash, Hurdis McCrary, Jug Earp, Arnie Herber (Photo courtesy Green Bay Press-Gazette)

---

toppling. Had Green Bay won, it is practically certain it would have agreed to visit Portsmouth Sunday, glad for the chance to strut on the Ohio gridiron, keenly partaking of the championship limelight. But with its crown not endangered. Such is the way of the cheese champions."

Portsmouth Coach Potsy Clark joined the chorus, calling the Packers' decision "a dirty deal all around."

Bystrom fired back in his *Press-Gazette* column before the week was over:

"In their righteous wrath, we wonder if sportswriters of the *Portsmouth Times* or Mr. Hooey took the time to learn true facts about the Portsmouth-Packer deal.

"We wonder if they know of Mr. Griffin's actions at the annual league meeting when schedules were prepared early this year. Or of his treatment of the Packers last year when they played the Spartans late in December. Or of the chances Green Bay would have had of getting a game with Portsmouth if the tables had been turned.

"Mr. Hooey, do you remember the game at Portsmouth last year? Do you remember the sleet and snow and raw, cold weather on that second Sunday in December? Do you remember how the Packers came on the field 15 minutes before game time and then were forced to wait 37 minutes after the stated starting time before the game got underway and when they protested to Coach Griffin, urging that he get the game started, he told them to go to __, and if they didn't like waiting to get off the field and sing for their guarantee? Did someone in Portsmouth mention sportsmanship?"

Bystrom went on to review events at the owners meeting early in the year when Lambeau approached Griffin to propose a home-and-home arrangement with Portsmouth, but was told the Spartans would not come to Green Bay.

The day after Bystrom's response, league president Joe E. Carr announced that the season was over and the Packers were champions since a Green Bay-Portsmouth game was not on the original schedule.

The Packers gave each player a $100 bonus, and Blood led the league in scoring with his thirteen touchdowns.

In non-football business, Green Bay drivers were chastised as the year ended because the National Safety Board, in its survey of forty-eight cities under 100,000 population, reported that Green Bay had the second-highest death rate from traffic accidents in 1931. Only Battle Creek, Michigan, was worse.

In an editorial, the *Press-Gazette* scolded:

"It indicates the necessity of education among motorists and pedestrians. We need to be reminded of the rules of the road, of the necessity of obeying traffic regulations, and that the world will not go to pieces if we happen to arrive at our destination a minute or two later than we expected."

***

December 31, 1931
"Another year of business depression ended. Did a little drinking but stayed under control at all times."

***

It was a changing and struggling world on December 31, 1931. But the Packers were champions for a third straight year.

Chapter 7

Bow to the Inevitable

There was no precedent, no template to guide a pro football team seeking to salve its disappointment after failing to win a fourth straight national championship.

So the Packers went to Hawaii.

Two days after their season and pro football reign ended with a 9-0 loss to the Chicago Bears at Wrigley Field on December 11, 1932, Curly Lambeau and seventeen players boarded a Milwaukee Road train for Chicago, to be connected to a Pacific Coast line to Los Angeles. From there, they sailed to Honolulu.

They had been invited to the island to play two Hawaiian teams before returning to San Francisco to play a charity game at Kezar Stadium against a collection of pro players.

The *Green Bay Press-Gazette* didn't send Bystrom or Calhoun on the trip, but told Lambeau to hire someone in Hawaii to cover the games and wire the stories to Green Bay. The paper also commissioned Johnny Blood to send columns concerning the team's travels and activities. Since Blood's reputation as the "Vagabond Halfback" also encompassed his non-football after-hours interests, it's likely some guidelines were established by the newspaper.

The send-off included an editorial:

> "The Packers have completed their eleventh year in the national professional football league and in the last four years of that period have established a record that will probably stand for a great many years to come.
>
> "They are on their way to far off Honolulu to spread the fame of their glory and, incidentally, that of the city and state

supporting them. It is a just reward for all their grueling efforts, and Hawaii paid them a fitting and proper tribute in inviting them in preference to those who have a little higher percentage for the current year."

The year ended far differently than how it began. For the Packers, January of 1932 brought a third straight winter of basking in the aftermath of a league championship.

Lambeau traveled to San Francisco for the East-West college football game, where he scouted, and found, new talent. Two weeks into the new year, he was able to announce that he had a commitment from All-American guard Herman Hickman of Tennessee, who had been impressive in the New Year's Day game. The *Press-Gazette* story included glowing predictions about Hickman.

Lambeau also announced he had a commitment from a second player who, although not on any All-America teams, had also caught scouts' attention in that game. He was fullback Clarke Hinkle, who had excelled at Bucknell. Pat Frayne, a sportswriter for the *San Francisco Call-Bulletin*, saw what Lambeau saw and wrote about it:

> "Why, for instance, was not Clarke Hinkle of Bucknell mentioned on more all-American teams? A great fullback, with more power than any fullback we have watched on the coast."

Hickman would end up with the Brooklyn Dodgers, not the Packers. Hinkle would be inducted into the Pro Football and Green Bay Packers halls of fame, and eventually have a Green Bay street and Packers practice field bearing his name.

Lambeau concluded his West Coast trip by visiting two of his players in the Los Angeles area: Nate Barrager, who ran a sporting goods store; and Russ Saunders, who was an assistant director at Warner Brothers Studios.

Football would come soon enough for Green Bay in 1932, but there was other news that identified the time. And there were women to date for my dad.

***

January 5, 1932
"Joan says we are going to be married some day. It's an open question."

(They were, but not to each other.)

January 18, 1932
"In eve covered murder and suicide at Motor Inn. Man shot woman, then killed himself."

February 18, 1932
"Japan sends ultimatum to China. Now watch the fun start. We'll all be at war in no time at all."

February 27, 1932
"Spent most of the day trying to run down story about meteor, which is supposed to have landed up in the Menominee reservation."

***

One news story concerned a war that ended sixty-seven years earlier. For several years, efforts were made to hold a joint convention to bring surviving veterans of the Union and Confederate armies together. But every time, the remaining veterans refused to attend.

A *Press-Gazette* editorial reflected on it:

> "We have turned that war into an affair of moonlight and romance. We have spun queer, misty haloes for the heads of those who took part in it.
>
> "We are at a safe distance from the war now. So the veterans regularly vote down plans for a grand get-together. And perhaps they are wiser than we are. The Civil War wasn't a knightly duel. It was a cruel, bloody and frightfully painful bit of hell on earth. The men who fought in it remember that fact."

Although a significant percentage of citizens and legislators remained loyal in their defense of the Eighteenth Amendment, the era of Prohibition was being more and more influenced by the Great Depression. The Wickersham Commission that had been appointed by President Hoover three years earlier, while sympathetic to the Volstead Act, had concluded that enforcement of Prohibition had become a sham. It was a bootlegger's gold mine.

With unemployment soaring in 1932 and the prospect of jobs being created if the liquor business could be revived, the energy in Green Bay and the rest of the nation was pointing toward repeal. It became a lively issue in the presidential campaign.

Roosevelt and the Democrats pounced on it, with Hoover maintaining his support for Prohibition. The November election was a foregone conclusion, with FDR winning the White House in a landslide.

The *Press-Gazette*, although supporting Hoover in the election, appeared to see the handwriting on the wall when it analyzed the president's treatment of the Prohibition issue three days before the November vote:

> "Mr. Hoover's attitude toward prohibition is supine and next to worthless. His term in office constitutes a record of running, hiding and dodging from this issue while 70 percent of his fellow citizens have implored for relief and assistance."

One of Hoover's last pre-election speeches was delivered at the University of Wisconsin Field House in Madison the Friday before Election Day. It was the start of Homecoming weekend in the capital.

Hoover tried to convince listeners that the country was on the road to recovery and said, "There should be no interruption in the policies that have brought this about."

Perhaps a sign of the futility in Hoover's campaign to stay in office was the fact that he stood too far from the microphone and much of his prepared speech couldn't be heard in the cavernous building.

The election was a rout. Roosevelt's landslide was reflected in Wisconsin, where he won 67 percent of the vote. He had a three-to-one advantage over Hoover in Brown County, where Green Bay is the county seat.

The biggest single news story of the year, and perhaps the decade, was the March 1 kidnapping of Charles and Anne Morrow Lindbergh's baby boy. The investigation included rumors, false leads, and attempted fraud before the baby's body was found two months later about four miles from the Lindberghs' New Jersey home. The story commanded headlines almost daily until September 1934, when Bruno Hauptmann was arrested and charged with the crime.

He was convicted and eventually executed.

***

March 2, 1932
"Col. Charles Lindbergh's baby kidnapped from New Jersey home. Plenty big news break. It's the story of the hour."

March 15, 1932
"That baby of Lindbergh's still missing after two weeks. Looks like they won't get it back."

May 12, 1932
"Lindbergh's baby found dead near Hopewell, N.J."

May 13, 1932
"Telegraph wires carrying nothing but news about the Lindbergh baby. That was a horrible crime. It's the biggest news break of the century."

***

It would be a memorable year all around. In the summer, 15,000 World War veterans marched on Washington, D.C., to demand that their promised bonuses from the government be paid immediately rather than deferred until the 1940s. It became a spectacle, with President Hoover refusing to meet with them and General Douglas MacArthur driving them out, and tearing down the huts and tents that housed them. It was a black mark for the government.

The year extended the drama of one of the nation's greatest miscarriages of justice. Nine African-Americans, ages 13-20, were accused of raping two white girls on a train near Scottsboro, Alabama. They were convicted by an all-white jury and sentenced to death. However, they were retried at the insistence of the U.S. Supreme Court, which ruled the nine hadn't received a fair trial. Despite one of the alleged victims admitting there was no rape, they were convicted again. The case would drag on and none of the defendants would be executed, but it would become the standard for unfair justice in the twentieth century.

Dad kept up with work, with national events, and effects of the Depression.

***

May 18, 1932
"Pay cuts at office but I only get 37 cents off. "

June 6, 1932
"In eve covered J.C.C. meeting. Lavvie Dilweg, candidate for dist. attorney and Packer football star, spoke."

June 14, 1932
"Republican national convention opens in Chicago. They'll vote for a referendum and will renominate Hoover, but he won't be re-elected."

June 20, 1932
"Busiest morning in months. One man killed, 16 injured in weekend accidents. Worked on the story until 2:30 and it made Page One."

June 27, 1932
"Democratic convention opens in Chicago. Roosevelt seems to be gaining strength."

June 30, 1932
"Al Smith addresses Democratic convention as band plays 'Sidewalks of New York.' But they'll nominate Roosevelt."

July 1, 1932
"Texas and California desert Garner and the Democrats nominate Franklin D. Roosevelt of N.Y. for president. Press-Gazette put out an extra."

August 3, 1932
"Rogers Hornsby ousted as manager of Chicago Cubs. Charlie Grimm succeeds him. In aft interviewed Jack Chervigny, former Notre Dame star halfback, now coach of Chicago Cardinals pro team."

August 26, 1932
"Johnny Blood signs to play with Packers again."

***

For many in and around Green Bay, football season couldn't come soon enough. Prior to their first league game, the Packers prepared to host a team called the Grand Rapids Maroons at City Stadium.

The *Press-Gazette* sounded the drum beat in an editorial the day before the game:

> "Football, which keeps Green Bay before the nation the next three months, makes its annual debut here tomorrow. From all over the state, followers of the Packers, and they are legion, will come to view the team in its opening contest.
>
> "For a city of our humble size to send forth an eleven that throws the gauntlet down before the lion ... and beats them all, can be ascribed only to planning, training and daring. The recreational and entertainment values of such an organization are self-evident. The commercial value is too far-flung to attempt to appraise."

The game was as one-sided as expected – the Packers winning 45-0 – and it proved the value of signing Hinkle, whose running and defense stood out.

***

September 11, 1932
"I saw Packers beat Grand Rapids, 45-0."

September 13, 1932
"In eve interviewed Jug Earpe, Packer veteran, and worked on Packer publicity at office."

***

It wouldn't be that easy a week later when the Chicago Cardinals came to Green Bay. There was a major change in the Cardinals roster in 1932. Ernie Nevers wasn't on it.

The Superior, Wisconsin, native broke his wrist in that San Francisco charity game the previous January. Declaring he was getting out "while I'm still in one piece," he announced his retirement as a player. He would become a college and pro coach, serve in the South Pacific during World War II, and join the charter class of the Pro Football Hall of Fame.

But he wouldn't play against the Packers anymore.

The game was played in a downpour in front of about 3,500 people, a highlight being Mike Michalski's recovery of a blocked punt for a touchdown. The Packers won, 15-7.

***

September 18, 1932
"Started for Two Rivers to play ball but never got there. Car piled up at Manitowoc and all 5 of us got hurt. Treatment at hospital. Dad came and got us. Hobbled to football game. Packers 15, Chi Cardinals 7."

September 19, 1932
"Car all smashed up so bought a new one, Chevrolet 1932 coach."

September 20, 1932
"Primary election day. Cast straight regular Republican vote, for Walter Kohler and all the rest. Furthermore, Kohler went in and the LaFollettes went out. Great day for Wisconsin."

***

The Bears traveled north the following weekend and played the Packers to a 0-0 tie, after which Lambeau said of the Bears: "It's the greatest Bear team we ever faced."

The game would eventually have a significant effect on the championship race.

***

September 25, 1932
"Picked up Joan and we came to Green Bay for football game. Chicago Bears held Packers to 0-0 tie."

September 30, 1932
"Cubs and Yanks back in Chicago. Bet the Cubs win that series yet. Looks bad though."

October 1, 1932
"Babe Ruth and Lou Gehrig each hit two home runs and Yanks beat Cubs in World Series 7-5."

***

Next to town were the New York Giants, and they also were absent a star of the past. Benny Friedman, the team's best player and quarterback, retired after the 1931 season, although he did unretire briefly to play some games with Brooklyn. Friedman would be inducted into the Hall of Fame in 2005, twenty-three years after he died by suicide.

Former Packer Bo Molenda was now on the Giants' roster, but spent the game on the bench. Hurdis McCrary and Hank Bruder scored touchdowns in the Packers' 13-0 victory.

***

October 2, 1932
"Saw Packers beat N.Y. Giants 13-0. Touchdowns by McCrary and Bruder."

October 3, 1932
"Yankees won World Series by beating Cubs in fourth game, 13-6. Lazzeri hit 2 home runs. Today I'm on telegraph desk again - plenty tired of it. Calhoun will be back on job tomorrow, saints be praised."

October 5, 1932
"Hoover and Roosevelt are putting up one great campaign for the presidency."

October 7, 1932
"Joan writes she can't give me date for Sunday, and I'm well pleased. But called Fritz and she can't either. Situation now is serious."

***

First place belonged to the Packers a week later when they rallied to beat Portsmouth 15-10, Hinkle scoring on a 22-yard run on fourth down in the final period. Al Rose scored the other touchdown for Green Bay when he recovered a blocked punt in the end zone.

***

October 8, 1932
"Interviewed Potsy Clark, coach of the Portsmouth Spartans."

October 9, 1932
"Saw a sensational football game - Packers rallied to defeat Portsmouth 15-10."

October 10, 1932
"In aft took Cal Hubbard and Verne Lewellen, Packer football players, to interview Mrs. Ada Wendt, 70, a Packer fan."

October 13, 1932
"Roosevelt seems certain to defeat Hoover in Nov. 8 election, but I'll vote for Herb."

***

The first road game awaited, and it was a rematch with the Bears at Wrigley Field. The Packers won 2-0 when Tom Nash blocked a Bears punt through the end zone. A key play occurred when Bronko Nagurski appeared to have an open field for a Bears touchdown, but was run down by Arnie Herber after 43 yards and the Bears were unable to score.

League president Joe E. Carr met with Packers executives at the Knickerbocker Hotel the day before the game and paid tribute to the team's head coach.

"To me, it is remarkable how Curly Lambeau continues, year in and year out, to consistently produce a winner," Carr said. "Around the league, the other managers are rating him as a gridiron magician."

One sidelight on that Sunday occurred when an elevated train on Chicago's north side jumped the rails and many Packers fans onboard escaped injury.

***

October 16, 1932
"Packers took great game from Bears at Chicago 2-0."

October 17, 1932
"Seems as though everyone is out of work now."

October 18, 1932
"Since 1924, when I started bowling, I have rolled 55 200 games. Highest scores - 267, 256, 247, 242, 235."

***

Victories over Brooklyn (13-0) and Staten Island (26-0) in Green Bay produced no surprises, the latter game being part of "Coach Lambeau Day," with Curly receiving a set of Bobby Jones golf clubs from the Packers organization.

That game was marked by a brilliant performance by Herber. The Green Bay native scored on an 85-yard interception return and threw two touchdown passes.

***

October 21, 1932
"Dad hard up these days and it keeps me flat keeping him in money."

October 23, 1932
"Went to game, Packers beat Brooklyn 13-0."

October 30, 1932
"We saw Packers wallop Stapleton 26-0, the main thrill being Herber's 85-yard run."

November 4, 1932
"In eve took Grace to see Greta Garbo and Joan Crawford in 'Grand Hotel.'"

November 5, 1932
"Calhoun and Bystrom both gone to Chicago so I put out sports extra by myself."

***

It was time, then, for the Packers to begin their season-ending stretch of seven road games, starting at Wrigley Field in Chicago against the Cardinals. The game was a showcase for Johnny Blood as the Packers won 19-9.

Bystrom wrote: "The Chicago Cardinals have a mighty good football team but they haven't a Johnny Blood – and that's probably the reason they lost."

Blood caught two TD passes from Herber and set up a Hinkle touchdown with another reception. Bystrom made note of the Cardinals' "colored halfback named Joe Lillard, who threw passes all over the field."

***

November 6, 1932
"Heard Packer game over radio. They beat Cardinals 19-9."

***

Among those watching the game was Heatley (Hunk) Anderson, who became Notre Dame's football coach after Knute Rockne's death, and was also serving as athletic director. This was almost eleven years after Anderson and two other Irish football players were suspended from all amateur athletics after being caught playing a game for the Packers in Milwaukee under assumed names.

***

November 7, 1932
"Election eve. It looks as though Roosevelt will beat President Hoover easily, but not on my vote."

November 8, 1932
"The whole nation goes Democratic, and our next president will be Franklin D. Roosevelt. Voted practically the straight Republican ticket."

November 10, 1932
"Started work on Calhoun's desk. He's left for east with Packers."

November 12, 1932
"Shifted to sports desk. Bystrom goes to telegraph. Helped him put out sports extra in aft."

***

In Boston, the Packers easily beat the Braves 21-0, with the *Press-Gazette* headline blaring "Braves Scalped by Green Bay Packers."

***

November 13, 1932
"Packers won at Boston 21-0. They're still undefeated."

November 14, 1932
"Had lunch with Rep. James Hughes, our newly elected congressman. Furthermore, he paid for it."

November 15, 1932
"The country is going wet. There's talk of legalizing beer soon."

November 17, 1932
"Packers are getting plenty of ink from the eastern papers."

***

On to the Polo Grounds in New York for a rematch with the Giants a week later, where Tim Mara, the team's owner, credited the Packers for the growing popularity of pro football.

"Just think," he told Calhoun in an interview the day before the game. "The (New York) *Sun* has never carried a line on professional football, yet they gave your club a few squibs last Thursday night."

Mara also issued a warning.

"You can tell my friends in Green Bay, including A.B. Turnbull and Dr. Kelly, that we are going to make things mighty interesting for the Packers this Sunday. I think my club has arrived... and there is going to be a lot of gloom in the Packers home town Sunday night."

His team backed him up, and the Giants ended the Packers' unbeaten streak, winning 6-0. In a telegram to team officials after the game, Packers President Lee Joannes said the team just couldn't get underway on the muddy field. Later, he said the team was overconfident, saying "The boys got too much publicity in New York."

Henry McLemore of United Press filed a unique story that Sunday night:

> "That was a ball game, pardoners. It had everything. At the invitation of Coach Lambeau, we watched the game from the Green Bay bench, swathed in one of those flowing canvas coats with sheepskin collar. Curly said, 'I just want you to see

for yourself whether or not professional players take the game seriously.'

"The answer is yes, they do. Those skeptics who think that the winning or losing of a game means little to the pros should have been with us in the Green Bay dressing room between halves. The gloom was ankle deep. You may think I'm lying but there were tears. Don't let anyone tell you the pros loaf and take it easy. If the pros have a tendency to dog it, why did Blood, still weak from an attack of the flu, pester Lambeau until he was sent in the game to get rid of him? That ends today's lecture."

***

November 20, 1932
"Heard football game on radio. Packers lost first game of season, to New York, 6-0."

November 23, 1932
"Packers have tough row to hoe if they are to win another championship."

***

Staying in New York, the Packers went over to Ebbets Field on Thanksgiving Day and beat Brooklyn 7-0. Prior to the game, Lambeau traded Herman Hickman to the Dodgers for $500 after the Tennessee lineman said he didn't want to play in Wisconsin because there were better pro wrestling opportunities for him in the east.

***

November 24, 1932
"Thanksgiving day, noon edition. Then football game over radio. Packers 7, Brooklyn 0. Touchdown by Hank Bruder."

November 26, 1932
"Money plenty tight these days. Another bank closed yesterday."

***

Three days later, the Packers ferried over to Staten Island to play the Stapletons. The game ended in a 21-3 Packers victory, and featured a near brawl involving fans. Blood intercepted a pass and returned it for a touchdown.

Here's how Calhoun described things:

> "As he crossed the end zone, he got a bit playful and some of his antics didn't sit well with the Stapleton fans who leaped the barrier and surrounded Johnny as if a scalping party was to be staged. Claude Perry was the first Packer to reach the scene of hostilities and he breezed head first into the mob.
> "Before the final whistle, a good many of this loyal Stapleton fans who had been shouting for Green Bay blood early in the game were goose-stepping towards the exits, meek as lambs."

***

November 27, 1932
"Listened to football game over radio. Packers rallied in second half to beat Stapleton 21-3."

November 28, 1932
"The Packers have two tough games ahead. Looks like there'll be a new national champion."

***

But too many Packer players were hurt. Hinkle, Herber, and Lewellen had to leave the game with injuries. Hubbard and Michalske had leg injuries, and Tom Nash and Harry O'Boyle were finished for the season.

With games remaining at second-place Portsmouth and the third-place Bears, the Packers were 10-1-1, Portsmouth 5-1-4, and the Bears 4-1-6.

The Packers moved on to Columbus to prepare for the pivotal game against Portsmouth. The strained relationship of the past between the Packers and their Ohio hosts took on a new chapter. The Columbus Board of Education barred the Packers from practicing on the Central High School field.

The Columbus American Association baseball team offered the use of its field and proposed that admission be charged and shared equally with the Packers. But Lambeau declined, saying it would leave a "money grabbing" image for pro football.

Finally, the Packers gained permission to use the field at Aquinas Catholic High School.

November 30, 1932
"Visited at hospital with Tom Nash, injured Packer football player."

December 2, 1932
"City all steamed up over crucial football game at Portsmouth Sunday."

***

The game in Portsmouth was one-sided, with the Spartans winning 19-0. In his report to the *Press-Gazette*, Calhoun said the Packers' "dash and fight was missing" and the team "only seemed to be a shadow of their real selves."

***

December 4, 1932
"In aft listened to football game. Portsmouth walloped Packers 19-0 and there'll be no pennant raised in Green Bay next fall."

December 5, 1932
"House of Representatives votes against repeal of 18th Amendment, and the whole nation wants it. City damned near in mourning after Packer defeat."

***

There were repercussions.

Lambeau complained to league president Joe E. Carr about the officiating. Turnbull let his feelings be known also.

"While the Packers probably would not have won the game anyway, I believe that the poor officiating had much to do with the piling up of such a lopsided score," Turnbull said. "The Spartans were offside one to two yards on practically every play, thus providing a great handicap for the Packers passers and kickers. If the head linesman had called these offsides, an entirely different complexion might have been placed on the game."

Dr. Kelly, who also attended the game, issued an extended comment to the *Press-Gazette* the following day:

> "Without attempting to establish any alibis, it may be said that the character of the decisions given by the officials contributed to the demoralization of the Packer team.

"The physical condition of the players was such that it required only something of this nature to turn the scales. While other teams have been playing 11 games, the assignment of the Packers has been 14 games. In other words, the team is pretty well battered and tired out, but we must not forget that they won nearly as many games as the Spartans and Bears put together.

"Another factor which must be taken into consideration as an explanation of Sunday's defeat is the attitude taken by the spectators. In all my connections with professional football, I never have seen a crowd so unsportsmanlike and insulting as the crowd at Portsmouth. From the moment the Packers arrived at the field until the time they left, they were subjected to a barrage of epithets and abuse which would have taken the heart out of any team. This unfortunate attitude was not confined to the male fans but was general among the women as well.

"It is hard to lose a championship but, after all, Green Bay has had its share, and as good sports we must bow graciously to the inevitable."

***

December 7, 1932
"Packers invited to play two football games in Hawaiian Islands."

December 9, 1932
"There are 15 million unemployed in U.S. Everyone is saying the country is finished. They are wrong. America will rise again."

***

The Spartans' scheduled season was completed with a 6-1-4 record, with ties not yet being counted in the standings. The Packers were 10-2-2 with a final game against the Bears remaining, so there was no way they could catch Portsmouth. What they could do, however, was beat the Bears at Wrigley Field and hand the championship to the Spartans.

They didn't.

The Bears won 9-0 in a game that Calhoun wrote featured no standout performances from the Packers. It left the Bears and Portsmouth tied for first with 6-1 records, since the ties didn't count. If the post-1972 rule had been in effect counting ties as a half-win, half-loss, the Packers would be the only professional football team to win four straight championships.

As it was, the Bears and Spartans played what was the league's first playoff game. It was scheduled for Wrigley Field, but extreme cold forced the teams to play in the indoor Chicago Stadium, on an 80-yard field. The Bears won 9-0 to capture the 1932 title.

The Packers went to the beach.

***

December 11, 1932
"Listened to Packer-Bear game on radio, played in snowstorm. Green Bay lost 9-0."

December 12, 1932
"Packers back home. They leave for Hawaii tomorrow."

***

There was some confusion over who the Packers would play in Hawaii. The *Honolulu Star-Bulletin*, sponsor of the games, had given Green Bay the impression there would be two games. The first would be against the University of Hawaii team, the second against a team called the Townies, made up of former prep and college players.

But things had changed by the time the Packers docked in Hawaii. The sponsors decided that a game between the Packers and a collection of former athletes from throughout the island's Kamehameha School District would draw better.

A second game would be played a week later against a team of alumni from Honolulu's President William McKinley High School, because it had just beaten the Townies 23-0.

Fans back in Green Bay would receive play-by-play through a unique arrangement. A man was hired to send the result of each play, through a wireless signal, from Honolulu to a location across the street from the Western Union office in San Francisco. The information would be walked across the street and translated to Morse code, then telegraphed to a radio station in Green Bay. Packer veteran Verne Lewellen, who didn't make the trip because he had duties as the Brown County District Attorney, sat in the radio booth and, recognizing the play, dictated information to the announcer who told listeners. Fans heard the result of each play about three minutes after it occurred.

The game against Kamehameha was played on Christmas Day and the Packers won 19-13. The story of the game, printed in the *Press-Gazette*, was written by Blood, who showed a talent for the written word.

"Playing on the beautiful island here was vastly different than on the frozen turf at Chicago, Green Bay and the east. But for a light breeze that swept down off the Oahu mountains where it was raining, the heat probably would have been repressive."

He also wrote about the touchdown pass he caught from Herber. Most interesting was the fact that the player who threw the 70-yard pass for the islanders' only score was Danny Wise, a 150-pound back at Kamehameha High School.

***

December 23, 1932
"House of Representatives passes beer bill. Now it's up to Senate."

***

Despite continued efforts by many to invoke optimism in the struggle for financial recovery, the year-end outlook in Green Bay wasn't good. Activities at the paper mills, tanneries, and railroads remained at a low ebb. A general surplus in labor prevailed in most area industries, with the closing of some shops impacting 3,000 workers.

Speaking of optimism, University of Missouri President Walter Williams, who started the school's journalism school, offered the following prediction as the year came to a close:

> "Hitler has reached the peak of his power. He is another William Jennings Bryan. Hearing him speak, you can see the crowd swayed by his eloquence even if you do not understand all that is said," he told an audience. "Hitler has gained a tremendous following through promises but when he fails to make good on those promises, he will start on a decline of his power. That time soon must come."

But not yet.

Green Bay Press-Gazette, December 15, 1932

$10,000 Loss in Blaze at Clisby Home

Three are Overcome by Smoke, One Cut by Broken Glass

Damage estimated at from $10,000 to $15,000 was caused and several persons narrowly escaped serious injury as the result of a fire that broke out shortly before 8 o'clock this morning at the three-story frame residence of W.B. Clisby, 913 E. Mason St, practically destroying the building and its contents.

Firemen from both east side stations fought the blaze for several hours, but were unable to save anything but the shell of the structure. Walls remain standing, and only a portion of the roof was burned off, but the entire interior was gutted.

Three persons sleeping in the house, which is a two-family flat, at the time the fire broke out, were overcome by smoke. They are W.B. Clisby, 72, Grace Messenger, 22, and John C. Messenger, 43. John M. Walter, 25, who lived with his grandparents, Mr. and Mrs. Clisby, in one section of the house, suffered cuts about the hands while engaged in helping other occupants to escape.

Firemen said that the blaze apparently originated in the basement near the front of the house, and then spread through the upper stories. So sudden was the spread of the fire that occupants were forced to don any clothes within reach and hurry to safety out-of-doors.

Walter and Mr. and Mrs. Clisby were on the third floor of the house when the fire was first noticed. Christine Weeks, a teacher at East high school, was on the second floor, and Mr. and Mrs. John C. Messenger, daughter Grace, and son John jr., were on the first floor.

Miss Messenger was overcome by smoke that seeped through the registers in the house. She was taken to the home of Mr. and Mrs. Harry W. Williams next door, where she was revived. Mrs. Messenger and John jr. left the house as soon as the alarm was given, Mrs. Messenger having first called the fire department.

Mr. Messenger was overcome by smoke as he was attempting to reach the rear door. He was helped to the door by Walter, who had been aiding Mr. and Mrs. Clisby to reach an outer door located between the first and second floors of the building in the rear.

Walter had taken Mrs. Clisby down to the landing and had helped her out of doors. He started back to get Mr. Clisby whom he cautioned to remain on the third floor until his return.

Mr. Clisby had started downstairs by himself and Walter found him between the first and second floor, overcome by smoke. After assisting Mr. Clisby to the outer landing and seeing that he was safely out of the house, Walter returned to find Mr. Messenger whop, although partially overcome by smoke, said that Mrs. Messenger and Grace were in their rooms.

Walter then returned to the first floor of the house and began a search for Grace Messenger and her mother. After he had failed to find them, he again returned to the main part of the house and it was then that he incurred his injuries. A door he had left open had closed while he was searching for the women, and in an effort to break through he smashed the glass, severely lacerating both his hands, losing the tips of the second and third fingers on his right hand.

He was taken to St. Mary's Hospital for first aid treatment.

***

December 15, 1932
What a day! House caught fire at 7:45 a.m. and we were all smoked out like rats. Total loss. Cut my hand on door, treated at hospital.

December 16, 1932
Everyone is being very kind but we took an awful beating on the fire. Fished out some of my clothes and sent them to the cleaners.

December 20, 1932
We are leading a hand-to-mouth existence. Plan to build new house but that'll take time.

December 24, 1932
Family moves into house we are renting at 515 S. Jackson St. It's pretty bare. Couldn't help feeling sort of blue in eve. First time since fire.

December 29, 1932
"Damn glad to see this year end."

December 30, 1932
"Got my last glimpse of a $54 pay check. We get cut 10% first of the year."

Chapter 8

Recovery Brewing

December 31, 1932
"1932 ends with world unhappy, trying to fight its way back to prosperity, and making a sorry job of it. The third consecutive year of world-wide business depression. Millions of men out of work, all salaries cut, prices down to rock bottom."

***

The lowest of times, for sure. At the very least, 1933 promised something different for Green Bay, as it did for the rest of the country. Roosevelt's election all but guaranteed that the bootleg liquor trade – a staple of sorts for many in the area – would be retired along with the Eighteenth Amendment.

It was not unexpected, as Roosevelt had made his intentions clear in the 1932 campaign. Wisconsin would be the second state to ratify the amendment on April 25, 1933, and it all became official on December 5.

There was tension in Green Bay when some members of the Brown County Tavern Operators Association pressured, unsuccessfully, to have saloons raise the cost of a beer from five cents to ten cents, hoping to take advantage of the public's rush for legal, and better, beer.

There were even a few incidents when windows of some establishments were broken in an apparent effort to coerce the bar owners to raise the price.

A *Press-Gazette* editorial implied that law enforcement could be more aggressive in its pursuit of the perpetrators:

"This is coercion. It is blackmail. It is gang warfare. It is a disgrace to this community. But isn't there really a greater disgrace in the community, the disgrace of inertia, of the do-nothing-about-it?"

Eventually, there were arrests and the tension eased.

What else the incoming administration could do to speed economic recovery was only speculation as the year dawned.

For the Packers, there was an island holiday interrupted briefly by a couple obligations. They played a game against a team called McKinley that managed to hold Green Bay to a 6-0 halftime lead before the Packers rolled on to a 32-0 victory.

Johnny Blood reveled in the fact that the game drew a crowd of 17,760 islanders.

"The team cuts into 50 percent of the gross so everyone is happy," he wrote. "They will relax for the next ten days."

Adding the obvious, Blood wrote that the players "were thoroughly relaxed Monday night."

Blood, Arnie Herber, Mike Michalske, Hank Bruder, Wuert Engelmann, Roger Grove, Al Rose, and Joe Zeller then played an exhibition basketball game against a Hawaiian team, and the football Packers put on a passing and kicking exhibition during their stay.

It was a positive public relations performance by the Packers and for Green Bay.

Honolulu sportswriter Red McQueen sang the team's praises in his column:

> "Naturally, we became personally acquainted with every member of the team and regarded them as the finest bunch of boys we ever would care to meet. The ordinary professional generally has a great opinion of himself and possesses plenty of ego, but not the Packers. They are regular guys all and look more like a college team to us than anything else. We're pulling for them to come back next year and several more years."

The voyage from Hawaii to San Francisco lasted ten days and over occasionally rough seas. Several teammates who had been unable to make the Hawaiian trip were waiting to greet them after their ship sailed beneath the Golden Gate Bridge: Cal Hubbard, Verne Lewellen, Hurdis McCrary, and Tom Nash.

Also greeting them was Harold (Red) Grange, the legendary Chicago Bears halfback who agreed to play with the Packers for the two west coast exhibition games on the schedule. Grange said this would be his final competition as a football player.

One national writer noted that Grange's retirement left Babe Ruth as the only remaining active athlete from among the six dominant sports performers of what was called the Golden Decade of the 1920s. The others were boxing's Jack Dempsey and Gene Tunney, tennis's Bill Tilden, and golf's Bobby Jones.

It would have made an interesting anecdote to the Packers-Bears rivalry – the Galloping Ghost playing his final games for the Green Bay Packers. However, Grange changed his mind and was on the Bears roster for two more seasons.

Blood, and likely several Packers, had dreams of greater fame, as he wired to the *Press-Gazette*.

"A contract for a short motion picture in which the Packer team would perform also has been proposed by Hollywood promoters, but it is not definitely set yet."

Nor would it be.

Meanwhile, back in Green Bay…

***

January 1, 1933
"Feeling fine. No hangover. In eve Fritz and I went for a long ride and I really think we're getting somewhere."

January 3, 1933
"Calhoun sick again so back I go on sports desk. Packers defeated McKinley team in Hawaii, 32-0. Am thinking too much about Fritz but can't help it. Went out to see Mary."

***

Sports editor Art Bystrom was Calhoun's substitute as telegraph editor. The job included the gathering of news from the various news sources transmitted by telegraph, then directing them to the appropriate news departments at the *Press-Gazette*.

No doubt, local readers found interest in a report by Register of Deeds Rigney Dwyer the same day that noted while there were fewer marriages in Brown County in 1932 (466) than in 1931 (515), there were 200 more babies born.

Meaning?

***

January 5, 1933
"Big news story breaks at noon. Calvin Coolidge, ex-president of U.S., dies."

***

One of the top sports stories that Dad handled that day was a report from the President's research committee on social trends. It included the "possibility that public interest may eventually shift from college to professional football because of the superior skill of the latter."

J.P. Steiner, a University of Washington sociology professor and a member of the committee, wrote: "If this happens, college football may follow college baseball and decline as a public spectacle, becoming a game of no more than local interest."

***

January 11, 1933
"Still on sports. Calhoun apparently is going to be sick forever."

January 20, 1933
"Bystrom sick so back I go on sports desk. Packers play Ernie Nevers' team at San Francisco Sunday."

(The back-and-forth assignments were not unusual for the time and, no doubt, Dad welcomed the variety and a break from his regular routine of picking up news at the fire station, police department, and hospitals.)

January 21, 1933
"Learned that Ginny has been dating and necking Bill. So, when we got together tonight, told her we were all through. She seems to like Bill pretty well anyway. Went to Anderson's. Had 12 beers.

January 31, 1933
"Scathing letter from Ginny, who says I am no gentleman. Don't ever remember pretending to be one."

February 3, 1933
"Adolf Hitler is the new chancellor of Germany, the poor devil."

(Dad was partially correct in attaching "devil" to Hitler. But the die had been cast for the immediate future for Germany and the millions of victims of Hitler's menace. Dad would soon realize that, also.)

February 16, 1933
"Assassin fails in attempt to kill President-elect Franklin Roosevelt but seriously wounds Mayor Anton Cermak of Chicago in Miami."

(The *Press-Gazette* published an Associated Press photograph of a woman who was credited with grabbing the would-be assassin's arm as he fired, thus diverting the shot. Cermak would die several days later, but the woman's actions prevented history from being revised and FDR served another dozen years.).

February 20, 1933
"Senate has passed bill repealing 18th Amendment. House passed it today. Now states must ratify it and the prohibition farce will be over."

***

The House approved the resolution 289-121 so the parade of state votes could begin. Few in Wisconsin could have expected the state to wait very long to make its decision.

Many were struggling to get a foothold in the midst of the Depression, and difficult decisions were required. The Green Bay City Council slashed the salaries of city administration officials by 5 percent.

Judge Henry Graass tried to stall creditors by announcing he wouldn't grant any property foreclosures unless an emergency made it imperative.

Farmers went on strike three times during the year in an effort to raise milk and dairy prices. More than 2,000 farmers met at the Columbus Club auditorium in February and voted to join the Wisconsin Cooperative Milk Pool, leading to efforts to block milk deliveries to creameries.

There were numerous incidents of milk being poured out on Brown County highways, and several cheese factories were forced to shut down temporarily. The Fairmont Creamery, Green Bay's largest, was only able to obtain 60 percent of its milk delivery during the strike.

One of the strike leaders, angry at the state for supporting dairy businesses during the strike, said, "You got no business putting an honest man like Al Capone in prison and letting these racketeers remain outside."

Hopefully, that wasn't his strongest argument.

Judge Graass appeared before the striking farmers in Green Bay and urged lawfulness.

"You have a perfect right to organize," Graass said. "You have a perfect right to picket and to use every means to peacefully persuade others to join with you in this effort. But as your circuit judge, I caution you to remain within the law, to refrain from violence."

There were few violent confrontations throughout the state.

A panic had set in after two eastern states declared bank moratoriums. Fears increased that many people would storm the banks to withdraw funds in anticipation of similar steps being taken in Wisconsin.

They were right. Acting Gov. Thomas O'Malley declared a fourteen-day moratorium for banks in Wisconsin. National banks protested, saying they were under federal control. A couple Green Bay banks (Kellogg-Citizens and Peoples Bank and Trust) provided some services. It lasted barely a week after newly inaugurated President Roosevelt called for a four-day national bank holiday.

***

March 1, 1933
"Green Bay banks reported shaky. Town is wrapped in gloom."

March 3, 1933
"Moratorium declared, closing all banks in Wisconsin. National financial crisis nears. No money in circulation at all. Banking system is paralyzed. City seems stunned. Nation turns to Roosevelt."

March 4, 1933
"National banking crisis. 40 states have closed all their banks. Franklin Roosevelt inaugurated as 32nd president of United States."

March 6, 1933
"President declares national banking holiday for 4 days, closing every bank in U.S. Mayor Anton Cermak of Chicago, shot by assassin Feb. 16, dies in Miami."

March 7, 1933
"Some banks permitted to reopen on modified status. There never was a time when so much history was being made, as today."

March 8, 1933
"Wisconsin banks reopen but try to get some cash."

March 15, 1933
"Banks all over U.S. opening up as holiday ends. Nation's sentiment seems much improved."

March 16, 1933
"Find myself damned interested in Ginny, Fritz, Joan and Trudy — and none of them interested in me."

(Apparently, the moratorium extended to Dad.)

March 18, 1933
"Saw Dad, who is trying to promote a brewery, now that beer is coming back."

March 22, 1933
"President Roosevelt signs beer bill, effective April 7, and the breweries are buzzing after 13 years of inactivity."

April 5, 1933
"Wisconsin also votes to repeal 18th Amendment, to be the second state to do so. Thirty-six states must ratify."

April 7, 1933
"Breweries turn open their doors and pour out beer for the first time in 13 years. Tested some in aft and it's great, much better than the bootleg stuff."

(The Rahr Brewing Company was the first brewery in Green Bay to receive its permit to manufacture, store, and bottle fermented alcohol, but it was under strict requirements not to remove any of it from its premises until a minute after midnight on April 7.)

April 8, 1933
"America, happy at return of beer, settles down to drink itself back to prosperity."

***

Green Bay planned its celebratory reunion with legal beer, scheduling a Beer Parade. But, with Holy Week approaching, city leaders decided to hold the parade on Easter Monday, April 17, rather than tempt the ecclesiastic fates.

The parade was billed as a funeral for the Depression and the Eighteenth Amendment, included seventy-five floats, and drew thousands to downtown Green Bay. Chances are, some beer was consumed.

***

April 19, 1933
"Joan writes, accepting date for Saturday, which she first refused, and I've asked Trudy. Sent a few special delivery letters to straighten things out."

April 20, 1933
"Now comes special delivery from Joan, saying impossible to see you Saturday. This sounds like a gag."

April 22, 1933
"Finances are approaching another crisis. Wonder how I'll pull out of it this time. If only Dad could take care of himself."

***

A further sign of the times – and an omen to the future – was the announcement that Bay Beach would remain closed to swimmers because of the excess quantities of pollution. City parks superintendent L. Earl Fogleson cited a decision by the Wisconsin Board of Health that declared:

"Until the pollution is abated and existing conditions are considerably improved, the public should be warned not to make use of Bay Beach for recreational bathing purposes."

He said it could take four or five years to get the beach back to a healthy swimming level. Close to a century would have been more accurate.

***

May 16, 1933
"Farmers, on milk strike, involved with militia at Shawano. Someone will get shot pretty soon."

May 27, 1933
"Covered state track meet, won by West Green Bay. Ralph Metcalfe, Marquette star, ran 100-yard dash in 9.8 seconds."

(Metcalfe, an African-American star at Marquette, ran exhibition races at the state high school track meet. He won the silver medal in the 100 meters at the 1932 Olympics in Los Angeles and would go on to place second behind Jesse Owens at the 1936 Olympics in Berlin.)

June 24, 1933
"Cleaned up drowning story. Missing orphan's body found. My biggest story in months, front page and A.P. two days straight."

(A sobering story. As many as seventy orphans from the St. Joseph Orphanage in Allouez – currently site of the Green Bay Catholic Diocese offices on Webster Avenue – had walked down the hill to the Fox River near the railroad viaduct to go swimming. Edna Bowers, 14, sank in deep water and efforts to rescue her failed. Her body was recovered the same day, but orphanage officials suddenly realized that her 15-year-old sister, Agnes, was missing. Almost two days later, Agnes' body was recovered beneath the viaduct.)

July 8, 1933
"Met Jim Crowley, new head football coach at Fordham U."

August 18, 1933
"Lou Gehrig of N.Y. Yankees sets new consecutive playing record of 1,308 games."

***

For the Packers, the 1933 season would be a transition as age was catching up to many of the players who led the team to the triple titles in 1929-31 and the near-miss in 1932.

Lewellen was retired. Gone also were Jug Earp and Tom Nash. Hubbard was thirty-three. Michalske, Blood, and Dilweg were all thirty. The new brood was an unknown.

The *Press-Gazette*, as usual, started the pep rally of print on the eve of the first game of 1933 against the Boston Redskins with an editorial:

> "The wonder continues to grow throughout the country that this comparatively little city can continue, year after year, to put on the field the greatest or nearly the greatest football team in the world. Could there possibly be any better publicity for this city? Could literature, speakers, statistics, history, conditions, any of them, create a more enviable reputation?"

To that moment, the Green Bay Packers had produced a record of 124-36-17 and outscored their opponents 2,879-791.

But cheering alone wasn't going to produce the number of victories that had become regular in the previous four years. The opening game found the Redskins holding the Packers to a 7-7 tie, and Bystrom wrote that Boston clearly outplayed Green Bay.

A rebound was hoped for the following weekend when the Chicago Bears came to town. It appeared to be a Packers victory, with Green Bay leading 7-0 with five minutes left in the game on a short touchdown run by Buckets Goldenberg in the second quarter.

But the Bears drove nearly the length of the field to score a tying touchdown. Then, when the Packers were forced to punt with under a minute left, the Bears blocked Arnie Herber's kick and recovered in the end zone. Chicago's 14-7 victory was secured after the ensuing kickoff.

Bystrom called it "the most heart-breaking defeat the Packers ever tasted," made worse for the fans by George Halas dancing on the sidelines. Halas said, "I've been waiting six years for this day."

The game was also memorable for a collision that occurred when the Bears' Bronko Nagurski tried to tackle Clarke Hinkle head-on and suffered a broken nose for his effort. The collision would become a staple of Packers-Bears lore.

For the first time in at least five years, the Packers needed a key victory to move their season in the right direction. It would have to come in Milwaukee, where the Packers would host the New York Giants at Borchert Field. It would be the eighth time the Packers played in Milwaukee, having never lost a game there.

However, the Giants won 10-7, and Bystrom didn't sugarcoat his report:

> "A crowd of 13,000 turned out for what they expected to be a great football game. They didn't see it. What they saw was the Packers playing one of their worst games, offensively, in many years. They probably retired to their homes convinced that there is a cog or two missing in the great machine that so many years was the Packers.
>
> "Somewhere between Green Bay and Milwaukee, the Packers lost the punch they showed against the Bears in Green Bay a week ago."

***

October 1, 1933
"Drove to Milwaukee to see Packers lose rotten game of football to New York, 10-7 at Borchert Field. Covered game, worked late."

October 3, 1933
"Guess the Packers are all through as a championship threat."

***

Of interest was a play in which referee Meyer Morris suffered a sprained hand and wouldn't let the game continue until Dr. Kelly came on the field to treat him.

Lambeau's mood was expressed in this paragraph passed on to the *Press-Gazette* later in the week in a story written by Calhoun:

> "Lambeau was disgusted with Sunday's exhibition from the offensive point of view and has read the riot act to several of his headliners who have been content to bask in the limelight and let others do the blocking."

The story didn't identify the headliners.

The Packers were looking up at the rest of the Western Division and had unbeaten Portsmouth coming to town next. Papers in Ohio were printing stories about the game with references to the "former gridiron monarchs," "slipping Packers" and "fallen champions."

Bystrom went out on a limb:

> "Curbstone critics and cigar store sages to the contrary, we believe the Green Bay Packers have got just about all the bad football they are going to play this year out of their system. And with that announcement, we boldly add that the Green Bay team will beat the Portsmouth Spartans Sunday by a score of 19 to 7. All right, wolves, climb on."

Bystrom missed slightly on his score prediction, but was spot on with the result. The Packers beat the Spartans 17-0 in a driving rain that had players' uniforms caked in mud so thoroughly that Herber accidentally blocked Goldenberg out of a play, thinking he was an opposing player. The Packers didn't attempt a single pass with the exception of a successful extra point.

***

October 8, 1933
"In aft saw sensational football game. The Packers did it again, smacking down Portsmouth 17-0. Got soaked to the skin but didn't mind a bit."

October 14, 1933
"Germany withdraws from League of Nations. Looks like Hitler is gunning for another war."

October 15, 1933
"In aft covered football game. Packers walloped Pittsburgh 47-0, with Buckets Goldenberg running 81 yards for touchdown."

October 16, 1933
"The Packers are making a determined comeback after a poor start."

***

An easy contest against the Pittsburgh Pirates the following Sunday – a 47-0 romp – set up a rematch with the Bears, this time at Wrigley Field. It bore a startling resemblance to the first meeting in Green Bay. The Packers led 7-0 with four minutes to play, but the Bears scored a touchdown and a field goal in the final minute to win 10-7.

Controversy centered on a play in which Clarke Hinkle appeared to cross the goal line on a short run. But the Bears' Red Grange knocked the ball loose and recovered it, and the referee overruled the head linesman's initial touchdown call and gave the ball to the Bears.

The last home game saw the Packers beat up on the Philadelphia Eagles – the former Frankford team – 35-9 before starting a six-game road trip. The game included a humorous episode when Blood tried to whisper to teammate Roger Grove that the play was No. 62. Repeated attempts failed until a defensive back for the Eagles shouted, "Blood says No. 62. Do you get it? Now let's play ball."

The road trip featured an ugly start. The Packers defeated the Chicago Cardinals at Wrigley Field 14-6, but it featured a near free-for-all when confusion among the officials got everyone worked up.

In the third period, a Cardinals punt was downed at the Packers 6-yard line, but umpire Meyer Morris mistakenly said a Packer touched it and was prepared to give possession to the Cardinals. Referee George Lawrie confirmed it.

Hubbard became irate and grabbed Lawrie by the shoulders. Both benches cleared and fans raced onto the field. Some punches were thrown, although wildly, before Morris said he got it wrong and it should be Packers ball. Lambeau reportedly had told his team that if the mistake wasn't corrected to leave the field in protest.

As a sign of the times, every reference in Bystrom's game story to Cardinals halfback Joe Lillard included the fact that he was a Negro.

The victory was a boost for the Packers, but only temporarily. They went on to Portsmouth and lost 7-0, then to Boston to lose 20-7, and finally to the Polo Grounds, where they lost to the Giants 17-6.

***

November 12, 1933
"Heard football game over radio. Portsmouth 7, Green Bay 0."

***

The wheels were coming off. Lambeau became so frustrated during a team practice prior to the Giants game, when several players appeared to be taking it easy, that he told them to leave the field and turn in their uniforms if things didn't improve. The practice pace picked up.

Then, the night before the game, Blood broke team training rules – specifics weren't divulged – and Lambeau suspended him. Reports indicated that Blood showed up for practice in no shape to do anything. Making things even worse, Hubbard fractured a thumb and finger in the game and was lost for the season.

Prior to its next league game, the Packers played a Thanksgiving Day game against the Staten Island Stapletons on the island. It didn't count, since Staten Island wasn't part of the league anymore. Lambeau had only seventeen players in uniform, but Green Bay won 21-0 against a team that included hired college players who had completed their eligibility.

In a column prior to the Packers' final two games, Bystrom wrote a revealing column:

> "Why, many ask, haven't the Packers won more games this year? We believe there are many reasons for the poorest season of the last six or seven years, but we can't see any cause for alarm over the situation.
>
> "The reason we don't believe fans should become alarmed over the season's record should be apparent to fair-minded fans. Sure, we want a winner here. But so do fans in the other cities, the players on the other teams, coaches and owners - and they are going to do everything they can to see that they get one. They have to for their own salvation.
>
> "In line with this reasoning, it can be assumed that the other clubs went out after real performers to strengthen their teams. Here's what we believe happened. The other clubs got to be quite a bit stronger. Green Bay did not. In other words, Green Bay practically stood still, with a team that was as good as the championship squads of a few years ago, but the leaders caught up, in fact passed them."

The Packers played the Eagles in Philadelphia three days later and won 10-0, then rushed to catch the train for the ride back to Green Bay.

***

December 2, 1933
"Sports page include AP All-America. Backfield includes Sauer, Nebraska. In aft with Grace to see Katherine Hepburn in 'Little Women.' Then beer.

December 3, 1933
"Didn't stir out of the house all day. Stayed by the radio and heard some interesting programs, including Russ Winnie's broadcast of the Green Bay-Philadelphia game, which the Packers won 10-0. No women on my mind. It's an off-season.

***

Lambeau gave his opinion of why the season didn't go well.

"We made mistakes," he said. "I've made them and willing to admit it, but don't think they'll occur again. To begin with, I called team together too late. Blood, Hubbard, Mike (Michalske) and Hinkle reported even later than the others. Hinkle's tonsils had to come out and he wasn't ready for the early games."

Lambeau also referred to a letter that Hubbard received from league president Joe Carr shortly before the Portsmouth game as being "untactful." Carr warned Hubbard that another incident similar to his contact with the referee in Chicago could jeopardize his chances of getting a job as a Major League Baseball umpire. Lambeau said Hubbard just wasn't the same after that.

Hubbard would go on to a very successful career as an American League umpire from 1936-51, and then as an umpire supervisor until 1969. He is the only person to be enshrined in both the Pro Football and National Baseball halls of fame.

Leading up to the final game against the Bears the following week, Green Bay attorney M.E. Davis notified Joannes that he would buy a $50 suit or overcoat for a Packer for every touchdown scored against the Bears. With that, he said he would also donate $50 for needy children through Associated Charities in Green Bay.

Then, a couple days before the Packers traveled to Chicago, Herber dislocated a hip and suffered lacerations to his face when the car he was driving slammed into a truck on the north boundary of De Pere. His season was finished.

***

December 6, 1933
"Final state convention ratifies 21st Amendment, wiping out the prohibition laws. Dropped into one of the new liquor stores to see what it's all about and bought great 1927 sherry. Tastes great.

December 10, 1933
"Taxi down to loop in a.m. visited Tribune Tower. In aft out to Wrigley Field to see Packers lose great football game to Bears, 7-6. Monnett ran 88 yards for touchdown."

***

    The Bears, who a week later would defeat the Giants for the championship, edged the Packers 7-6 at Wrigley to end the Green Bay season at 5-8-1.
    Many members of the team traveled to St. Louis a week later to play a team there called the Gunners, but the Packers Corporation notified the players they were on their own for their expenses. They beat the Gunners 21-0.

***

December 18, 1933
"Nasty hangover, worst I've ever had. Mouth feels like the inside of a dead pelican."

December 19, 1933
"Have started new sports column in Press-Gazette, entitled 'Do You Remember?'"

December 21, 1933
"Charles and Mrs. Lindbergh back in U.S. after tour of Europe, Africa and South America."

December 23, 1933
"Got assignment from Columbia News Service to cover feature on Green Bay blind woman who regained her sight.

December 25, 1933
"Seventeen below zero. Ran into big fire. Oldenburg-Krippner building burned with loss of $64,000. Covered whole story. Plenty cold and tired.

***

The *Press-Gazette*, whose editorial page was known to favor Republican policies over Democratic ones, took stock of the world as the year closed, comparing 1933 to pre-1933 life:

> "If we judge solely and alone upon the physical differences of the situation presented, we have made great improvement. Those who want to thank Mr. Roosevelt for it may do so. Those who wish to ascribe it to natural causes may have their say-so.
>
> "No fair person, however, will deny to the President full credit for the death of Prohibition and the life of our banking system, both major props to a better and more orderly society. Anyone with eyes can see improvements so evident upon every hand.
>
> "And, perhaps, better still, American confidence is bubbling over again."

***

December 31, 1933
"Attended church in a.m. The parson will recover. Listened to radio all evening, completing a mild but economical New Year's Eve."

Chapter 9

Two Cents and a Rubber Nickel

Many of 1934's events became the stuff of movies and legends.

There was the highly publicized removal of criminals from American soil. First, it was the

Clyde Barrow-Bonnie Parker team ambushed by federal agents in Louisiana in May. Two months later, federal agents gunned down John Dillinger outside a movie theater in Chicago. In October, Pretty Boy Floyd died in a gunfight in Ohio, and in late November, agents finally caught up with the villain known as Baby Face Nelson in a shootout in the Chicago suburb of Barrington.

It was also the year that Adolf Hitler, now in complete dictator mode in Germany, got rid of some high-level military personnel he considered a potential threat to him. Most notable was the killing of SA Commander Ernst Rohm during a series of days later identified as "The Night of the Long Knives."

A woman named Oliva Dionne gave birth to quintuplets (five girls) in late May in Ontario. And an arrest was finally made in the two-year-old Lindbergh baby kidnap-murder case when Bruno Hauptmann was apprehended in September.

Locally, in the hopeful but pipe dream category, predictions were being made that pollution in the Fox River could be cleaned up within four to five years with the construction of sewage treatment plants between Lake Winnebago and the river's mouth at Green Bay.

State sanitary engineer L.F. Warrick told commissioners of the Green Bay Metropolitan Sewerage District that the Fox River was the next major objective of the Wisconsin Board of Health.

For Dad, there was continued interest in education, entertainment and ... other things ... as he watched the world events unfold. It was a year that found him playing an increasingly active role in the *Green Bay Press-Gazette's* coverage of the Packers.

***

January 1, 1934
"No chasing around last night so woke up without headache this morning."

January 2, 1934
"Democrats confidently await opening of Congress tomorrow, certain that Roosevelt will continue to crack the whip."

January 3, 1934
"In Wisconsin, stalwart and progressive Republicans unite in fusion ticket, attempting to wrest control of state from Democrats next fall. They'll never do it. I am going to devote myself to getting myself entirely out of debt."

January 4, 1934
"Roosevelt announces U.S. deficit of nine billion dollars. Don't know much about it but that sounds like a powerful lot of dough. Spent some time getting my sports column 'Do You Remember?' up to date."

January 7, 1934
"Came home to listen to radio, including political talk by Will Rogers and unusually good program by Jack Benny and Mary Livingston on the Chevrolet Hour. They did a burlesque of Cinderella that was a scream."

January 8, 1934
"Roosevelt may ask Congress to ratify the St. Lawrence waterways treaty. That'll mean a fight as the Senate is opposed to it."

January 9, 1934
"Bid Gage, who has been out of work about a year and a half, landed a job at the Bay West Paper Company."

(Bid Gage was a close friend of Dad's, a groomsman at his wedding, and a co-conspirator in numerous beer drinking episodes. The job he landed at Bay West was in sales promotion. He became a sales manager, then general manager, and in 1970, was named president of Bay West. He made an impressive recovery from the Depression.)

January 10, 1934
"Attended German class at Vocational School. I am very fond of anything German, except Adolf Hitler."

January 13, 1934
"I predict a war between Japan and Russia soon, probably this year. There's plenty of trouble brewing in Europe too."

January 23, 1934
"Gov. Schmedeman demands action from Wisconsin senate, but it's nickels against doughnuts he doesn't get it. May God keep me out of politics."

January 24, 1934
"I am going to try and make a trip to Germany, probably in 1936 or 1937."

(Spoiler alert: Guess what didn't happen.)

January 31, 1934
"Talked with Dad. He is optimistic about plans for a new distillery and brewery here, but I'll believe it when I see it."

February 4, 1934
"Saw Fredric March, Miriam Hopkins in 'All of Me.' A fine show, but Mother wouldn't have liked it, as two young ladies approached the sacred portals of motherhood without observing the customary rites of wedlock. Personally, I like babies."

February 7, 1934
"Today is the 40th birthday of George Herman (Babe) Ruth, the Sultan of Swat, who will smack "em again for the New York Yankees this summer. The Bam is still good enough to rate a $35,000 salary this season."

March 8, 1934
"The firemen played another joke on me by putting a bomb under the hood of my car. It was fake, of course, but it scared the hell out of me."

March 9, 1934
"Have developed quite a case on Margaret Sullavan, the screen actress. For two cents and a rubber nickel I'd write her, which would be a crazy thing to do. But who said I wasn't crazy? Would like to try for a job in Chicago, much as I hate the place."

***

Pursuit of Dillinger was a story that captured the attention of many. Listed as Public Enemy No. 1 by the FBI, Dillinger made a dramatic escape from the Crown Point, Indiana, jail using a wooden gun, and readers feasted on the story.

In late April, he and several of his henchmen and girlfriends spent a long weekend at the Little Bohemia Lodge in Manitowish Waters in far northern Wisconsin. Federal agents were tipped off and converged on the lodge the last Sunday evening of the month.

It was a botched raid. A Conservation Corps worker was shot by one agent who mistook him for a member of the Dillinger gang, and one FBI agent was also killed in the shootout.

Dillinger and several others escaped out the back of the lodge and through the woods, commandeered a car from a nearby property owner, and fled the area.

Three women who traveled with them were arrested, but refused to give their names.

Emil Wanatka, proprietor of the lodge, told agents he knew who his lodgers were.

"Sure, I knew it was Dillinger," he said. "I played cards with him every day. Those Chicago cops couldn't find him and in Indiana they couldn't hold him. So why should I have tried to take him? Say, he had a roll of money big enough to choke a cow."

It was an embarrassment for the FBI, but Dillinger's days were numbered as he left Wisconsin.

***

May 9, 1934
"The Press-Gazette is going to print a 150-page edition in June to commemorate Green Bay's 300th birthday. It means top-heavy work for all of us until then."

May 11, 1934
"There is going to be a lot of fun in Europe one of these days. All nations are armed to the teeth, only 20 years after the beginning of the World war."

Associated Press correspondent DeWitt Mackenzie seemed to share the same sentiments:

> "Grim fear impelled country after country to disregard the terrible ravages of the protracted economic depression and saddle already overstrained budgets with huge sums in a feverish rush to military preparedness.
>
> "Europe is mainly concerned but distrust spreads around the neurotic world to the Far East. Even the United States feels the influence.
>
> "In Europe, the panic was caused largely by the insistence of numerous countries that Germany was preparing for conquest and already had rearmed to a point where she was a menace to her neighbors."

***

July 11, 1934
"Now they have me writing fillers for the Press-Gazette Tercentennial edition, which comes off the press next Tuesday. It's fun, and I enjoy reading up on Wisconsin history."

July 12, 1934
"Today is my father's birthday. Gave him some cigars. He's had tough sledding the past few years and the future looks discouraging. Must have given him a few thousand dollars in the past few years."

July 14, 1934
"Babe Ruth, the old bambino of swat, hit the 700th home run of his major league career."

July 18, 1934
"The Press-Gazette's Tercentennial edition, 216 pages, the largest paper ever published in the midwest, issued today."

July 23, 1934
"Federal agents in Chicago kill John Dillinger, notorious bank robber and fugitive, as he leaves loop theater. It's a sensational news break."

(Prior to catching up with Dillinger, the FBI had arrested his girlfriend, Evelyn Frechette of Menomonie, Wisconsin, and charged her with conspiracy to harbor and conceal him.)

July 25, 1934
"Engelbert Dollfuss, chancellor of Austria, is assassinated, and Europe is mobilizing. There may be another war, but my guess is there won't - right away."

August 2, 1934
"Von Hindenburg, greatest of the Germans, is dead, and the nation is fearful of its future. It may well be."

August 3, 1934
"Germany today looks across the bier of her dead president into an uncertain future of super-Hitlerism. The chancellor has usurped all power, and he may even strike for the throne, a la Napoleon."

***

The highlight for Green Bay residents in 1934 was the August visit by President Roosevelt to help commemorate the community's tercentennial. FDR's visit came less than a month after the *Press-Gazette* published its 216-page Tercentennial Edition.

Roosevelt arrived by train shortly after 8:30 a.m., was transported to Bay Beach after parading through sections of the city, and then delivered a prepared speech about the values of the New Deal before an estimated 36,000 people. A special platform had been constructed on the park grounds for the occasion.

Dick Holznecht, a twelve-year-old *Press-Gazette* carrier boy, was escorted to the platform by Secret Service agents so he could shake Roosevelt's hand, representing the youth of the city.

By mid-afternoon, Roosevelt's train was already in Chicago on its way back to Washington, D.C.

***

August 4, 1934
"Green Bay anxiously awaiting the arrival of President Franklin Roosevelt next Thursday. Had a chance to serve on his guard of honor, but had to turn it down because the Press-Gazette will issue an extra that morning."

August 9, 1934
"I saw the president twice today, once as he arrived at the C&NW depot, and once along the line of parade. He is badly crippled, can hardly walk. While at station, I saw and shook hands with Senator Robt.

LaFollette, Senator F. Ryan Duffy, Governor A.G. Schmedeman and Rep. James Hughes. It was quite a thrill seeing the president. He's my idea of a great guy."

August 10, 1934
"In eve worked on Packer publicity, then covered a supremely boring three hour session of the Green Bay common council. I'll bet people have died of council meetings."

***

The business of hosting a president and celebrating history finally completed, the city could train its mind back on its favorite topic – the Packers.

The disappointment of the 1933 season increased the motivation to make more roster changes prior to the 1934 season. The most important move involved Johnny Blood. In early August, the Packers sold him to the Pittsburgh Pirates, a move no doubt prompted by Blood's behavior in New York the previous fall when he showed up for practice so hung over that he was suspended.

Bystrom wrote about the split between the Packers and one of its greatest stars:

> "We are going to miss Johnny Blood this fall … perhaps not miss him as far as the game itself is concerned, but for other reasons. Johnny was always colorful. He was good copy and volumes could be written about his exploits, both on and off the gridiron.
>
> "Blood was an 'on-and-off' performer last year but we believe if he gets down to business and quits a lot of his foolishness, he still has a year or two of good football in him."

Gone also was Hubbard, who decided to take a job as line coach at Texas A&M. There were fourteen new players who weren't on the 1933 roster. Most significant were veterans Tiny Engebretsen and Swede Johnston, and rookies Joe Laws and Ade Schwammel.

The Packers warmed up for their regular season by playing a game against a team from Fort Atkinson, Wisconsin, called the Blackhawks. Green Bay won handily, 28-7, with Laws and Johnston making impressive debuts.

***

August 28, 1934
"There seems to be a change in the air. Maybe I'll get a job in St. Louis. Would hate to leave Green Bay but am very restless."

August 31, 1934
"Heard radio account of football game between Chicago Bears and American All-Stars before 80,000 at Soldier Field, Chicago. Scoreless tie. The year's largest crowd for a sporting event."

September 4, 1934
"The Packers are assembling what appears to be their greatest football team, featuring some marvelous new material."

September 7, 1934
"With the football season underway, I'm now doing considerable sport work with Art Bystrom, which I like very much."

September 9, 1934
"In aft took play-by-play at Packer football game. The team opened its season by walloping the Fort Atkinson Black Hawks, 28-7. Monnett scored two touchdowns and the others went to Grove and Chet Johnson. Was kept plenty busy on the sidelines, as didn't know all the new men."

***

The Packers then beat the Philadelphia Eagles 19-6, but learned that Johnston might not be with them for the rest of the season. Johnston had played for the St. Louis Gunners in 1933 and signed a contract with them at the end of the season. Thinking the Gunners would no longer field a team, he signed with the Packers. But the Gunners held him to his contract and threatened to fine him $125 for every game he played with the Packers.

A sidelight to the Eagles game, according to Calhoun's notes, was the fact that Arnie Herber, Claude Perry, Swede Johnston, and Buckets Goldenberg played parts of the game without head gear, which Calhoun noted, "isn't always a good idea."

***

September 16, 1934
"Covered play-by-play of Packer game in aft. Green Bay looked impressive as it won from Philadelphia Eagles, 19-6. Most of the scoring

was done by the eminent Mr. Monnett, formerly of Michigan State, who got two touchdowns, an extra point and a field goal. Adolph Schwammel also booted a field goal. Davis' statistics were all wrong, as normal, so had to figure out correct ones at office."

September 17, 1934
"Letter from Robert Ambruster, St. Louis. Things don't look so bright for a job down there right now, and that means I'll hang on with the Press-Gazette for a while at least. Am pretty much pleased to do so. That isn't sour grapes either."

September 20, 1934
"They've captured a man named Bruno Hauptmann in New York, who apparently knows quite a lot about the Lindbergh kidnapping of March 1, 1932."

***

Then it was time for the Bears' annual visit to Green Bay, and the result was similar to the prior season. Tied 10-10 after the third period, the Bears scored twice after that, one on a 34-yard run by Bronko Nagurski, to win 24-10. With a record crowd of 12,582 watching, the Bears unveiled a new threat in back Beattie Feathers.

In his notes, Calhoun pointed out that Hinkle once had to punt from beneath the goal posts, which were located at the goal line. He noted that teams usually had a gentleman's agreement to let punters move away from the posts, but the Bears made him stay put.

Also, striving to give readers the most important details, Calhoun wrote this about an early version of tailgating:

"Many fans came in the morning, bringing their lunch to eat while they waited for the game to begin. One good-natured gentleman sat eating a pot of beans with a spoon; another had three pints of milk to keep his appetite satisfied."

***

September 29, 1934
"Just like a bolt out of the sky came a note from Managing Editor Kennedy: 'Effective October 1 your salary will be $125 per month instead of $108. Keep this confidential.' This considerably changed my immediate financial outlook."

***

Having played so poorly in the 1933 game against the New York Giants at Milwaukee's Borchert Field, the Packers redeemed themselves by beating the Giants 20-6 at the new field at State Fair Park.

***

September 30, 1934
"In aft heard great football game over radio. Green Bay Packers defeated New York Giants at Milwaukee, 20-6. Green Bay touchdowns by Grove and Goldenberg and points after touchdown by Monnett, two field goals by Monnett. It was a real triumph for the Packers."

***

But that performance preceded a 3-0 loss to the new Detroit Lions when Glen Presnell kicked a 54-yard field goal.

***

October 7, 1934
"In aft covered play-by-play at Packer-Detroit game. Glenn Presnell's 54-yard place kick beat Green Bay, 3-0. It was a disappointing contest to watch."

***

Then, after a cakewalk 41-0 victory over the Cincinnati Reds in Green Bay, the Packers boarded a train to Milwaukee to watch Dizzy and Daffy Dean pitch in a baseball exhibition. It was also the prelude to another game against the Bears, an exhibition at midweek obviously arranged to pick up some capital from Milwaukee fans.

***

October 9, 1934
"The unbelievable Dizzy Dean shut out the Detroit Tigers, 11-0, to give the St. Louis Cardinals the baseball championship of the world."

October 14, 1934
"Took play-by-play at Packer game in aft. Green Bay 41, Cincinnati 0. Hank Bruder played sensational game."

***

In a somewhat bizarre incident during the Bears' 10-6 exhibition victory, Packers fans in Milwaukee became so enraged at head linesman George Lawrie when they thought he was ignoring several offside infractions by the Bears that they surrounded him at the end of the game, with one spectator knocking him to the ground. Nothing came of the incident.

When Laws scored the Packers' touchdown as the gun sounded ending the game, fans rushed on the field. Bruder attempted an extra point kick with a couple young fans standing about five feet away.

The public address announcer was Rocky Wolf, a member of the Bears publicity staff who enjoyed getting Packers fans riled by exaggerating gains by Bears players.

***

October 17, 1934
"Drove to Milwaukee in aft with Torinus and Art Bystrom. Ate at Old Heidelberg. Then out to State Fair Park where Packers lost tough game to Chicago Bears, 10-6. Joe Laws got the Green Bay touchdown. Drove home right after game. Bed at 2:30 a.m. Torinus has a fine radio in his car, which helped make the trip pleasant.

October 21, 1934
"In aft took play-by-play of football game between Packers and Chicago Cardinals. The Packers played fine ball to win, 15-0. Touchdowns by Hinkle and Grove, both catching sensational passes from Herber."

***

Bystrom cheered: "They hit hard and often, charged like smashing pile drivers and tackled as if it were to be their last stand for life."

So, there were flickers of optimism as the Packers traveled to Wrigley Field to meet the unbeaten and two-time league champion Bears.

It would be a milestone of sorts for Dad, as he not only took a couple game photos from the sidelines but was also assigned to write the lead game story for the first time.

The Bears won 27-14, but that didn't stop John M. Walter from finding a silver lining in his game story lead:

> "Proving beyond all doubt that Green Bay is represented by a fighting football team, the Packers held a brilliant Chicago Bears eleven to a 27-14 score here yesterday before more than 15,000 people.

"No one can say that the Packers didn't give all they had to win. No one can say they didn't battle these Bears right down to the last chalk line. And no one can say, truthfully, that the Bruins, twice National champions, are weakening."

***

October 28, 1934
"Arose at 11:30. Dinner at Drake Hotel with Mrs. V.I. Minahan and Torinus. Delicious crab meat in Cape Cod Room. Then out to Wrigley Field to see the Chicago Bears take a great game from the Packers, 27-14. The boys put up a great battle. Snapped a number of grafted pictures."

October 29, 1934
"Wrote lead story on Packer game. My pictures turned out swell."

***

Calhoun contributed several notes to go with Dad's game story. Included was a comment from Lambeau that he considered the Bears the greatest professional football team he had ever seen, and a mention that Hinkle and Bruder played the entire sixty minutes of the game.

But Calhoun went after the officiating, too:

"The Bears, particularly Hewitt, had been offside all afternoon but they weren't called on it until the Packers had little chance to even up the ball game. It's a queer business, if you ask me.

"The Bears, who are past masters of holding, exercised all their talents in yesterday's game. A blind man could detect some of the offenses, but not the officials. On Feathers' 47-yard run for a touchdown, half of the Packers were being held by the Bears. The officials either will have to call these penalties or else the Packers will have to start practicing some holding plays."

Calhoun did get a comment from referee Bobby Cahn who made the observation that "the Bears have 22 good players and the Packers about 14."

***

The Packers, My Dad and Me

October 31, 1934
"Attended tryouts for Little Theater play 'Three Cornered Moon.' Would love to play the part of Allen Stevens, if they have a good leading lady. Went by myself to see fine motion picture, Claudette Colbert in 'Cleopatra.' It really was a magnificent spectacle."

November 2, 1934
"In eve first rehearsal of 'In the Money' Elks Club musical comedy. I play the lead."

November 5, 1934
"Handling the sports desk while Calhoun is east with the Packers. Trudy's acceptance of my invitation assures me of the best looking date at the military ball. Never saw her when she didn't look gorgeous."

November 6, 1934
"Election day. Voted for Gov. Schmedeman and practically a straight Democratic ticket, although Wisconsin went back to the LaFollette Progressives. The nation turned in a Democratic landslide.

***

A 10-0 victory over the Boston Redskins helped, but the Packers were beaten in New York by the Giants, 17-3, and then shut out by the Chicago Cardinals in Milwaukee, 9-0.

***

November 16, 1934
"Two letters. One from Trudy saying I may take her to the football game Sunday. The other from Muriel, saying I may take her to the football game Sunday. Even my non-mathematical mind can see that this is a poor situation, as two and one don't make two. Everything happens to me."

November 18, 1934
"Quite a long day. Left Green Bay at 8:15 a.m., picked up Trudie at Sheboygan and continued to Milwaukee. Then out to State Fair Park in West Allis to see soggy football game on a muddy field. Cardinals 9, Packers 0. Green Bay playing terrible ball. Back at Schroeder talked to Bob Jones, Les Peterson and Mike Michalske of the Packers."

***

Part of the *Press-Gazette's* report on the loss to the Cardinals was revealing:

> "The Cardinals had plenty of fight and that's what won the game. On the other hand, the Packers, that is most of them, seemed content to just go through the motions and let matters take care of themselves. If they managed to win, that was all right. If they didn't win, that was all right too. That seemed to be their philosophy."

***

November 23, 1934
"Calhoun left for Detroit with the Packers so I'll be on the sports desk for the next 10 days.

November 24, 1934
"In aft saw Fred Astaire, Ginger Rogers and Edward Everett Horton in 'The Gay Divocee,' a highly amusing picture enlivened by Astaire's marvelous dancing.

***

Then, unexpectedly, the Packers went to Detroit and stunned the unbeaten Lions 3-0 when Hinkle kicked a 47-yard field goal in the fourth quarter.

***

November 25, 1934
"In aft heard sensational football game over radio. No one expected them to do it but the Green Bay Packers rode to a brilliant victory over the Detroit Lions, 3-0, on Clarke Hinkle's 50-yard field goal. Felt very elated over it all. The boys outplayed the Lions decisively. Am plenty flat and no pay day until December 1. Rather tough, just when I seem to be getting somewhere with Mary. Wish she were a little more human. She's far too good a girl for me."

***

Calhoun soaked up the Detroit surprise:
"Anybody who saw last week's exhibition against the Cards in Milwaukee would have hardly believe that it was the same football machine. Looking like the Packers of old, the Bays deserved the victory as they battled the chesty Lions from the opening whistle.

"Pregame odds at several of the betting establishments were offering 8 to 5 on the Lions and some of the short enders were smiling from ear to ear at the unexpected turn of events."

But joy was temporary as the Packers dropped a 6-0 decision to the Cardinals three days later on Thanksgiving.

***

November 29, 1934
"Thanksgiving Day and more to be thankful for than last year. For one thing, I'm still unmarried. In aft kept statistics of football game over radio. Packers lost to Chicago Cardinals, 6-0. Then helped present 'The Courtship of Miles Standish' over radio station WHBY, taking the part of John Alden. In eve stayed home and listened to radio, including fine program by Fred Waring. He featured a new song 'June in January' which probably will be a sensational hit.

***

The Packers ended their season with a 21-14 victory over the St. Louis Gunners.

The team finished with a 7-6 record, and while Lambeau said one or two games were disappointing, he deemed the season a success.

What remained to be learned at the end of 1934 was whether the Packers were on their way up or down.

It seemed to be the same for Dad.

***

December 4, 1934
"Heard Dad is hard up for clothes. Must do something about it immediately. Feel very unsettled about Dad. It would be almost impossible for me to support him entirely, and he's doing almost nothing for himself."

December 5, 1934
"Dad has smashed his car and now he has to use mine part of the time. Letter from Muriel, asking me down. She was injured falling off a horse. Never thought much of those animals anyway."

December 10, 1934
"Surprise Christmas savings check for $20 arrives. That's Mother's doings, and it comes in plenty handy. New York sprang a big upset

yesterday to beat the Chicago Bears for the national professional football championship, 30-13, scoring 27 points in the last quarter."

December 20, 1934
"Here's a jolt. Dr. Nadeau funds my sinuses full of infection and an operation seems imperative. Nothing like ending the old year right. If I have to have another operation, am all for getting it over with."

December 21, 1934
"Spent miserable morning at hospital. Injections into my sinuses. The x-rays showed they are badly infected and there's more stuff in them than there is at the bottom of the Chicago River."

December 22, 1934
"One of those days to forget. Operation on nose and sinuses by Dr. E.G. Nadeau in a.m. at St. Vincent Hospital. Under local anesthetic but suffered plenty.

December 29, 1934
"The old year is sliding to an end. It finds the nation making great strides toward working its way out of five years of business depression. Next year should be the best since 1929. People are getting out and spending money, factory payrolls are increasing. In general, the road is open again."

December 31, 1934
"And the year 1934 ends. It hasn't been such a hot year. It saw me in three hospitals, and battling all the time with financial troubles. One bright spot was the handsome salary raise I got in October. Had a few thrills but no steady girl during the year. In general, worked hard and improved my position at the Press-Gazette."

***

A big change awaited in 1935. For Dad and for the Packers.

Chapter 10

Fall and Rise

Pat Ringer worked at Rothe Foundry, but this was a Sunday and a perfect time to spend $2 and bring his son, Lloyd, to a Packers game. It was September 26, 1931, and the Brooklyn Dodgers were the opponent at City Stadium.

Father and son found their seats in the top row of the bleachers at the northwest corner of the stadium. Early in the game, a play at the east end of the field caused spectators in front of the Ringers to stand. So they stood, too. But something was different when they prepared to sit down.

"I went to sit down, kind of backed up, and the board was gone" Pat Ringer would later testify. "I fell kind of that way and caught myself on one of those hooks, and I slid down the board to help (Willard) Bent.

It was an incident that almost brought the Packers to ruin. Willard Bent, age fifty-one, was seated on the same top row of wooden bleachers as the Ringers. The bleacher seat became dislodged when everyone stood to see the play, and when Bent went to sit down, he was unable to avoid falling twelve feet to the pavement. He sustained injuries to his vertebrae, muscles, and tendons, and was transported to St. Mary's Hospital on South Webster Avenue, a few blocks away.

A year and six days later, Bent filed a $20,000 lawsuit against the Packers, claiming the corporation was liable for failing to provide clamp devices to keep the wooden plank secure. The civil suit claimed that Bent suffered "great bodily injury, breaking his vertebrae, breaking and tearing his muscles" that he was "so maimed and permanently injured and has endured great pain and suffering."

Bent was represented by Arthur Fontaine of the Silverwood & Fontaine law firm in Green Bay. The Packers' defense was handled by its attorney, Gerald Clifford, whose law firm included former Packers receiver Lavvie Dilweg.

The trial began February 23, 1933, before a jury of eight men and four women. They were: D.D. Clark, Mrs. A.J. Reinhard, John Tauscher, Mrs. H. O'Neill, William Van Oss, George Barth, Leroy Hoberg, Lucio Christensen, Ida Wintgens, Joseph Hermes, Charles Kehl, and Mrs. Louis Arndt. Kehl was chosen as foreman. Judge Henry Graass presided at the Brown County Courthouse.

Clifford countered Bent's claim by telling the jury that the Green Bay Board of Education had custody and control of the bleachers, and the Packers had no ownership there.

Dr. Webber Kelly, former president of the Packers Corporation and still on its executive committee, was president of the Green Bay School Board at the time of Bent's accident. Asked by Clifford if there was any contract between the Packers and the school board pertaining to the football facility, Kelly said no.

Clifford also contended that Bent's condition was impacted by "continuous, excessive, not only use, but abuse of intoxicating liquor over a lifetime."

Under cross-examination, Clifford continued to focus on Bent's use of alcohol, implying that Bent's physical issues weren't necessarily the result of the fall.

"Isn't it a fact that you have been drinking to excess for a long period of time immediately preceding this trial?" he asked.

"No, I ain't been drinking steady," Bent said.

"Isn't it a fact that you have been told by your physician that (head trouble) has been aggravated by your continuous and excessive use of intoxicated liquor?" Clifford said.

"I believe he did say something like that."

When Bent said his back hadn't recovered from the fall from the bleachers, Clifford asked, "Your trouble didn't interfere with your walking down to Anderson's saloon and back in the past six months, did it?"

Clifford pressed Bent repeatedly about his drinking, and his history of accidents and injuries. But it was testimony from Dr. John R. Minahan that opened a different line of questioning as Clifford tried to zero in on a specific infection that he claimed was at the crux of Bent's continued poor health.

With Minahan on the stand, Clifford asked: "Didn't you say to Mr. Leland Joannes Saturday when you were going out of the courtroom that the trouble with this son of a B is that he is full of syphilis?"

"I said he had it," Minahan replied.

In cross-examining Bent, Clifford asked: "Don't you know, as a matter of fact, that you have a very serious infection now?"

"No, I don't know it," Bent said.

The trial lasted a week. The jury decided that the Packers were more responsible than Bent for the accident, and awarded him a total of $5,544.10.

When the insurance company that held the Packers' liability safety net went out of business, the Packers had no choice but to go into voluntary receivership while they appealed the verdict to the Wisconsin Supreme Court.

Judge Graass made the benevolent appointment of Frank Jonet as receiver. Jonet had connections with the Packers dating back to 1919. At the time of the trial, the franchise was in Joannes's name, a move approved earlier in the year by the league.

Joannes, who was team president from 1930-1947, loaned the Packers $6,000 and was the force behind getting the corporation back on its financial feet.

The long and complicated legal journey finally wrapped up in the Wisconsin Supreme Court on January 8, 1934, nearly two-and-a-half years after Bent's fall. First, the court concluded that for legal reasons the bleachers must be considered a public building, and Bent, as a ticket buyer, was not required to assume risk sitting on the bleachers.

Justice John Wickhem explained why the Green Bay Packers Corporation had to pay the man $4,775, a figure arrived at upon appeal by the Packers. He wrote that the "safe place" statute applied equally to religious and charitable institutions as it did to others. Since the Packers fell into the non-profit basket, they had to pay.

Following the high court decision, Joannes promised the corporation "will leave no stone unturned" to meet its financial obligations, adding that more fans may be given the chance to buy into the club.

But he admitted the situation was critical.

"Just what effect the Supreme Court decision will have on the future of professional football in Green Bay is, of course, unknown at this time. The situation has been brought about by events over which the football corporation officials have had no control. The 1933 season, in spite of the fact that the club lost quite a number of games and encountered bad weather at home, will show that it operated without loss.

"Yet it is almost a certainty that under these kind of times the club cannot operate with much, if any profit, certainly not enough to liquidate the claims standing against it. Some plan will be worked out to be presented to the fans and Packer supporters for their final decision and approval."

There were rumors. One included a scenario that would have the franchise transferred to Milwaukee, where a larger number of potential fans and investors were located.

The initial trial garnered very little publicity – the verdict warranting just a two-paragraph story on an inside page of the *Green Bay Press-Gazette* – but it would have a significant impact on the Packers' future.

What followed eleven months later were events that remain among the most critical in the history of the Green Bay Packers.

Twenty-five top business leaders of Green Bay met on a Friday evening at the Joannes Bros. company offices on South Washington Street. Lee Joannes, the Packers Corporation president, laid out the details of the financial crisis confronting the fifteen-year-old team.

"You have been invited here tonight to decide whether the Packer football team shall be retained here, or whether you want to throw it overboard," he said.

"Green Bay is the smallest town in the National Football League but, with careful management and a comparatively low overhead, we have been able to compete with such cities as New York, Chicago, Boston, Philadelphia, Brooklyn and Detroit, and up until a year ago keep going without a deficit. As a matter of fact, over the last 12 years the club has made money, enough to build City Stadium, which represents a permanent investment of more than $20,000, all paid by professional football.

"However, the club did not make any profit this year due to the team – handicapped by weather, injuries and lack of sufficient first-class material – did not make such a good showing and was not as good a drawing card as in previous years.

"We reduced expenses to a minimum and operated economically the last two seasons in the hope that we could make enough to pay off the claims against the corporation and to lift the receivership. Due to several circumstances we have been unable to do this. So we are laying our cards on the table and are asking you whether you consider the team of sufficient value to Green Bay to be continued."

This was a major crossroad for the corporation.

"We cannot go on operating when the club is losing money," he continued. "The court will not permit it. We must either raise enough money to lift the receivership and reorganize the corporation or close up shop. Under present conditions, we are handicapped in signing players, contracting for games and in many other ways. It is an unhealthy condition all the way around and cannot possibly go on."

The Packers had $12,322.46 in outstanding claims that included the court-ordered settlement with Bent. Joannes said it would be vital to raise $10,000 within thirty days to keep the corporation out of bankruptcy.

"Do you think it is worthwhile to attempt to do this, or do you want to pass the whole thing up?" he asked. "Personally, in view of the worth of the team to Green Bay as an advertising medium and as an entertainment feature during the fall, I think it would be a crime to let the Packers leave Green Bay without trying to do something about it. I am confident that if we once clean up these liabilities and build up our team to the 1929 and 1930 standards, we could keep our heads above water for many years to come."

Lee Joannes, president of the Packers Corporation, led a crucial meeting of Green Bay business leaders to discuss the continued viability of the team. (Photo courtesy of the Green Bay Packers)

Jonet spoke next, reporting that the corporation had $99,586.01 in receipts and $102,992.33 in disbursements in 1934. The bulk of expenses went to player salaries, guarantees to visiting teams, and traveling expenses.

He said the corporation was in the black at midseason with $9,000 on hand and that "things looked fairly bright. However, we got three tough breaks in succession, two rainy Sundays and a poor crowd at the Cincinnati game here, and we dropped approximately $12,000. We finished the season with a deficit, not a large one, but large enough probably to cause the court to order the corporation into bankruptcy unless the claims outstanding are cleaned up. The present situation cannot go on."

Then Andrew Turnbull, the former corporation president and publisher of the *Press-Gazette*, spoke.

"The situation is not hopeless," he said. "I've seen years when conditions looked much blacker and we came through all right. We have a good ball club, but in order for Green Bay to stay in the National league, we must have an extraordinarily good ball club and we can't have that kind of club without more first-class players. We have a good coach, too, one of the best in the league, and if we have the money we ought to get the players. The Packers will again be up there fighting for the championship."

The speeches finished, Green Bay Association of Commerce president Frank P. Vaughan made a motion that the $10,000 be raised to support the Packers.

It passed unanimously and Joannes immediately appointed a committee to draw up a plan to solicit the funds. Those in attendance on that history-setting night were:

J.I. Christopherson, C.A. Straubel Cheese Co.; Emil Fischer, Atlas Cold Storage; Barney Walters, Green Bay Hardware Company; Lawrence Balza and J.E. Bryson, Balza Pickle Company; Ray Leicht and Genere Leich, Leicht Transfer and Storage; Frank Bogda, Bogota Motor Company; Harry Golden, J.H. Golden Company; Raymond Decker, Green Bay Food Company; Forrest Plott, Fairmont Creamery; A.E. Winter, Morley-Murphy Hardware; Milton Larsen, Larsen Canning; M.E. Davis, attorney; Harvey Lhost, F. Hurlbut Company; James Stathas, Brown County Motors; Paul Burke, Northwest Engineering; Frank Vaughan, Bay West Paper Company; D.V. Pinkerton and L.G. Wood, Northern Paper Company; Ceil Baum, Baum's Department Store; and R.C. Smith, Farmers Exchange Bank.

Unable to attend, but sending their support for the Packers were: J.M. Conway, Hoberg Paper and Fibre Company; A.C. Witteborg, Beaumont Hotel; Charles Raasch, H.C. Prange Company; and Fred Cobb, Cobb's Sunlit Bakery.

Press-Gazette sports editor Art Bystrom sat in on the meeting and wrote about it several days later:

> "There will be no adoption of the Packer professional football club by Milwaukee or any other city. Having nursed and fretted over her 'baby' for twelve years, coddling it along through sick, lean years when it looked like it and the league it played in would not survive, Green Bay is not ready to disown it after such a minor setback as has been experienced the past two years.
>
> "Would Green Bay step down at this time after weathering much worse storms when the future was dark because of a few thousand dollars? The answer came at a meeting here the other night. They (business leaders) voted unanimously to extricate the football corporation from its present financial difficulties to build up the team for another championship."

The meeting set the course to get the franchise out of debt. Reorganization occurred a month later with Joannes remaining as president, Fred Leicht elected vice-president, Jonet as treasurer, and George Calhoun as secretary.

The executive committee included those men plus Turnbull, Clifford, H.J. Bero, and E.R. Fischer. Significant was the election of a board of directors that included many of the financial backers and ticket subscribers. They were H.J. Wintgens, D.V. Pinkerton, Harvey Lhost, John D. Moffatt, Ed Schuster, Leslie Kelly, Charles Mathys, F.O. Walker, H.G. Stolz, Fred L. Cobb, A.A. Reiner, J.E. Peep, and Arthur Schumacher.

The meeting at Joannes Bros. was held just sixteen days before the Rose Bowl game that would showcase the talents of an Alabama wide receiver named Don Hutson.

Nobody knew it then, but the decision by those Green Bay business leaders made it possible for the future Hall of Famer to choose Green Bay as his post-college destination.

Chapter 11

Hope and Hutson

It was just a coincidence, of course.

But there was interesting symmetry on February 22, 1935. It was the day Dad received news that would soon propel his impact on the Green Bay sports scene to a new level. It was a day that also took him to a new movie.

***

February 22, 1935
"Big news at the office. Bystrom may get a job with the Associated Press and I might – and I say I might – get his spot as sports editor. I'll know before March 11. It would be a great break. Went to see Mary Boland in 'Pursuit of Happiness.' Story was laid in 1776 and concerned that happy but, unfortunately, dead custom of bundling, which involved getting in bed with a woman, fully dressed, when the house was cold. Never went at it just that way."

The aforementioned coincidence had nothing to do with bundling. But the top headline on the *Press-Gazette* sports page that day read: "Green Bay Packers Secure Don Hutson."

Dad's six and a half years as sports editor, before being activated by the army, included the launch and prime of Hutson's showcase pro football career that was instrumental in making what writers at the time called the "overhead" offense a staple in the game.

The two men became good friends.

That day in February wasn't Dad's first introduction to Hutson, however. He heard what many Americans heard nearly two months earlier.

***

January 1, 1935
"Climbed out of bed at 9 a.m. after 12 hours of sleep — certainly was one tame New Year's Eve, but it didn't cost me a dime, and with my flat pocketbook, I should register gratitude. Came home in aft and listened to thrilling football broadcast from Rose Bowl. Dixie Howell led Alabama to victory over Stanford, 29-13."

***

Howell was indeed an individual star, but his two wide receivers would leave a greater mark on the football landscape.

His right end was Paul Bryant, whose deification in the Crimson Tide culture – they called him Bear Bryant – would be eternal. The left end was Hutson, who caught two touchdown passes in the game and would live long enough to see his name attached to the indoor practice facility of the Green Bay Packers.

Alabama coach Frank Thomas called Hutson the best all-around performer he had seen in years. Georgia Tech coach William Alexander described him as the best end the south had seen in a decade.

Lambeau wasn't at the Rose Bowl, instead scouted college players at the Shriners Benefit game in San Francisco the same day. One of the players who caught his eye was the right tackle from Minnesota named Phillip Bengtson who, although never to wear a Packers player jersey, would one day carry the same title that Lambeau carried in 1935.

Another player in that benefit game was the center from Michigan, Gerald Ford, whose impact would be made later outside of football.

As the year dawned, *Press-Gazette* sports editor Art Bystrom added his wit to the season with some proposed resolutions:

> "To Coach Lambeau – to get two of the best tackles in the country for next year's Packer team. To the National Professional football league and game supporters – to stop harping about officials and do something before next season about getting competent ones. To Mike Michalske – to quit making six-heart bids doubled and vulnerable (at least when he's my opponent.)"

After the holiday football schedule was put to rest, the country obsessed over the trial of Bruno Hauptmann, who faced a deluge of evidence that pointed to him as a key figure in the kidnapping and murder of the Lindbergh baby in 1932.

***

January 8, 1935
"They're drawing the net tighter around Bruno Hauptmann, who is on trial for kidnapping the Lindbergh baby. Phil LaFollette was inaugurated governor of Wisconsin yesterday - he didn't get in on my vote."

***

The trial would last five weeks. Hauptmann would be convicted primarily on circumstantial evidence, and sentenced to be executed. His appeals failed and the sentence was carried out fourteen months later.

There was encouragement for the Green Bay business community a week into the new year when *Forbes Magazine* listed the city as one of the fifteen best in the country for its continued recovery in 1934 from the Great Depression.

"From July to September business declined less rapidly in 1934 than in 1933," the magazine cited. "In September and October it rose more rapidly, and since October it again declined at a slower rate than in the previous year."

It was a time in history when a slower business decline was seen as progress.

Then President Roosevelt approved a two cent per-hour raise for common laborers in the paper and pulp mills. It didn't affect the male workers in the three Green Bay mills as they maintained their 40 cent per-hour rate. But women in the mills saw their hourly pay go from 33 to 35 cents.

Equal pay for equal work was sexist in the business world in 1935. But Dad got some good news.

***

January 15, 1935
"The Press-Gazette nudged my pay up another $5 a month today – I'm now getting $130 monthly."

***

The Green Bay City Council approved an ordinance to restrict what it called "come-on girls" from soliciting drinks from men in taverns unless they were already acquainted. If caught, they could be assessed a fine or given jail time, and the tavern's license could be suspended. The ordinance made no reference to "come-on guys."

The Packers made news in early February when they signed Southern California tackle Ernie Smith and Kansas State tackle George Maddox. At the same time, the corporation formed an executive board that included Lee Joannes, Fred Leicht, Frank Jonet, Dr. Webber Kelly, Andrew Turnbull, H.L. Bero, and Emil Fischer.

Curly Lambeau met with the board and described the difficulty of trying to compete with the Chicago Bears, Boston Redskins, and Detroit Lions, who were able to offer more money.

"The Chicago Bears offered Cotton Warburton, the West Coast Flash, $5,000 a year," Lambeau said. "But he is worth that to the Bears. His name alone will draw many extra customers into the big Chicago park. If we had him, we could not count on extra customers to pay such a high salary."

Warburton, who starred as a running back at Southern Cal, never signed with the Bears. Instead, he took a job in Hollywood as a film editor and began a career that peaked when he won an Academy Award for editing the 1964 movie *Mary Poppins*.

Lambeau told the board he had his eye on two Alabama players.

"Hutson and Lee, end and tackle respectively, are rated as real performers," he said. "I contacted both, only to find that Brooklyn is also trying to land them. The eastern club has offered them attractive contracts, but they have not come to definite decisions."

Six days later, Lambeau had Hutson's signature on a contract. Speaking to Bystrom, Lambeau said Hutson "should be an outstanding performer within a year or two."

Or sooner.

Dad didn't have to wait long to get confirmation of his promotion at the *Press-Gazette*.

***

March 1, 1935

"Starting Monday, March 11, I shall be sports editor of the *Press-Gazette*. So says Managing Editor R.A. Kennedy. This is the break of breaks for me, and it's going to mean some terrific work. Have a million ideas to improve the page."

March 2, 1935
"Laying plans for taking over the sports desk. Kennedy wants me to run a 'Looking Up' column every day. The contacts I'll make in that work will be practically limitless."

March 5, 1935
"When I go on the sports desk, I'll be on the hospital run no longer. And may the saints be praised."

March 7, 1935
"Conferred with E.L. Lambeau, coach of the Packers, and picked up considerable material for my column."

***

With the promotion, Dad began a relationship with Lambeau that tested both of them, as both were strong-willed and driven. A few years later, Dad would confide in his diary that he and Lambeau weren't on speaking terms for a period of time, a relationship that eventually required Turnbull to intercede and mediate.

But, when he stepped into his new position, Dad found that Lambeau was a prime source of information. A news tip during Dad's first week in the editor's chair was a good start.

***

March 17, 1935
"Coach E.L. Lambeau has informed me that the Packers expect to sign George Sauer, Nebraska's great All-American fullback. It would be a great stroke of business."

March 19, 1935
"Broke the Sauer story all over the sport page, using plenty of ink. Scooped the Milwaukee papers nicely by neglecting to answer their telephone calls in the morning."

March 28, 1935
"There is a helluva situation in Europe. Germany is rearming under Hitler, and France is cementing a powerful alliance with Russia."

***

Hitler's rise to power was drawing caution from many in the U.S., and a *Press-Gazette* editorial reflected the concern:

> "Are we to believe in Adolf Hitler's peace speeches? Dr. Jacob Gould Schurman, former American ambassador to Germany, says we should.
>
> "Yet the whole philosophy of Hitler and the Nazis is based upon the belief that force and violence are necessary in foreign as well as internal policies.
>
> "It is plain that the Nazis propose to recreate the spirit of aggressive militarism and there is not much doubt that they also propose to rearm Germany to a much larger extent than the right of equality would justify. Hitler has said frankly in his autobiography that he cannot see any future for Germany without a new war."

***

April 1, 1935
"The early success of my work on the Press-Gazette sports desk has set buzzing an ambition which those five years in the rut nearly ended. This break is just what I needed."

April 8, 1935
"All the nations of Europe are preparing for war. They never learn. Neither do we. We'll probably have to fight it for them."

April 11, 1935
"Breaking out of a clear sky comes word from Managing Editor Kennedy that my salary has been raised to $150 per month. He wrote, 'You're getting along very well on your job and this increase is, in a measure, a slight appreciation of that fact.' This isn't a raise. It's a godsend."

***

His daily sports columns covered much more than Packers news, as high school and college sports were still more popular than professional sports for many people. But the Packers were already a year-round topic of conversation.

April 17, 1935, column

We have no intention of attempting to build up synthetic, non-existent team spirit, but any real fan of the Green Bay Packers cannot dodge the fact that interest in the squad is running higher at the present time than any similar period in recent years.

John Walter

"I don't want to wish away the summer," one man remarked the other day. "But I'll certainly be glad when the football season opens again."

Relief of the pressure on the team's treasury, and signing up of some of the best freshman pro football material in the country, probably are the prime reasons for the current enthusiasm, and the changed attitude is being reflected by the players, both old and new.

"I'm tired of being second string fullback to Bronko Nagurski," Clarke Hinkle writes in from Toronto, Ohio. "I want to be the best fullback in the league next fall."

Clarke is working for the Weirton Steel company, coaching its baseball team as its playing manager and clerking in the mill.

Cal Hubbard has resumed his chores as umpire in the International Baseball league, and he writes in to say that his resignation at Oklahoma A & M college has not gone through yet. It's no secret that the Packers are carrying on extensive correspondence with the giant tackle.

***

April 21, 1935

"Easter Sunday. Attended church with family. Everyone was there, most of them in new clothes. But there were many who didn't have any. These people have lived through the worst depression in the country's history and you can see it on their faces. I admire them."

***

May 8, 1935, column

Since the Packers corporation was reorganized, it has received 50 percent more applications from college men interested in signing with the team, according to Coach Curly Lambeau. The boys know now that the club is on a sound footing and many of them would prefer to play and live in a smaller city.

May 10, 1935, column

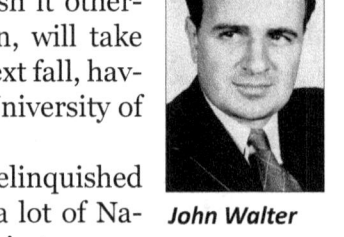

John Walter

Although some of the Packers might wish it otherwise, Earl Clark, Detroit's Flying Dutchman, will take one more fling at the professional gridiron next fall, having turned down a coaching offer from the University of Colorado.

Dutch's return to the gridiron, which he relinquished during the season of 1933, is bad news for a lot of National Professional league teams, but is certain to mean added cash at the gate, for Clark is one of the most colorful, and at the same time, one of the best players in the circuit.

In deciding to slip on the harness once more, Dutch declined a contract from the University of Colorado as basketball coach and assistant football coach at a salary somewhat less than $3,000. He will return to the Lions at a reported salary of $6,500 and a promise of steady employment in Detroit when the season is ended.

May 15, 1935, column

When the representatives of the National Professional Football league meet in a special session at Pittsburgh Sunday, the question of officiating will be a major issue, along with discussion of means for its improvement throughout the midwestern section of the league.

Last fall there was squalling all along the National league battle front, because of alleged mishandling of important football games. The answer unquestionably is – better officials.

Who are the best officials in the midwest? With a few exceptions, they are the men who work games of the Western conference, and that group, with Major John L. Griffiths , commissioner, is hostile to professional football. It has a rule which prohibits its officials working pro contests.

How can the National league obtain the services of these crack referees, head linesmen and umpires?

By getting the Big Ten rule changed, which appears to be an insurmountable obstacle, or by raising the pay of professional football officials – those are the answers.

It probably wouldn't be necessary to give the officials more money per game than the Western conference. If the scale were raised in the pro league, we are certain that many outstanding midwestern officials would prefer to work 14 games per season for the league than seven or eight annually for the Western conference.

Eastern National league teams are not faced with this problem. There the colleges and universities cooperate to such an extent that the best officials are permitted to work both collegiate and professional contests.

The eastern colleges are smart. They know that the moneyed eastern pro clubs could out-purchase them in the matter of obtaining officials and they prefer to play ball the right way.

May 21, 1935, column

Notes taken by Curly Lambeau at the Pittsburgh meeting of the National Professional Football league:

Half a day was spent discussing officiating, and the results of the conference to be reflected in improved officiating next fall.

The Packers officials will work in teams, with the referee in charge. Meetings will be held twice annually to discuss rules, as the league wants all officials to be experts.

Most important, salaries of officials will be increased, the circuit thus definitely committing itself to obtaining the best officials available. Men working the 1935 games, realizing that they are under the closest scrutiny and facing almost certain criticism for every mistake, won't be apt to make so many.

Lambeau reported that Clarke Hinkle drove over from his home in Toronto, Ohio, and expressed great enthusiasm for the coming season. Clarke should. With the dynamite they have lined up for the next season working at his side and ahead of him, the veteran fullback will be expected to turn in his best year since he joined the Green Bay squad.

The league is looking for an outstanding man to handle the circuit's publicity and will make a decision at the June 16 meeting of the National loop. That session will be held at Chicago, when the 1935 schedule will be drafted.

***

The major purpose of the pro football owners meeting in Chicago was to come to agreement on the 1935 schedules. They couldn't do it and finally had to leave the matter in the hands of league president Joe Carr. A new home-and-home schedule format was being put into place and it created some significant changes. For example, the Packers' twelve-game schedule in 1935 wouldn't include games against the New York Giants, Boston Redskins, or Brooklyn Dodgers because of the new home-and-home format.

Another topic at the Chicago meeting, one that received little attention, was a discussion of the future of the Green Bay franchise. An item near the back of the *Chicago Tribune* sports section included the following:

"Considerable discussion is understood to have been held over the Green Bay franchise, which a group of sportsmen are attempting to have transferred to Milwaukee. No action was taken on the matter, but it was reported a number of club owners favored placing the team in Cleveland if the franchise is taken from Green Bay."

Among those attending the meeting, in addition to Joannes and Lambeau, were: Arthur Rooney, Pittsburgh Steelers; Jack Mara and Steve Owen, New York Giants; Bert Bell, Philadelphia Eagles; Charlie Bidwell, St. Louis Cardinals; Dan Topping, Brooklyn Dodgers; George Halas, Chicago Bears.

***

June 10, 1935, column

There's at least one new Packer who is looking forward to his stay in Wisconsin and its opportunities to enjoy life outdoors, and that's Ernie Smith, former USC tackle who has been signed for the 1935 season.

John Walter

Smith writes from Los Angeles that he is anxious for his first glimpse of Wisconsin. He has been keeping his weight down to 225 with a strenuous program of ice skating, riding, hiking, sailing, swimming, fishing and occasionally football.

"As to professional football," says Ernie, "the toughest team I ever played against was the Packer squad of 1933. I have played against three pro teams – the Packers, Bears and Cardinals – all in post-season games.

"I have heard so much about the wonderful fishing around your territory that I shall expect to participate in this sport soon after my arrival in Green Bay."

"I understand from Curly Lambeau that we have quite a number of good players to help bring Green Bay the championship this season. You can rest assured that if it is within our power, we shall surely do so."

Ernie is remembered as one of the most versatile USC students of all time. He was an All-American football tackle, starred in intra-mural sports, played ice hockey, was in the Trojan band and glee club, and led an orchestra for two years. He is married.

***

Despite the growing fan support for the Packers and pro football, it was baseball that garnered the most attention from sports fans. In June, local baseball enthusiasts were able to announce that two Major League teams – the Pittsburgh Pirates and St. Louis Browns – agreed to play an official game in Green Bay in early August.

Exciting fans even more was the fact that both teams were managed by baseball legends. The Pirates were led by Harold (Pie) Traynor and the Browns by Rogers Hornsby, nicknamed "The Rajah." Fellow hall of famer Honus Wagner served as a coach for the Pirates.

***

June 20, 1935, column

Dreams do come true, and on the afternoon of Monday, August 5, you probably will be one of a great crowd which jams into Green Sox park to see the Pittsburgh Pirates and St. Louis Browns make the first appearance of big league baseball clubs here in nearly 30 years.

They don't drop around Green Bay way very often, do these major league teams, but when they do, it's a good attraction. In 1908 Chicago's White Sox came in for a game with a picked W-I league club, and this year you can't register any objections to a Pirate-Brown setup.

The Brownies have been doing poorly in their league, true, but they have plenty of color and their lineup is studded with important names.

So is that Pirate lineup, but Pittsburgh, on the other hand, is engaged in a hectic battle for first place and at the present writing is struggling with the St. Louis Cardinals for the runner-up spot behind the New York Giants.

You are going to see the Waner brothers, Pie Traynor, Rogers Hornsby, Sam West and a dozen other men whose names go into record books in important places.

It will be a real occasion in the city's athletic history, and it will bring in as many people as a Packer-Bear game.

***

As summer settled into July, Packer player contracts were being signed. Most significant was news that Cal Hubbard would return to play for the Packers. He left the team before the 1934 campaign to be on the coaching staff at Texas A&M, then left the university to be an umpire in the International Baseball League. He would rejoin the Packers when the baseball season ended in early September.

Late in the month brought the annual stockholders meeting at the county courthouse. Lee Joannes was re-elected president. A major topic was an upcoming season ticket campaign in which Joannes set a sales goal of 3,000 tickets, saying it was vital so the corporation has enough funds to keep pace with teams in the larger cities.

The Packers also announced they would play four exhibition games in nine days against teams in Merrill, Chippewa Falls, and La Crosse, replacing scrimmages that were held in previous seasons.

Lambeau made his pitch.

"The Packers may not be in the playoff for the title next fall," he said, "but we will always be in the running. If we get as many good breaks next fall as we received bad breaks last year, we'll be on top at the end.

"Detroit is spending a lot of money and has a great organization, but the Bears are our barometer. They are our natural rivals."

Praising the new batch of players under contract, Lambeau said this about Hutson: "A very fast man who is great at snaring passes but who may need a little toughening before he is ripe for full-time work."

Apparently, the toughening was fast-tracked.

Speaking to the Green Bay Lions Club at the Beaumont Hotel a few days later, Lambeau said the league's goal of complete home-and-home scheduling means it would have to reduce the number of teams from nine to eight.

"Green Bay must not be the team to be eliminated," he said. "There never was a time when the Packers were more greatly in need of their fans' support."

Joannes echoed the sentiment.

"This is a crucial hour for professional football in Green Bay," he said at the first meeting of the season ticket canvassers. "We must have a good financial nest egg to start off with as our team expenses this year are considerably higher than in other seasons."

**

July 22, 1935
"Called in by Lee Joannes, president of the Packer football corporation. He says I may be able to get the Packer publicity job this fall. It would mean an additional $100 a month, which I certainly could use. Covered corporation meeting of Packers in eve. Joannes re-elected president. Some day I hope to be secretary of that outfit. Maybe not so many years in the future either. This publicity job, if I get it, would be a stepping stone."

July 30, 1935, column

With sultry, muggy weather settled over the city like a damp shroud, and the temperature fit for little in an athletic way, but swimming or boating, this department today swings to the promise of another football season.

John Walter

Hemmed in on all sides of the National league front by the formidable array of the most powerful elevens in the history of the circuit, the Packers nevertheless are counted upon to make a strong showing, and upon the likelihood that they will do just that rests the hopes of a corps of season ticket salesmen who today, perhaps, will ask you to arrange for your permanent 1935 reservations.

Why should you accommodate these volunteer workers? You can write your own answers, but here are a couple them.

1. Your purchase will help keep the Packers in Green Bay. Facing year by year a great financial outlay, and competing with bankrolls as impressive as the fourth period temperament of the Chicago Bears, the team absolutely cannot do without the 100 percent support of every one of its fans. It would be a dull Sunday afternoon in the autumn without a Packer team in Green Bay.

2. Your purchase will assure you the same seat for every one of the six home games, which brings to Green Bay the cream of the professional football league. By a new arrangement at the Packer ticket office, you may obtain special accommodations for special guests – thus, if your party is increased by one or two on the eve of the game, your seats will be changed so that the entire group may sit together.

3. Your purchase will enable you to see the Packer-Bear game, probably the outstanding annual clash in midwestern professional football, at no advance in price.

July 31, 1935, column

A little work with pad and pencil reveals that the probable Packer squad of 1935 not only will be the heaviest in Green Bay history, but will rank among the greatest squads of the National league in the matter of tonnage.

If all the men who are expected to report late next month do so, the Packer line will average 224 pounds; the ends will hit the scales for a 202 pound average; and the backfield will reach the unusually high average of 196 pounds.

Now this is beef.

Look at your probable tackles. Cal Hubbard is good for 263 pounds, Ernie Smith weighs 224, George Maddox is the same, and Tar Schwammel does 226.

The guards won't be so big. If Bob Jones reports, with his 218 pounds, he'll hit pretty close to the average for the position. Others will be Champ Seibold, 235 pounds; Bob O'Connor, 215; Tiny Engebretsen, 240; Mike Michalske, 206; and Lon Evans, 212.

At ends you'll have Don Hutson, 196 pounds; Bob Tenner, 211; Milt Gantenbein, 202; and Al Rose, 201. Centers will be Nate Barrager, 208; George Svendsen, 214; and Frank Butler, 227.

Riding behind this pile of beef will be one of the heaviest and speediest backfields in football history. Just look at these statistics.

Joe Laws weighs 180 pounds. Roger Grove is good for 182; Buckets Goldenberg hits 212; Hank Bruder 199, Arnold Herber 204, Bob Monnett 183, Clarke Hinkle 204, Herman Schneidman 200, Swede Johnston 197, and Sol Kramer 210.

Beef, all beef.

August 5, 1935, column

A helping hand for the corps of salesmen which is attempting to sell 3,000 season tickets to maintain the franchise of the Packers in Green Bay, appears at the bottom of this page.

It's a form you can use to express your appreciation of the work being done by the new Packer corporation, and of the efforts in lining up the best home schedule in the history of Packer football.

If you fill out the form and mail it to the Packer ticket office, Columbus Community Club, Green Bay, you will guarantee yourself excellent seats for six home games, and your price range is $6, $7.50, $9, $12 and $15.

Every seat in City stadium will be reserved. You'll have the opportunity of securing permanent reservations for all six of those home games unless your party is reinforced by additional guests before game time, in which case the corporation will gladly shift your seats so that your entire party may sit together.

It has been a long time since you have been offered a better bargain.

***

The cynic in me suspects that Dad was putting on a full-court press for that Packer publicity job.

A labor crisis descended on the city the last day of July when the

Green Bay Clothing Manufacturers on Main Street discharged two female employees after they tried to organize support for the Amalgamated Clothing Workers Union. It led to an immediate strike by sixty other seamstresses and the situation got ugly in a hurry. Strikebreakers were hired and had to be escorted to and from the building by police officers. There were instances of hair pulling, face scratching, and slapping.

Company president Arthur Fogel was initially unbending.

"If we have to have a union shop here, I can state as president of the company that the Green Bay plant will be closed down," he said. "I have nothing against organized labor but this is not the class of goods made in union shops. It is made by colored labor in the south and by sweatshops labor in the east, and if we are to stay in business we meet the competition."

The strike lasted almost three weeks before Mayor John Diener and former Packers president Dr. Webber Kelly negotiated a settlement with Fogel that made union membership optional and gave employees a ten percent pay increase. The plant remained in operation in Green Bay.

***

July 31, 1935
"The European situation, governed by a powerful set of dictators – Stalin in Russia, Hitler in Germany, and Mussolini in Italy – is rapidly approaching a climax. My guess is that there'll be a war before November."

***

Ticket prices for the Pirates-Browns baseball game were set at $2 for box seats, $1.65 for grandstand, $1.35 for bleacher reserved, and $1 for general admission.

The contract required both teams to play their starters and Green Bay officials hoped to fill all 8,423 seats at the baseball park. The teams bused into Green Bay a few hours before the game, with the Browns checking into the Beaumont Hotel and the Pirates into the Northland Hotel.

For Dad, a lifelong baseball fan, the highlight was meeting Traynor and Hornsby. He asked each manager what they thought of the playing field.

"It's terrible," Hornsby said. "That skinned infield will give you many an error."

"It's great," said Traynor. "It'll be a well-played game."

Mayor John Diener threw the ceremonial first pitch, with Honus Wagner intentionally swinging and missing. It was a game that had to contend with drizzling rain, and the Pirates took a 6-3 victory. Fortunately, the heavier rain didn't start to fall until later in the day when 2.13 inches fell in a 24-hour period. The attendance was estimated at 3,500 and both clubs bused out of town immediately after the game.

***

August 5, 1935
"Covered the big league game at Green Sox park. Met the managers of the clubs – Rogers Hornsby of the Browns and Harold (Pie) Traynor of the Pirates. One of the Pirate coaches was old Honus Wagner, star of stars in a day gone by. Pittsburgh won 6-3."

August 7, 1935
"Clarke Hinkle, the Bucknell battering ram, signs to play with the Packers again."

August 8, 1935
"President Roosevelt is being hit hard by scores of critics, and by adverse decisions of the Supreme Court. The Republicans see success in 1936 – but they're wrong."

***

August 9, 1935, column

Although the annual football game between the Chicago Bears and the College All Stars is a joke as far as providing a test between college and professional football is concerned, the game August 29 will have considerable significance to Green Bay Packer fans.

The annual clash is, in fact, an all-professional engagement, being a battle between old veteran hands at the pro game and youngsters untried at the same sport. There never was a bona fide college team in history which contained a star-studded lineup equal to that of Coach Frank Thomas and his assistants, and there never will be.

John Walter

But the All Stars, with Thomas as head coach, and his two leading assistants all disciples of the so-called Notre Dame system of play, will be schooled in that style, and the Bears, to meet them, will be forced to combat the Notre Dame offense.

That's just where the Packers come in. Coach Curly Lambeau is going to have a great preview of just what he can expect in the way of defensive measures from the Bears this fall, and two prospective Packers, Don Hutson and George Maddox, will be playing for the All Stars.

Bob Tenner, another Packer recruit, was offered a chance to play with the All Stars, but turned it down. He is an intern at a Minneapolis hospital, and while he is obtaining a leave of absence to play with the Packers, he didn't feel like extending his time for the Chicago contest.

***

August 9, 1935
"Mae De Wan came over in eve and she read my cards, making a number of interesting predictions. I am going to try a new line of work; I am going to be interested in a very dark young lady; a man in my family will die before winter; I shall get into a fight with someone before long. All very interesting and all unlikely."

(And all wrong. Had the wrong cards, probably.)

August 12, 1935
"Attended Packer ticket sales meeting at Joannes Brothers. It doesn't look like I'll get that publicity job – this year, anyway. Talk with Coach Curly Lambeau learning about the football setup."

***

There was major news midway through the month. Roosevelt signed into law the legislation establishing the Social Security Administration, providing retirement nest eggs for all U.S. working citizens. But there was also tragic news.

***

August 16, 1935
"The news break of the year — Will Rogers, the great humorist, and Wiley Post, famous round the world flier, are killed in plane crash at Point Barrow, Alaska. The entire nation is truly shocked. Rogers was loved by everyone."

August 20, 1935
"Am beginning to be impatient for the arrival of the football season."

August 21, 1935
"It's going to be an exciting autumn — girls, trips, and Dad as my only major problem. Life is waking up for me after those dull depression years."

August 22, 1935
"The Packers are beginning to arrive. Saw Buckets Goldenberg, Bob Monnett, Arnold Herber, Joe Laws, Herman Scheideman, and George Sauer, Nebraska's great all-American fullback. Got the Packer publicity job after all – or part of it anyway. I'm to work with Calhoun and will get $150, which will be much appreciated. There also was the definite indication that I'll get more next season."

August 23, 1935
"The Packer football team is assembled and ready to leave for the Rhinelander training camp."

***

The Packers of 1935 chose to hold their training camp in Rhinelander, Wisconsin. As the players prepared to board the bus taking them north, they were greeted by Johnny Blood, who had been sold by the team a year earlier and most recently signed to play for the Chippewa Falls (Wisconsin) Marines in hopes of convincing the Packers to re-sign him.

Heading north, the team stopped for dinner at the Muskie Inn near Elcho, then settled in at the Pinewood Lodge at Lake Thompson, just south of Rhinelander.

***

August 22, 1935, column

The Packers are going to have a lot of fun at Lake Thompson during their training week, which starts Saturday and ends with a night game at Merrill Aug. 31. But they're going to be under real training camp discipline.

Coach Curly Lambeau's list of instructions to his players, released today, made this very clear. For instance:

The first workout will be held Saturday afternoon at Rhinelander. The second will be held Sunday afternoon, and after that two workouts will be held daily.

While the squad makes its headquarters at Pinewood lodge, everyone is expected to be in bed at 11 o'clock or before. Breakfast will be served at 8 o'clock.

There will be no smoking when in uniform, and absolutely no drinking at any time.

Football pants must be worn at every practice.

Dr. W.W. Kelly is the club physician, and all injuries, regardless of how trivial they seem must be reported to him.

This list of rules and instructions follows the Packer policy to leave no stone unturned in seeking a winning football team. Players, as well as the coaches, realize the critical nature of the approaching season to football fans of Green Bay and Wisconsin.

They'll be in shape.

John Walter

August 24, 1935, column

Football hopes of Green Bay moved northward today, with the opening of the Packers' training camp at Pinewood lodge, Lake Thompson, and the team's fans already are looking over road maps with an idea to getting first previews of the 1935 season.

The previews will take the shape of exhibition games at Merrill, one week from tonight; at Chippewa Falls, Labor Day; and at Stevens Point September 6. The Stevens Point contest will be played at night.

With some concerted driving, the Green Bay fan can attend all three of those games, and become familiar with the new players before they make their home debut against La Crosse September 8.

Here are the suggested routes to the three cities: Merrill, Highway 29 to Wausau, then north on U.S. 51 to Merrill; Chippewa Falls, west on Highway 29 all the way; Stevens Point, Highway 54 to Waupaca, then Highway 10 to the destination.

If you decide to follow the team, you'll cover 110 miles one way to Merrill, 183 miles to Chippewa Falls, and 93 to Stevens Point.

August 26, 1935, column

Green Bay is indebted to Rhinelander for the hospitality which has been extended the Packers football squad, and for the interest which the northern Wisconsin city is displaying in preparations for the 1935 season.

Sprawled across the entrance to Rhinelander is a noisy banner, proclaiming the city is the training headquarters of the Packers, and the gateway Pinewood lodge, the training quarters, bears the words "Green Bay Packers - Welcome."

The arrival of the football team was the chief topic of conversation on Rhinelander streets and in Rhinelander homes Saturday. Hundreds of people were on hand to witness the workouts on the high school field, their principal difficulty being identification of the players.

"Which is Laws?" "Who is Bruder?" were typical of the numerous questions Green Bay visitors had to answer. Rhinelander displayed an increasing interest in the entire personnel, and the Packers gave them an excellent show.

Pinewood lodge itself is ideal as training headquarters. The players are being fed all they can eat, which is plenty, and every accommodation is being made for them. Pleasure games of every kind are on hand, there are boats and fishing equipment, and all the room in the north wood.

August 27, 1935, column

Although the Green Bay Packers are providing a variety of a new type of entertainment for the people of Rhinelander and northern Wisconsin, probably the outstanding event on their own recreational program will occur tonight when the players will be guests of the management at a local motion picture house.

The entire squad will leave Lake Thompson immediately after supper and will move into the city to walk the aisles in front of a packed house. Rhinelander has seen nothing of the Packers except at the actual practice sessions, when the team is brought to the high school field by bus, and is whisked away again, as soon as the customary sprints are run.

The writer has attempted to contact most of the squad members, to get an actual line on the team's morale, and without exaggeration or unnecessary ballyhoo it may be reported that the spirit could not be improved. The older players are satisfied that Green Bay will be in a position to make a great stand against national league opposition this season, and the younger men have adopted a "What Chicago Bears?" attitude.

A shortage of newspapers has handicapped the Packers somewhat, and all are eager for news from Green Bay. How are the fans taking the team this year? Are they interested in the progress the squad is making at training camp? (The mail delivery is nothing to write home about, and Saturday's paper had not been received at camp by Monday night.)

August 29, 1935, column

Notes from the training camp of the Green Bay Packers:

Swimming has been crossed from the recreational schedule of the squad at Pinewood lodge, because Lake Thompson is several degrees colder than the Arctic circle just now...the Packers remain muffled in sweaters when they are not practicing, but the weather is just what Coach Lambeau ordered, being an advance specimen of the coming football season.

The Packers call Al Rose "Junior"...and they pronounce Bob Monnett's last name as though it were spelled "Mo-nay"...Clarke Hinkle is called "Hink" and they refer to Buckets Goldenberg as "Buck"...Arnold Herber is "Herbie" and Dominic Vairo is "Nick"...incidentally, this Vairo is a swell pass receiver.

Everyone with whom you discuss the Packers here asks you if the high school setup isn't perfect...it's close to it, at that...the school is perched atop a hill overlooking the athletic field, a la Manitowoc Lincoln...an elevated highway runs along one end of the field and this always is crowded with cars when the Packers are practicing...across the field from the high school stand the bleachers.

A Rhinelander Boy Scout troop has obtained the concession at the practice field and sells soft drinks, candy and incidentals to fans watching the team work out.

August 30, 1935, column

This chilly football weather, cold as a head lineman's heart, may be just what Coach Curly Lambeau ordered for his Green Bay Packers, but it is proving very tough on itinerants, CCC workers and sports writers.

The wind here is as nerve-wracking as a Lake Michigan breeze in mid-summer, and any man, woman or child who ventures into the streets without being securely bundled and with an extra sweater in tow, is promptly locked up.

This may sound like an exaggeration, but the writer yesterday locked two front teeth attempting to use a frozen tooth brush, and had to hurry in from Lake Thompson for repairs.

The Packers are doing pretty well under the October blasts. There are a few sniffles and a couple of rather impressive colds, but no one is missing practice and Curly is satisfied with the team's condition.

It's a pleasure to watch the Packers backfield in action. The boys are heavy, and they pack power. Green Bay will have its biggest group of backs since the days when Charles de Langlade was good for five yards anytime through Braddock's line, and Jean Nicolet was an all-Fox river valley selection.

Lambeau is working hard with Champ Seibold, the giant Oshkosh boy. Seibold had a private skull drill yesterday with the coach, Milt Gantenbein and Bob Monnett putting on the demonstration.

***

Sometimes, a newspaper's purpose is to quash rumors. Apparently, someone pulled a prank with a fake radio setup at a Green Bay tavern that convinced listeners that Bears fullback Bronko Nagurski had been killed in an automobile accident. The *Press-Gazette* sports desk was deluged with phone calls seeking confirmation of the report.

Nothing had happened to Nagurski.

But there was real news to report. The Packers ordered new kelly-green team jerseys with gold on the arms and shoulders and gold numerals. At the same time, veteran end Lavvie Dilweg, who was fourth on the team's all-time scoring list at the time (behind Verne Lewellen, Blood and Lambeau) announced his retirement to become a full-time attorney with a Green Bay law firm.

The Packers then began what was their preseason schedule of 1935 – four games in nine days against city teams in Wisconsin.

***

August 31, 1935
"Drove to Merrill, 18 miles north of Wausau, and covered game there in evening. The Packers crushed a weak Merrill team 34-0 before a hostile crowd."

September 2, 1935
"Covered football game in afternoon. Packers defeated Chippewa Marines, a stubborn outfit, 22-0. Arnie Herber did some good running and some great passing. Score was only 3-0 at the half."

September 4, 1935
"Covered football game. Packers ran wild over Stevens Point 40-0. George Sauer scored two touchdowns. Bed felt wonderful and have a sneaking hunch I am going to have a real battle to stay out of it. You can't burn too many candles at too many ends."

September 7, 1935
"Visited Don Hutson and George Svendsen at Hotel Northland. Then

to bed, flat on my back with this cold, a great spot to be in with the Packers' opening home game tomorrow."

September 8, 1935
"Covered football game in afternoon, Packers 49, LaCrosse Old Style Lagers 0. The team looked good, yet there is an undercurrent of pessimism concerning its chances for the season. Monnett scored three touchdowns and kicked five extra points."

***

August 31, 1935, column

Night before last the Bears of gridiron talent, playing without benefit of Brumbaugh and without courtesy of collegians, won the second annual clash between veteran professionals and young men just breaking into the pro game.

John Walter

The game was popular —so popular that nearly 80,000 people sat in the rain to watch it progress. The result proved nothing insofar as the professional vs. college controversy was concerned, but as a spectacle it rang the bell.

Next year again football fans of the nation will be asked to express their opinions of the cream of American football, and their ballots will send a tried squad of gridiron talent to another battle with a professional team, probably the Chicago Bears.

Why the Chicago Bears? Why not against an all-professional team, selected by professional football fans to oppose the College All-Stars, who have abandoned the amateur ranks?

If anyone is looking for a real test between young football players just out of college, and veterans of the professional game, an all-star selected team from the National Football league would possess power and experience enough to satisfy the most rabid backer of the collegiate gridiron.

Or if the collegians must face one team instead of a selection of men capable of settling once and for all the question of relative merits, why not let the National league champions draw the assignment? The Bears may have won more games than any other league team last year, but they were outsmarted and neatly thumped by the New York Giants in the playoff, and it doesn't seem fair to permit one team possessing no title, to bask permanently in the spotlight of one of the nation's greatest football spectacles.

September 4, 1935, column

STEVENS POINT – A destructive running attack, with such men as Joe Laws, Clarke Hinkle, Hank Bruder, Bob Monnett, George Sauer, Buckets Goldenberg, Swede Johnston and Arnie Herber hauling the freight, will be one 1935 goal of the Green Bay Packers, now marking time here in preparation for tonight's game with Stevens Point.

Statistics of the first two practice games reveal that, given proper support from a strong line, the Packer backs should be able to pick up plenty of inches from scrimmage. With the opposition scrawny, they piled up 252 yards against Merrill Saturday, from scrimmage only, and against much tougher going at Chippewa Falls those backs were good for 137 yards.

September 5, 1935, column

STEVENS POINT – A football team decided to play football here last night, just about the time that the Packers trotted out on the field for the second half of their game with the College All-Stars, and the result guaranteed Green Bay fans colorful, open football for the entirety of the home season.

It's a beautiful thing to watch a football team click on every play, and that's what happened through most of the second half. The actions of the backs were timed to a split second with the openings in the line, and as a result the big, heavy Packer ball carriers pounded through for one first down after another, many of them on successive plays.

The passing as yet is somewhat short of expectations but the talent is there, and Green Bay fans probably will see this branch of the game equal to or surpass the running attack. Ends and backs have been having trouble getting to the right spot for reception, but their difficulty is no greater than might be expected for so early in the season.

Stevens Point was much better than Merrill and not as tough as Chippewa Falls. It made the old Packer fans homesick to see Eddie Kotal stepping around again. Kotal looked fast and shifty, and possibly might be good for a National league position yet, if he were interested in trying for it.

Green Bay fans haven't had much of a chance to see the Packer players this season. The squad will appear on the stage of the Bay theater Friday evening, and will be introduced individually to the audience, along with appropriate organ music.

September 9, 1935, column

You didn't need much football knowledge – you only required the interest which the casual fan is expected to have toward the Packers – to realize that there are several young men, very new to the city, who probably will be calling Green Bay their home.

It's hard to remember when a crop of newcomers to the Packers attracted more attention than did several of the 1935 candidates as the team whistled through the La Crosse Lagers at City stadium yesterday afternoon.

Much of the chatter centered around the lengthy George Svendsen, Minnesota center who bobbed up from nowhere on three occasions to intercept two passes and scoop up a fumble, running for touchdowns on two occasions. The fans are going to like Svendsen, and his appearance in the lineup will mean a little more pressure at the gate. He has color.

Bob O'Connor and Ernie Smith are going to be a pair of consistent stumbling blocks on the left side of the line, and when Milt Gantenbein is posted on the outer end, the three look pretty close to impregnable. It'll be interesting to see how the combination develops.

Dominic Vairo, Bob Tenner and Don Hutson, added to Gantenbein and Al Rose, give the Packers a strong potential end corps. It's a matter of development and experience as to which improves the fastest. Stocky Sol Kramer and Curtis McDowell are a couple of other newcomers who worked hard and caught the coach's eye.

Herman Schneidman kept moving in and out of the plays with speed despite his 195 pounds. He may be the answer to the search for a blocking quarterback of sufficient talent to permit Goldenberg to be used at halfback.

September 10, 1935, column

Coach Curly Lambeau of the Packers gets lots of freak mail. One that arrived this morning carried a note of encouragement from a real Packer fan in Milwaukee, member of a growing sports fraternity.

He signed it "Packer fan" and said "Interest in the 1935 Packers at a mighty high pitch here. Am driving to Green Bay with a party on the 22nd for the Bear game and we've decided that we don't mind if your team loses every other game on the schedule. But beat those Bears."

You don't have to live in Milwaukee to voice these sentiments. Just the same, Curly is worried most right now about the Cardinals. The Packers have enough good backs on the injured list to make any all-America team. Although only Bruder and Hinkle definitely will be unable to play against the Cardinals, half a dozen others are far from top shape.

***

Then, another major news story. Louisiana Sen. Huey Long's reign as the political muscleman of Louisiana was ended when the son-in-law of one of Long's enemies shot him in the corridor of the State Capitol in Baton Rouge.

***

September 9, 1935
"Huey Long, dictator of Louisiana, is wounded by a would-be assassin in Baton Rouge. He is reported near death and few will mourn his passing. Lunch at Northland with Ernie Smith, the new Packer tackle."

September 10, 1935
"Huey Long dies, as the sane-thinking people of the nation cheer. Sic temper tyrannous, or wasn't that misused when Abraham Lincoln died? Tonight's Packer feature was on Don Hutson, the all-American end from Alabama who was catching Dixie Howell's passes in the Rose Bowl last New Year's Day. He'll never be a pro all-American. He can't block and is too brittle. Very fast though."

***

It's one of the more memorable entries from Dad's diaries. A slight miscalculation.

It was a journalistic whiff.

The dining room in our De Pere home included a framed, autographed picture of Hutson throughout the 1950s, a clear indication of where the man from Alabama stood among Dad's Packer memoirs.

Interesting that Hutson took second fiddle to Long in Dad's diary of the day. But the feature story shared some personal and statistical details about Hutson. He was a commerce major at Alabama, ran the 100-yard-dash in 9.7 seconds, and although not married, "gets special delivery letters" from someone.

The *Press-Gazette* editorial commented on the Long assassination:

> "Although engaged in the very act of further prostituting his government to his personal ends at the time he was shot, every American will abhor the violence leveled at Senator Long

because brute force in controversies of this kind never accomplish lasting results any more than the use of war in national disputes. The blame for Huey Long is Louisiana."

With the opening regular-season game just nine days away, the Packers re-signed Blood, who had performed for both Chippewa Falls and La Crosse in the exhibition games against the Packers. His presence was needed, in part, because of injuries to Hinkle and Bruder. But his return to the Packers was fitting.
This wasn't a replacement. This was Johnny Blood.

***

September 11, 1935
"In evening attended chicken dinner for Packers at Beaumont Hotel. Sat between Don Hutson and Dustin McDonald. Cal Hubbard, the Packers great 265-pound tackle, on hand for first time."

September 12, 1935
"My office relations with George Calhoun, the telegraph editor, are becoming very strained. He thinks I am trying to muscle in on his job as Packer secretary, in which he is entirely correct. Dropped in to Northland to visit with several of the Packers. George Maddox, George Sauer and Lon Evans."

***

The opening game was a disappointment as the Chicago Cardinals beat the Packers 7-6 at City Stadium, the difference being the extra point the Cards made and the Packers missed.
Dad's headline was a classic case of shining a bright light on a dark space: "Packers Hold Cardinals Team to One-point Win."

***

September 15, 1935
"Discussed the Packers with A.B. Turnbull, the Press-Gazette general manager. In afternoon covered Packers' first National league game of season. Cardinals defeated Green Bay 7-6. Team looked very disappointing. Swede Johnston scored the Packers touchdown and Bob Monnett kicked the extra point...almost. Filed story for the Associated Press from the field."

September 16, 1935, column

John Walter

Although the Packers might have escaped with a tie at City stadium yesterday afternoon, your real fan agreed that any team capable of holding the Cardinals to one point this season is going to play a lot of real football.

Possibly the greatest factors in the Packer defeat were the group of crippled backs who witnessed the contest from the bench, and an unwillingness by the Bays to block and tackle at important moments in the game when a particularly direct effort might have saved a lot of trouble.

The presence of Hinkle in the backfield, affording a threat to keep the Cardinal backs closer to the line, would have aided the Green Bay aerial attack, particularly if Herber had been in shape to throw passes accurately.

Arnie made a game effort when he entered the game in the fourth period, but he had all he could do to stand up, and the mauling he got from four or five Cardinals, who broke through the Packer line on the first pass play, didn't improve his physical condition a bit.

There's one thing to remember: even though they only did lose by a single point, the Packer team which yesterday battled the Cardinals is far from the team which, its injured players once again available for service, should be ready to meet National league opposition during the October schedule.

A word to the wolves – don't sell the Packers short.

***

September 16, 1935
"The Packer fans are disgruntled about the showing of the team yesterday. Issued a warning 'Don't sell the Packers short' in my daily sports column. No one sees it yet but the team will come back against the Bears next Sunday."

September 18, 1935
"Took the afternoon off and saw a couple of pictures. Fredric March and Greta Garbo in 'Anna Karenina' and Stan Laurel and Oliver Hardy in 'Bonnie Scotland.'
***

Not your typical double feature, but unique and contrasting views into foreign culture, I'm sure. And something to take your mind off the fact that the powerful Chicago Bears were coming to town.

Chapter 12

Herber to Hutson

It was time for repair and recovery.

The news came from Washington, D.C., that Green Bay and Brown County would get $41,187 from the government as part of the Works Progress Administration program to help put more people to work and spiffy-up the area landscape.

The money would be used to replace or repair sidewalks and street curbs, painting and grading at the metropolitan sewerage district plant, along with making some school playground improvements and the like.

The Packers set about to do their own version of repair and recovery as they looked ahead to the Chicago Bears' invasion. They re-signed Mike Michalske for another season, and then named him and Cal Hubbard as assistant coaches. Michalske would coach the defensive line, Hubbard would coach the offensive line.

But injuries hovered over the team, as Dad wrote three days before kickoff.

"Just how much Arnold Herber and George Sauer will be to the team Sunday is problematic but both probably will get into the game."

In his diary, Dad took a prophetic position:

***

September 19, 1935
"Football fans are getting excited about Sunday's Packer-Bear game. It'll be a classic."

September 21, 1935
"Picked the Packers to beat the Bears in my column, although the odds favor Chicago."

***

The Bears played a team in Kenosha in an exhibition contest, freeing George Halas to attend the Packers-Cardinals game and scout his first league opponent.

"Halas left Green Bay after scouting the Packers in the Cardinal game, fairly optimistic. He had been assured by friends that Hinkle, Sauer, et al. would not be ready. But now that they are back, he is genuinely apprehensive," wrote George Strickler in the *Chicago Tribune*.

The game became a Packers archival staple.

Arnie Herber returned the opening kickoff to the Packers 17-yard line. Strickler wrote what happened next:

> "Hutson raced up the field past Beattie Feathers, took a pass from Herber, and raced 45 yards to the goal. Blame for the defeat will rest largely with Feathers, regarded as one of the fastest men in the league.
>
> "Standing in midfield, he waited for Hutson to race up to him and allowed the end, the fastest man on the squad of 43 All-American college men last month, to get past him. Feathers was close enough to touch him in a lunge but it was useless to give chase."

The Packers won the game, 7-0. Dad led his game story accordingly:

> "Lifting 14,000 spectators from their seats with an 83-yard touchdown play as their first effort after the opening kickoff, the Green Bay Packers protected their margin through 59 minutes of bruising football which followed."

One can imagine the frustration of devoted Packer fan Carl Holznecht, who had missed just two home games in the Packers' seventeen seasons. He was at the game in charge of the sales force selling *Who's Who in Major League Football* magazines.

Holznecht watched Herber returned the kickoff, then was called to the sales office in the rear of the stadium to provide more magazines to one of the salesmen.

That's when Herber-to-Hutson happened.

A young Don Hutson poses for this promotional shot early in his career. (Photo courtesy Green Bay Press-Gazette)

September 22, 1935

"Bear day in Green Bay, the usual high pressure excitement. The Packers, playing brilliant ball, defeated the Chicago Bears 7-0 before 13,000 wildly cheering fans. Herber passed to Hutson for a touchdown on the second play of the game and Hutson outran the Bear secondary to the goal line. It was an 83-yard gain and the stands went crazy. Down to the office for more than seven hours of work, writing the play-by-play, compiling statistics, getting my story in shape and mopping up heads and copy on the other games."

***

September 23, 1935, column

Through sixty minutes of eight long games extending back three years, this writer has waited with thousands of Green Bay Packer fans to see the last five minutes of a football game wherein the mighty Bears

Green Bay native Arnie Herber takes to the air in this classic publicity photo. (Photo courtesy Green Bay Press-Gazette)

of Chicago, backs to the wall as the shadows fell across the field, carried dark despair and failure in their faces.

You saw the expressions yesterday afternoon at City stadium when eleven of those Bears, veterans of many a conquest over the Packers in recent years, realized that they had shot their last ounce of effort and braced to ward off the final crushing advance of the victory-crazed Green Bay team.

Very different, that setting, than the jubilant closing minutes of recent games when whooping Bears rode over beaten Green Bay teams which had given their best against superior odds.

John Walter

The Packers were the superior team yesterday, and you are going to see them superior in many a future contest.

Many a Green Bay fan is moaning today because he was late yesterday afternoon. Men who have witnessed hundreds of football games asserted unhesitatingly that the touchdown play which broke on the second play of the game was the most spectacular effort they ever had seen on a gridiron.

It took the experience of Arnold Herber and the skill of Don Hutson and the savage blocking of nine other Packers to execute it perfectly – timed to the split second.

It was the play of the season.

***

September 23, 1935
"That sensational football victory of yesterday is the one topic of conversation, dwarfing even the impending European war."

***

September 24, 1935, column

The decision by clubs of the National Football league to increase the player limit from 22 to 24 players will prove a boon to coaches of the circuit. It has always been a tough problem for coaches to cut their squads to 22 men after the third game.

This season, with almost half the pro teams operating under new pilots, the leaders will have a better chance to see their men perform in league competition and an injury or two will not deplete the reserve strength to cripple the squads.

The coaches this season are about equally divided between those who have come from the playing ranks and those who entered the pro game from the realm of college coaching. Led Wray, Philadelphia Eagles tutor, can be claimed by both sides, since he put in his apprenticeship with Frankfort and Buffalo before turning to college coaching at Pennsylvania.

The appointment of Milo Creighton as playing coach of the Chicago Cardinals enabled the coaches from the ranks to maintain equal balance, as Joe Bach of Notre Dame turned from coaching at Duquesne to piloting the Pittsburgh Pirates.

Among the other coaches from college ranks are Potsy Clark of Detroit, who formerly worked at Kansas and Butler; Eddie Casey, ex-Harvard, now with Boston; and Paul Schissler of Brooklyn, one time at Oregon State.

Curly Lambeau of Green Bay, Steve Owen of the championship New York Giants, and George Halas of the Chicago Bears all came directly to their coaching positions from the playing ranks.

Radio broadcast over a Chicago station last night described the Packers touchdown play against the Bears. The announcer said "Don Hutson has lifted Beattie Feathers' crown as being the fastest man in the National league."

September 28, 1935, column

A decade or two from today, several thousand people will relate, with great enthusiasm but with exaggeration, all the details of that much publicized touchdown play which burst in the face of Beattie Feathers last Sunday at City stadium.

The people who saw the play rapidly are coming to the belief that they were in at ringside on a very important event, which may go down in professional football history as one of the greatest plays of the game.

It has been described on the radio, written and re-written in the press, and yesterday it even was diagrammed, slightly altered at the discretion of the Packer coaching staff, in a Chicago newspaper.

You won't see another one just like that play, probably – but you'll see a great many passes, forward and otherwise, when the Packers meet the world championship New York Giants tomorrow. Aerial dynamite in the New York backfield will be matched with that of the Green Bay bombing squadron from start to finish, for the Packer-Giant games always are featured by the rain of forward passes.

It's anybody's ballgame, and almost any score looks good. We like 10 to 7, Green Bay.

September 27, 1935
"Lunch with Milt Gantenbein and Tiny Engebretsen of the Packers. They say they are going to win Sunday. There are a few thousand fans who will say amen to that. But New York looks very tough."

***

There was an unusual introduction prior to the Packers' game against the New York Giants. It was a dog, a Yankee Terrier, someone's idea of a team mascot for the Packers. It didn't have a name yet, but some of the suggestions were Champ, Zip, Packs, Toughey, Yank and Luck.

***

September 29, 1935
"In afternoon covered spectacular football game. The Packers did it again, rallying in the fourth period to defeat New York, 16-7. Touchdowns by Hank Bruder on a 65-yard run and Cal Hubbard, who played one of his greatest games."

***

September 30, 1935, column

It's remarkable what an efficient mascot can do for a team. It's remarkable, too, what consistent blocking, hard running and plays that click can do.

This isn't meant as a knock to the Packers pup, who took his first workout as mascot yesterday snoozing under the Green Bay bench, but it's meant to point out again to the delighted Packer fans who witnessed the rout of New York, that Green Bay is represented by a real football team.

It's going to take a great squad to beat this rising Green Bay outfit. Held scoreless in the first half, although they outgunned the Giants, the Packers seemed to be saving their real punch for the closing minutes, and when they turned it loose, the Giants faded and broke just as did the Bears under the same pressure.

Every Packer fan remembers the last few minutes of games in recent years, when Green Bay rooters sat in cold fear that the team would break under the strain of the closing period.

Many a Packer fan yesterday thrilled to the realization that this team, which finishes its football games with a pounding drive against whichever enemy is on the field, is going to take the place of the Chicago Bears as the quad with a last period complex.

It's a great sensation to watch the home team chasing a beaten enemy in full flight as the final gun cracks over the stadium.

***

In addition to the introduction of a team mascot, the game also featured a new promotional stunt by the Packers. During halftime, a plane flew over the stadium and dropped souvenir hats for some lucky spectators.

It was a gimmick that had a short lifespan.

***

October 1, 1935, column

Pickups from the Packer-Giant football game, which still has the town gasping.

Metropolitan newspapers and news services credited Milt Gantenbein with the sensational block which carried out the only two possible tacklers on Hank Bruder's 65-yard touchdown gallop ... the blocker, however, was Tar Schwammel and the man who is telling everyone Schwammel did it is Gantenbein.

John Walter

The new Packers were amazed at the ease with which they were able to play against the Giant line. The New York team was back on its heels in the fourth period, looking just like a bunch of old men against the young and driving Packers. One Green Bay player just out of collegiate ranks reported that the Giants were no tougher than a strong college team, but they were doing plenty of holding.

Everyone noticed the new deception in the Packer backfield. Bruder's fake punt from the Packer goal line, which ended with Blood slamming around left end, was perfect. And the boys used their heads. Once a Giant punt bounced high in the air above a New Yorker who was trying to down it. Bob Monnett leaped up and tapped the ball volleyball style to Laws, who got off a neat return.

Eighteen of the Packers were entertained at dinner Saturday noon at the Wisconsin state reformatory, where they made a great hit with the inmates, and no cracks. Johnny Blood served as master of ceremonies.

October 3, 1935
"Invited Johnny Blood, the Packer halfback, up for supper some night next week."

***

With a weak Pittsburgh Pirate team coming to Green Bay the following Sunday, Lambeau decided to rest several of his top players. Hubbard, Michalske, Hinkle and Bruder didn't play a down, while Gantenbein, Goldenberg and Rose saw limited action. But Hutson played and scored two touchdowns as the Packers drubbed the Pirates 27-0.

The Packers used the game as a marketing tool by inviting all high school coaches and players in Wisconsin and Upper Michigan to attend the game for just 50 cents. And, to satisfy the baseball enthusiasts, they provided inning-by-inning of the day's World Series game between the Detroit Tigers and Chicago Cubs. The Cubs were the primary team of choice for most area baseball fans of that era. The public address system played a live radio broadcast at halftime. The Cubs won 3-1, but the Tigers captured the series the next day.

***

October 6, 1935
"Covered football game. Packers 27, Pittsburgh 0. Feature was some spectacular pass receiving by Don Hutson, who is the fastest man in pro football. Hutson scored two touchdowns, George Sauer got one and Joe Laws one."

October 10, 1935
"In evening we entertained George Henry Sauer, the Packers great halfback, for dinner. Sauer is a prince of a fellow."

October 11, 1935
"Lunch with George Sauer. The team is confident of defeating the Cardinals on Sunday, but expects a tough game."

***

<u>October 12, 1935, column</u>

People have been blaming the fourth quarter enthusiasm of the Green Bay Packers onto youth and excitability, but there might be one factor we're all overlooking.

You get the idea, if you read the college roster of the young players who are starring with the team this fall.

George Sauer represents that great Nebraska eleven of 1933.

Bob Tenner and George Svendsen came from the unbeaten, untied, un-everything else team that pounded out of the University of Minnesota last fall.

Ernie Smith played great football with the mighty Southern California machine which ended Notre Dame's long string of victories.

John Walter

Don Hutson's undergraduate prominence resulted from his play with undefeated Alabama, Rose Bowl champion.

Bob O'Connor represents the powerful Stanford team of 1934, terror of the Pacific coast.

These boys just aren't used to getting trimmed. Maybe that's why they go crazy in the fourth period when the game is pretty close.

Maybe they're just what the veterans have been needing. If so, they're a potent tonic, because the old timers of the Packer machine never played better ball.

That's the kind of ball they'll need tomorrow. Make it 14 to 0, Green Bay.

***

The Packers then played two straight home games at State Fair Park in Milwaukee, first against the Chicago Cardinals. They outgained the Cardinals 91-7 in the first half, but lost 3-0 when Paul Pardonner drop-kicked a 17-yard field goal.

There was a hint of controversy that was never seriously pursued. According to Dad's story and column, Lambeau twice sent instructions in to attempt a field goal, and both times he was ignored. The likely villain was Blood, who was calling the plays. Both times the Packers failed to score.

Later in the week, Lambeau referred to the issue in a conversation with Dad about the team's offense as it prepared for the Detroit Lions:

"We hope to perfect an attack which will carry the ball deep into Detroit territory for possible touchdowns. If we can, we'll score the touchdowns, but if we can't, we'll kick."

Then Dad wrote:

"The mixup at Milwaukee, when the Packers didn't kick for almost certain points which would have won the game, has been straightened out satisfactorily. Somebody apparently didn't understand somebody else correctly but Lambeau emphasized that the situation wouldn't occur again."

Blood didn't finish the game as he was hit in the head making a tackle and was taken to a Milwaukee hospital in an ambulance, where he was treated for a concussion.

There was a bit of humor in the game. The Cardinals' Phil Sarboe tried an end run and was tackled by Ernie Smith, and the whistle blew. But Sarboe decided to get up and keep running and Smith decided to chase him, tore off the Chicago player's helmet and threw it at him, hitting him the head. The play was called back.

Imagine the viral online video of something like that today.

Oh, and movie actor George Raft was at the game, although there was no explanation of why.

***

October 13, 1935
"Packers pushed the Cardinals all over the field but lost a heartbreaker, 3-0 on Paul Pardonner's 17-yard drop kick. Packers played great football but received the most miserable breaks. Terribly disappointing."

***

October 14, 1935, column

You never felt more sorry for a bunch of fighting men than you did for the Packers during the fourth period of that game in Milwaukee. The boys were losing a heartbreaker and they knew it. It showed on every one of their faces. But they had the stuff to toss those Cardinals back twice on the goal linear the end of the game.

Tough to pick out individual stars. The team never worked harder. You never saw more breaks go the wrong way. You were glad when the final whistle blew.

The Packers seemed to be taking such an unnecessary pounding through that last period. It made you forget the yardage they piled up during the first half, enabling them to outgain the Cardinals by more than 100 yards for the game.

You were resentful about the team's failure to attempt goals from the field when in scoring distance. Twice orders to kick were sent in and disregarded while Lambeau raged along the sidelines. Maybe the Cardinals looked too soft.

You hated the Cardinals through the last half, for no other reason than they looked like a great ball team. You wished the Packers could click and keep clicking. You forgot for the moment that some day you'll watch this same gang of young Packers tear apart a powerful opponent for the championship of the National league.

You hoped that game wouldn't be played on the 13th of the month.

***

October 14, 1935
"Went to meeting of Ambassador club and gave talk on the Packers. Lavvie Dilweg, one-time All-America end, also was there and gave a better talk."

***

October 17, 1935, column

A couple of very interesting – and very different – football personalities are Lavvie Dilweg and Dave Woodward.

Probably they've never met. Undoubtedly, they've heard of each other. One probably possesses as great an interest in the Green Bay Packers as any other person, and the other will develop a feeling nearly as strong.

Lavvie spoke to the Ambassador club the other night, giving an interesting and enlightening discussion of the Packer team as you'd ever be able to hear. He wasn't afraid to call a shovel pass a shovel pass, but when he finished you felt very optimistic about the future of Green Bay's greatest sports unit.

You have to love the game to play it well, says Lavvie, who ought to know – he never knew how to play poor football. He mentioned Milt Gantenbein, Verne Lewellen, George Sauer – three players from different eras of Packer football – as men who obviously liked to play the game, irregardless of injury or pay check.

Dave Woodward doesn't know much about the Packers, except from hearsay, but he'll soon be as well acquainted with all of them as anyone. He's just been secured as athletic trainer for the squad, which will enable him to rub shoulders – and legs and knees – with the best of them.

Quite a pride Dave takes in his work. The trainer, he says, stands between the specialist and the coach. The specialist knows when the player shouldn't play, the coach wants him to play, and the trainer must satisfy both.

But the real assignment, Dave admits, is up to the athlete himself.

October 19, 1935, column

Green Bay interest in the feud which will send two powerful football units smoking into combat at Milwaukee tomorrow afternoon has dimmed local interest in another engagement, which may be of great importance, eventually, to the pennant hopes of the Green Bay Packers.

John Walter

The Brooklyn Dodgers will meet the Chicago Bears at Wrigley Field.

Brooklyn has every chance – almost better than an even one – of defeating the Bears, and doing the Packers a great turn in the quest of the latter team for the championship of the west. The Dodgers outplayed both New York and Boston, to which they lost close decisions, and thumped the Detroit Lions in a game which caused Packer pennant stock to advance a notch.

If you think it over, you'll take the Dodgers, with battering Stan Kostka, Minnesota's powerhouse, Bill Lee of Alabama, greatest tackle of the South last year, and brilliant Ray Fuqua of Southern Methodist, the gentleman who very nearly signed a Green Bay contract.

The Bears' physician says Bronko Nagurski, an individual the Chicago team has needed desperately this season, must continue to ride the sidelines.

So keep an eye on the Dodgers.

We can't – we'd rather watch the Packers.

We like that score at 6 to 0, Green Bay.

***

It was a bit closer than that, but the Packers won 13-9 after trailing 3-0 at the half. In the third quarter, Frank Christensen's punt was blocked by Tar Schwammel and, as Dad's game story noted, "the one person the Packers wanted to be near the ball landed on it."

It was Hutson who scooped it up and, benefitting from a Schwammel block, ran 25 yards for the touchdown.

One of the key Lions players, whose name wasn't even listed in the program because he had just joined the team, was former Centenary College alum Buddy Parker. It was the Packers' Hubbard, also a Centenary alum, who suggested that Parker try out with the Lions, telling him that the Detroit team was a better fit for him than the Packers.

Parker would last two seasons with the Lions, then went into coaching. Eventually named Lions head coach in the early 1950s, he guided Detroit to two championships before retiring in 1957.

October 20, 1935

"Covered football game at State Fair park in afternoon. Packers played brilliant ball, rallying in the second half to defeat the Detroit Lions, 13-9. Don Hutson picked up the ball after Schwammel blocked a punt and ran for a touchdown."

***

October 21, 1935, column

Now you can reverse your field, disregard those troublesome Cardinals for the moment, and turn your attention to Chicago, where another of those titanic struggles between the Packers and the Bears is in line for next Sunday.

Nobody expected Pittsburgh to defeat the Cardinals, but no one expected Braddock to take Baer either, and Sunday's lacing of Detroit by the Packers sets the stage for what probably will be the greatest game of the National league season to date, at Wrigley field next Sunday afternoon.

The Packers may get another miracle play, such as defeated the Bears here early this season, or they may be able to beat George Halas' team on straight football. If they do win, they'll go into first place, and you can set it down as a lead pipe fact they they'll be very, very hard to dislodge.

John Walter

Green Bay, of course, respects the Bears tremendously. The Chicago team has a passing attack which is as distracting as a split skirt on a bowling alley and as irritating as a mouse in a mince pie. The Bears, despite their defeat by the Packers, still are the rough, tough outfit which has been spread-eagling the opposition around National league circles for several seasons.

It's going to be the game of the season.

October 23, 1935, column

People ask occasionally just why the Green Bay Packers, or the West high school football team, or the East high squad, is credited with having gained only 204 yards in a certain game when they, the questioners, having been sitting right there in the stands, know perfectly well that the team actually made better than 300 yards, and perhaps close to 400.

In other words, the statistics are all wrong.

The matter comes to the front, probably, because all of the published statistics on certain games don't jibe, some of them to the detriment of the home team, and persons who make knocking an avocation realize that someone is drastically wrong.

Which results in a discussion of the form of statistics used for *Press-Gazette* coverage of all sporting events.

The yardage credited by the *Press-Gazette* to the Green Bay Packers, which is accepted as the official total by the press bureau of the National Professional Football league, in nine cases out of ten is correct almost to the inch.

The statistics are computed from the play-by-play, which are taken by three persons on the sidelines at each game. One of the workers follows the ball carrier, noting the type of play, direction and yardage gained. A second staff member takes note of blocking and a third watches the tackling.

When this play-by-play is written, the statistics are computed from it with great care. All first downs are noted in the copy, all passes are placed under the headings of attempted, completed or intercepted, the penalties and fumbles are tabulated and from the completed list the individual gains are obtained.

Once in a while something goes wrong. On one occasion a sheet of copy paper was lost, and the gains had to be approximated for the statistics, but this was a rare occurrence.

Just check that play-by-play yourself.

***

October 24, 1935
"In evening, Mother and I entertained Tar and Mrs. Schwammel at supper. Tar is the great Packer tackle, and we had a nice time of it."

October 25, 1935
"The Packers will be on the spot Sunday. If they lose, the Green Bay franchise will be in danger. If they win, they'll probably go on to the National league championship. But the Bears are big and tough."

***

I don't know if the future of the franchise hung in the balance during that game, if Dad was given some warning from someone with inside Packers connections, or he was just prone to exaggeration.

But there was no doubting the level of excitement leading up to the game. A *Press-Gazette* reporter went along Walnut and Washington streets and asked as many as fifty people for their opinions on the game's outcome. Here is what he wrote:

> Football conversation has been more rampant here this fall than in any season since the championship years. The old time spirit has returned, and smoke from the fire of sideline quarterbacks' arguments and Monday morning guesses are helping warm these October mornings.
>
> The train of thought runs along three tracks. There is the out-and-out Packer fan who does not give the Bears a chance. There is the dissenter who selects the Bears, sometimes with apologies. And there is the wisher and hoper.
>
> Among the comments:
>
> William Drew, jeweler: "The Packers. They are approaching the peak and should win this one.
>
> Ralph Moeser, clerk: "My good wishes are all with the Packers but I'm afraid that the Bears will win. With a man who can kick like Jack Manders, I can't see any other result."
>
> Rigney, Dwyer, Register of Deeds: "The Packers, with my fingers crossed."
>
> Roger C. Minahan, attorney: "The Bears. The Packers won the first game on a break that they won't be able to repeat."
>
> Fred Cone, meteorologist: "The Bears by two touchdowns. They have power where the Packers haven't. It will be hard to fool them with a miracle play again."
>
> Harry Flatow, merchant: "The Packers aerial attack will give them victory. With Hutson, they have a constant threat."

***

October 26, 1935, column

George Halas, Curly Lambeau and a varied assortment of Packers and Bears know that tomorrow afternoon's football game at Wrigley Field is going to be decided by breaks.

They know, and several thousand fans know, that the engagement is going to be one of the most bitter struggles ever waged on a professional gridiron, and that's just why, weather granting, better than 30,000 people will be present to witness it.

There are several reasons why the Bears should win, and several more why the Packers should come through.

The Bears are still the Bears. They lost at Green Bay early this year (refer to section H of the Packer alphabetic list – Herber, Hutson) but they since have been going as hot as a stadium light but at July beauty contest and they have their eyes dead set on the championship. They want to put on those rubber shoes and beat the New York Giants next December.

John Walter

The Packers are younger. They are bigger. They had the Bears on the dead run up here last September, and it was only the luck of the all-Americans that the Bears didn't buckle under another touchdown at the end of the game. The Packers are also aiming at the title and if they win tomorrow it'll be full steam ahead and buckle your chin straps.

All this would deaden any forecast.

Ours is 10 to 7, Packers.

Chapter 13

More Like Fiction

October 26, 1935
"Boarded a Milwaukee Road train, Chicago-bound, with the Green Bay Packers. Rode most of the way with Johnny Blood and Bob O'Connor."

October 27, 1935
"In the afternoon, the game, one of the most sensational of all-time. Trailing 14-3 with but two minutes left to play, the Packers suddenly went crazy. Don Hutson took a pass and ran 69 yards for a touchdown. Ernie Smith then recovered a fumble on the 13-yard line, Sauer hauled it to the 3-yard line, and a Herber-to-Hutson pass put it over, the Packers winning 17-14. Home with that great football team at 12:30 a.m."

***

The Packers had beaten the Bears in rather dramatic fashion in September when Herber passed to Hutson for the game's only touchdown. They doubled down on the drama at Wrigley Field on that last Sunday of October. George Strickler explained it in his *Chicago Tribune* report:

> "Fourteen plays and three-and-a-half minutes from the end of yesterday's game, the Chicago Bears were a swaggering, smug aggregation out in front 14 to 3 and seemingly unstoppable on their march to another championship.

"Fourteen plays later, they left the field, beaten 17-14 by a Green Bay team that staged one of the most sensational finishes in the history of football.

"Exits and parking lots around Wrigley Field were jammed with spectators. Green Bay players began to pick up blankets and headgears for the dash to the clubhouse."

Part of Dad's game story included this paragraph:

"The story of the game should be written in one solid book which would read more like fiction than any storyteller would dare to write."

It certainly looked gloomy after Johnny Sisk's 55-yard touchdown run gave the Bears their 14-3 lead with four minutes left. After the kickoff, the Packers had an incomplete pass and a three-yard loss before Herber connected with Hutson for a 68-yard score. Ernie Smith kicked the extra point.

On the first play after the kickoff, Bernie Masterson fumbled and Smith recovered at the Bears' 13-yard line. Sauer carried it to the 3-yard-line and Hinkle was held for no gain.

In the huddle, Hutson told Herber, "I can outrun Molesworth in case you want to try fifteen to the left."

"Fifteen it is," Herber said.

Fifteen had Hutson running parallel to the line of scrimmage, where he took Herber's pass and fell into the end zone as Keith Molesworth piled into him.

The game ended when Joe Laws intercepted Beattie Feathers' desperation pass.

Strickler wrote:

"The mistakes Masterson made were not as responsible for the loss as the superb passing of Herber and the matchless receiving of Hutson. The combination has defeated the Bears almost single-handed twice this year for the only setbacks the former champions have suffered. It's the most feared aerial attack and matches the Green Bay Lewellen to Blood combination which ruled the National league five years ago."

Jim Gallagher, *Chicago American*:

"The Chicago Bears won't see Arnie Herber and Don Hutson again this season. And that's all right with the Bears."

Marvin McCarthy, *Chicago Daily Times*:
"If you had seen this game in the movies or read it in a book, you would have been vastly annoyed and impatient with the author. You would have resented the imposition on your credulity and intelligence. This game simply couldn't happen, not even in imagination."

Frantic finish

Here is the play-by-play of last few minutes of the Packers-Bears game at Wrigley Field:

Herber punts to Molesworth, who returns to Bears 45-yard-line.
Sick runs untouched over tackle for 55 yards and touchdown. Manders kicks extra point.
Bears 14, Packers 3

Manders kicks off to Hinkle, who returns to Packers 30. Bears offside penalty declined.
Herber pass to Hinkle incomplete. Bears offside penalty.
Sauer fumbles, recovers for 3-yard loss.
Herber passes to Hutson for 65 yards and touchdown. Schwammel kicks extra point.
Bears 14, Packers 10

Schwammel kicks off through end zone for touchback.
Masterson fumbles, Smith recovers at Bears 13-yard line.
Sauer gains one yard up the middle
Herber pass to Tenner incomplete, interference penalty on Bears puts ball at 11-yard line.
Sauer gains eight yards.
Hinkle runs for not gain.
Herber passes to Hutson for three yards and touchdown. Smith kicks extra point.
Packers 17, Bears 14

Hinkle kicks off to Feathers, who returns to Bears' 40, laterals to Johnson who runs to Bears 41.
Masterson runs for loss of 10 yards, tackled by Rose and Kiesling.
Feathers' pass intercepted by Laws at Packers' 15, return to 25.
Game ends.

Tony Walter

October 28, 1935, column

On the Packers coach en route from Chicago to Green Bay ... the happiest man on the train is Buckets Goldenberg... If we get to the championship, says Buckets, I won't feel any better ... maybe it was my fault Ronzani got that touch ... guess he hid behind the line ... never saw him until he went past me ... but it was great to get in there and crack 'em at the end ... one minute I hoped the game would go on forever and the next I thought it would never end.

John Walter

I was a nervous wreck before the game, says Clarke Hinkle ... Me too, says Milt Gantenbein ... thought I'd outgrow it, but it got worse ... you should have been out on that field this afternoon ... Out on that end, says Clarke .... boy, they were pouring it onto me back of that line.

Bob Tenner's sound asleep, and looks good for the trip ... George Svendsen wanders up and down the aisle, swaying with the train ... finally settles down to read a book ... Hinkle starts a crossword puzzle ... hot bridge game in the smoker ... Johnny Blood and Walt Kiesling versus Ralph Smith and Verne Lewellen ... Kiesling got the football after the game ... wouldn't sell it for anything ... plans to have it framed.

Good-bye to Goldenberg and Arnie Herber at Milwaukee ... Buckets leaves with words of praise for Ernie Smith, who recovered that fourth period fumble ... a great tackle, says Buck ... and getting better ... Everyone comments that the game was similar to that 1933 last minute trimming the Bears gave the Packers at Green Bay.

Now we'll sit down and watch the others fight it out for a week, someone says ... great buildup for November 10 ... ought to fill the stadium up home ... Bob O'Connor figures Pittsburgh will be tough ... it took Boston today.

In comes Bud Jorgenson, Packer equipment man ... he listened to the fourth period in a downtown hotel and went crazy.

November 7, 1935, column

Football fans probably realize it, but there's no harm in calling attention to the fact that there is an unusual setup on tap Sunday in the professional gridiron battle between the Green Bay Packers and the Detroit Lions.

For one thing, the struggle probably will decide the championship of the National league's Western division, particularly in view of the throat-slicing parties scheduled between Chicago's Bears and Cardinals.

For another, Packer followers will have their first opportunity to see their team, at full strength in mid-season, tackle a powerful, contending opponent.

This is an important point. The Packers have appeared before home crowds later in the season than November 10, but always against comparatively weak opposition such as Stapleton, Philadelphia, or similar teams. Consequently, although the team had developed its ball handling and offensive maneuvers to a fine point, it never was called upon to display the entire repertoire against its home opponent.

Sunday's situation is vastly different. The Packers are playing their best ball of the season, and they face an opponent so dangerous that the upmost skill and power will be required to snatch a victory.

So critical is the setup that a victory will more firmly cement Green Bay in first place – while a defeat may topple the Packers to last place.

That's the Western division for you.

***

November 10, 1935

"In afternoon covered football game. The Packers came through with a brilliant passing attack to hand the Detroit Lions the worst defeat of their professional football history, 31-7. Johnny Blood scored two touchdowns, others went to Hutson and Sauer. Clarke Hinkle kicked a 30-yard field goal. Herber's passing was sensational."

***

November 11, 1935, column

This department never before has made a yip about officiating, and the writer privately has felt that no little of the chatter about offsides, roughness and similar tactics has been exaggerated but you have to admit that the boys slipped up in the third period yesterday ... standing on the goal line, Blood was set to receive Herber's long pass ... Frank Christensen wrapped his arms around Johnny, and the ball bounced off his tummy ...everyone looked expectantly at Field Judge Dan Tehan and when that official shook his head, indicating that no interference ruling would be made, the crowd went wild.

***

Tehan was also criticized for his role as time keeper since this was before scoreboards had the game time visible to fans. A *Press-Gazette* story detailed the issue:

> "There were a number of Packer fans today who weren't certain that Dan Tehan, field judge and time keeper, is any too accurate in the matter of holding the watch.
>
> "One stopwatch carried by a Packer fan in the stands who requested that his name be withheld, indicated that the second period went nearly 30 minutes, and that Detroit scored its touchdown after 21 minutes had elapsed. The period is supposed to last 15 minutes.
>
> "There was consternation on the Packer bench when Tehan announced 'Five minutes to play' after the Packer stopwatch indicated that play already had gone a minute and a half overtime.
>
> "A check of the official play-by-play reveals that 36 plays were run off in the first period, 42 in the third period, 35 in the fourth period, and 56 in the second period."

A few words about Tehan. First, he remains the longest-serving official in the NFL, having worked thirty-two seasons, his last one being 1965. So he clearly earned his stripes.

But he was blamed, at least in our house, for a call or non-call in the Packers-Bears game at Wrigley Field on November 10, 1957. The Packers, taking advantage of a Bill Forester interception, had the ball at the Bears' 30-yard line late in the third quarter with the game tied 14-14. It was third-and-22 and Bart Starr threw a long pass to Joe Johnson, who juggled it and appeared to catch it as he fell at the goal line with linebacker Bill George on top of him.

The officials ruled that Johnson slid out of bounds before catching the ball. Both the *Press-Gazette* and *Chicago Tribune* ran a sequence of six Associated Press photographs of the play in the next day's editions, which seemed to show that Johnson caught the ball inbounds. *Press-Gazette* sports editor Art Daley made it clear in his game story what he thought of the call. Even *Chicago Tribune* sportswriter George Strickler wrote that the sequence "undoubtedly will hang over every bar in Green Bay today, accompanied by a noose reserved for officials."

The Bears eventually won 21-14.

Dad blamed Tehan, who was working the game, and there might have been a reference to Tehan being in Halas's pocket, although he was from Cincinnati.

Tehan died in 1980, so he can't defend himself today. The Packers only won three games that year anyway, but Dad's reaction reflected the impact of the Bears-Packers rivalry on him from his days as a sportswriter and a fan.

***

November 13, 1935
"Rather griped because I won't be going to Detroit with the Packers. Not that I expected to. The company always has had George Calhoun cover the Eastern trips. But I'm trying to muscle in."

***

November 13, 1935, column

Some years back when the writer, perched upon a fallen willow in the denseness of the forests surrounding the old Bishop's lot at Van Buren and Cass streets, was waling the identity out of a stale birch tree in an effort to complete his second class Boy Scout tests, the late Rudolph Valentino came through with a picture, depicting the instability of life in the bull ring, which was entitled:

"Blood and Sand."

It remained for the Green Bay Packers and the Detroit Lions, bitter rivals from the days they were smacking each other into the Ohio river down Portsmouth way, to write the sequel to that tense descriptive title, and as a result Potsy Clark of Detroit won't eat his spinach – because he has sand on it.

The Lions, who looked as though they could have used a little spinach themselves Sunday, have been basking in the sympathy of Detroit fans since that game, and listening to the squalling of radio stations which have been heaping deprecations on the Packers for luring the innocent and unsophisticated Lions upon a sandy surface for their pro league game.

The aftermath permits Potsy to keep his reputation as the world's outstanding alibi expert. The Detroit team would have lost to the Packers Sunday if the teams had met on the front sidewalk of East High School, on the bottom of the Fox river or on the top of the Minahan building weather tower. They were beaten, licked and pounded into the ground by a superior football team and all the crying alibis in the world can't alter the fact.

They merely lead to the suspicion that the Lions, the big, brave team which can dish it out all over the National league, just maybe can't take it.

Tony Walter

***

November 14, 1935

"Watched the Packers practice at West High field. They'll be on their way tomorrow. The boys have lots of fight and are hopeful of defeating Detroit again. In evening Mother and I had George Sauer and Lon Evans of the Packers up for supper – swell chicken dinner which the boys much enjoyed. They stayed most of the evening."

***

November 14, 1935, column

Occasionally those who support the Green Bay Packers – and what real sports follower here does not? – are called upon to do something for the team rather than patronize the games.

Usually, when those occasions arise, the pleas are unnecessary, because the fans would have performed the required service anyway.

Such an occasion will occur tomorrow. The Packers, somewhat dented from their encounter with the Detroit Lions last Sunday, will head for the Eastern gridiron wars tomorrow noon, and the people of Green Bay are requested to go down to the station and see them on their way.

It's a cinch. Every Packer fan who can get away would be there anyway, and the presence of the city band, with the "On Wisconsin" and that peppy Packers marching song, will provide additional color for the noon-time ceremonies.

John Walter

Nevertheless, the fans are reminded that they have a great opportunity tomorrow to show the team just how completely its splendid fighting performances this season have won the hearts of the city's people, and if the prediction from this corner is correct, they'll be hanging out the SRO signs very early at the Milwaukee Road station.

See you there = we'll all be on hand to justify that often-used and seldom abused nickname – the pro team with the college spirit.

***

November 15, 1935

"With much blowing of whistles and cheering of fans, the Packers move out of town to the eastern football wars. Down to the station to see them off at noon, along with more than 1,000 other people. After

Green Bay Packers 1935 Team

First row: Mike Michalske, Bob Tenner, Nate Barrager, Ade Schwammel, George Svendsen, Russ Letlow, George Sauer, Bob O'Connor, Bob Monnett.
Second row: Buckets Goldenberg, Joe Laws, Tiny Engebretsen, Clarke Hinkle, Arnie Herber, Roger Grove, Hank Bruder, Milt Gantenbein, Herm Schneidman, Swede Johnston.
Top Row: Curly Lambeau, Johnny Blood, Al Rose, Frank Butler, Champ Seibold, Cal Hubbard, Walt Kiesling, Claude Perry, Don Hutson, Ernie Smith (Photo courtesy Green Bay Press-Gazette)

---

a lapse of three years, the city again is gripped in football hysteria. This great team won't let us down. It will smash ahead to the National championship."

***

Not quite. The Lions dominated and won 20-10.

Calhoun's lead sentence in his game story: "Old Man Over-Confidence and several costly fumbles coupled with a brilliant exhibition of football by Bill Shepherd set the stage for the Packers to meet defeat."

Later in the same story, Calhoun added this: "The excitement was so intense in the final period while the Lions were on the scoring spree that one Detroit rooter who was parked up in the East stands suffered a heart attack, and he succumbed before the stretcher bearers removed him from the stadium."

***

November 17, 1935
"Church in morning with Mother. Never could figure out why I go to church. I get so little out of it. Rather a habit, I suspect. In afternoon took play-by-play of Packer-Detroit game over radio from Detroit. The Lions pulled a surprise and upset Green Bay 20-10, in a muddy

game. Milt Gantenbein got the Packer touchdown, Ernie Smith kicked one extra point and a field goal. The Chicago Bears were upset by New York, 3-0, so we're tied for first place. Took Calhoun's story at office in evening. The Packers, it seems, were very smartly shellacked."

***

November 18, 1935, column

It was gratifying wandering around town after listening to that Packer-Detroit game yesterday, to find that the chatter generally was not favorable to the Green Bay team.

You always expect a volley of alibis and beefing whenever the home team loses, but the fans seemed pretty smart last night. They realized that they live in Green Bay, not Detroit, and they were leaving the alibis to Potsy Clark.

John Walter

Sure, we were licked, was the consensus. We were licked very smartly, and the Detroit team was the better of the two teams on the field yesterday. The stadium may have been muddy, but that didn't stop the Lions. They beat us, and beat us badly.

So what?

So the Packers are going to take everything out upon those Pittsburgh Pirates, the team that stands next in their path. So they will land upon Chicago and the Cardinals Thanksgiving day, and have their chance of chances to prove they are a championship team. So the Bears, facing two games apiece with Detroit and the Cards, are going to drop at least one more.

So the Packers still are the favored team in the National league, still in first place, and because the fans still stand solidly behind them, have the entire support of their city as they roll, checked only momentarily, to that championship playoff.

That's what.

***

November 18, 1935

"The Packers, much chagrined at their unexpected defeat by the Detroit Lions, came home today and prepared for a week of training in preparation for their at Pittsburgh next Sunday. Don Hutson, Packer end, is in the hospital with appendicitis."

***

Don Hutson played the Detroit game with a 100-degree temperature from a swollen appendix, but apparently didn't tell anyone he was so uncomfortable. Dr. Kelly had him check into St. Vincent Hospital, but said no surgery was planned and that Hutson could be on his feet by the weekend.

Dad met the Packers when their train arrived in Green Bay that Monday, but few fans showed up. One player said, "What must we do? Win all of our games?"

The door was opened for the Packers to make a run at the championship when Brooklyn upset the Cardinals in a mid-week game.

***

November 20, 1935
"The Packers are in undisputed first place in the National league's Western division because Brooklyn upset the Chicago Cardinals last night."

November 21, 1935
"Last day on my sports desk for awhile. Calhoun is going east with the Packers and I'm going on telegraph, a spot I cordially dislike."

November 23, 1935
"A new era of air transportation opens with the first flight of the China Clipper, a 25-ton mail plane, from San Francisco to Hawaii. From now on there will be regular mail service, and later passenger service, across the Pacific."

***

November 23, 1935, column

If Green Bay had continued its 1935 series of assaults on Detroit last Sunday, and had rubbed the Lions' noses in the muck of the University of Detroit stadium, your knowing fan would have hesitated to risk much on tomorrow's Packer-Pirate game.

As it is, the prevailing opinion holds that the Packers are going to pour things all over Pittsburgh, taking out their disappointment of the Detroit defeat on the Pirates.

Don't bet on too big a score. Pittsburgh is vastly improved over the

Tony Walter

demoralized outfit which succumbed to Green Bay 27 to 0, and has proved it by dumping over several formidable opponents, including the Chicago Cardinals and the Brooklyn Dodgers. The Packers probably would enjoy their greatest measure of success through the air, as the Pittsburgh pass defense is sloppy, for if the Pirates get the Bays in the mud tomorrow, things be tough.

The Packers should be an impressive team on a muddy field. They're great in the sand. At Detroit, when they had an excellent opportunity to make use of their superior weight and power, they bogged down and lost, but there were psychological factors in that defeat, which transcended the condition of the field. It was Detroit's day.

It should be Green Bay's day at Pittsburgh tomorrow.

***

November 24, 1935

"In afternoon took play-by-play of Packer football game over radio. Green Bay defeated a rather stubborn Pittsburgh team 34-14. George Sauer and Johnny Blood each made two touchdowns. Clarke Hinkle got another. At Chicago, the Bears and Detroit played to a 20-20 tie. This means that Green Bay can clinch the Western division championship by winning the last two games."

***

November 25, 1935, column

The Packers are looking right down the throats of the other teams in the Western division today, as a result of their victory at Pittsburgh yesterday, and the tie between the Bears and Detroit Lions at Chicago.

It's hard to see how the Packers could have benefited more than by that knotted contest at Wrigley field, the last period of which was played in almost total darkness. The shroud of dusk which descended upon the combatants probably spelled the end of their championship hopes, because the Packers, their fans, and the law of averages all combine to predict a Green Bay victory over the Cardinals Thanksgiving day.

If the Bears had won yesterday, someone else would have had to knock off George Halas' team before the Packers could be assured of their Western division title. If the Lions had copped, then Detroit would have remained in a commanding position.

Of course, the Packers must win their last two games. Nothing unusual about that. You rather expect championship teams to win their games. If the team rode through to an undisputed first place with but two contests to play and then dropped one of them, it wouldn't deserve the title.

The Packers could be in good shape for a great effort next Thursday. George Henry Sauer, after he blazed his way to two touchdowns, was carefully wrapped in oilcloth and cellophane and kept upon the bench. He was injured slightly. Don Hutson hugged his appendix and didn't get a minute of action. The other regulars were maneuvered carefully and should be ready to earn turkey and dressing for Thanksgiving evening.

Pick the Cardinals, if you want, and give us the Packers – by 13 to 6.

***

November 26, 1935
"Very irritated about my plans for tomorrow. They won't let me off early enough to leave at noon, so I'll have to take the mid-afternoon train. You have to be a confirmed drunk to get any privileges around that place."

***

November 28, 1935, column

The writer of this column, who never landed at Plymouth rock, or never had any ancestors who did, still observes the rituals of Thanksgiving day, and at the present writing is thankful.

That the Packers play three games with the Chicago Cardinals this season instead of two.

That George Henry Sauer has two legs, and has only injured one of them.

That the people who, after the Cardinal game, said "Well, this isn't our year" – "We aren't going any place this season" – are hard to find.

That appendicitis is such a small thing in the life of Donald Hutson.

That the team's opponents, having to keep careful watch on Donald and on Johnny Blood, have forgotten from time to time, to notice Milt Gantenbein.

That the basketball season, which involves covering games from a warm, comfortable seat, is begun.

That not one single football game involving a Green Bay team was played in the rain this season – yet.

***

To keep their championship hopes alive, the Packers would have to finally beat the Cardinals, and they'd have to do it without either Herber (injured ankle) and Hutson (that appendix).

The game would come down to a field goal attempt in the final minute at Wrigley Field. Trailing 9-7, Packer Tar Schwammel's kick from the 23-yard line passed over the right upright, so close to call.

Chicago Tribune's George Strickler wrote: "It lofted high over the upright and to the 7,500 who sat bundled in blankets it appeared Green Bay had duplicated its sensational finish against the Bears. But Referee James Durkee shook his head and signaled failure. The ball had curved outside the upright by a foot."

Dad described the game as part of a "dismal jinx" that the Cardinals had over the Packers. On Schwammel's kick, he wrote that "Durfee started to raise his hands, hesitated and then wrecked the Packers hopes with a negative gesture ... gave the Green Bay men the bitterest disappointment of any season. It's anybody's guess as to whether it was in or out."

***

November 28, 1935
"Sat around and talked with the Packers for awhile. Then to Wrigley Field, for football game which wrecked the Packers' championship hopes. The Cardinals won, 9-7, although Green Bay outplayed them almost constantly. Bob Monnett made a touchdown on a 60-yard run. Tar Schwammel attempted a field goal with 55 seconds left to play in the game and it was ruled no good, costing the Packers the title. Felt very badly."

November 29, 1935
"Arrived on sleeper from Chicago at 3:00 a.m. A terrific jam on the sports desk, which kept me occupied until 2 p.m. Much discussion over Schwammel's goal kick. The Press-Gazette photographer got a shot which shows the ball apparently crossing the bar. Used it on the page, which will provoke a storm of comment."

***

In truth, the picture was inconclusive, but was certainly fodder for fans to bemoan the outcome during the long offseason.

***

November 29, 1935, column

Fifty-five seconds from the end of the Packer-Cardinal game at Wrigley field yesterday afternoon there was brewed a storm which will rage all through the winter, and for many a season to come, wherever there are droves, fireplaces, taverns or any other place conducive to conversation.

"And I'm the sucker!" bitterly cried big Tar Schwammel, his face smeared with mud and his uniform a soggy mess, as he trudged off the field in the gathering dusk of Chicago's north side gridiron, his attempt at a goal which would have spelled sensational victory ruled a failure.

Tar blamed himself, because he is as conscientious a football player as ever played the game, and because he blamed himself he further proved his status as one of the most dependable, hard working and honest men on the Packers' great team.

He played a grand game all day, smashing through offensively time after time to lead the way for the Packer ball carriers, and being instrumental in that last desperate scoring drive which fell short at the end of the game.

John Walter

Tar said that in his honest opinion the kick crossed almost directly over the right post, slightly favoring the inside. Keeping his eye on the kicking spot, he didn't "look up until the ball was beyond the crossbars and maybe then I looked up too soon."

Referee Durfee said the kick was a failure. He probably gave his honest, unbiased opinion, and he stood behind Schwammel, slightly to the left of the kicker. The officiating was fair all afternoon – the Packers received a couple of good breaks from the officials; in fact, worked the ball down for the kick on an interference ruling.

It could have been in – it could have been out – it was called out, and it will go down in Green Bay football history as one of the toughest, bitterest breaks of all time.

When we said the officiating was fair, we meant it probably wasn't prejudiced. There were a couple of weak spots. On Schwammel's first attempt at a field goal, a Cardinal jumped prematurely across the line of scrimmage. Frank Butter, seeing the chance at a penalty which would have given the Packers a first down, deliberately passed the ball wildly to Blood. But Dan Tehan, the head linesman, failed to call the offside and Bill Smith recovered the fumbled lateral.

Tehan rapidly is becoming one of the most disliked and unpopular officials in the league, not only for his poor work at Green Bay, either. A storm of abuse broke over his head from the Chicago spectators when the game ended. One man walked right up and referred to him in a manner which implied no respect for his family.

***

November 30, 1935
"Green Bay's fading hope for a Western football championship depends upon a Brooklyn victory over Detroit tomorrow. Very doubtful."

***

November 30, 1935, column

John Walter

A few muddy scraps from the Packer-Cardinal game at Wrigley field Thanksgiving day:

The impression Bobby Monnett made on the crowd by scampering 60 yards through the Cardinal secondary for his touchdown... the spectators gasped and settled back... every time Monnett got his hands on the ball thereafter, everyone howled for someone to grab him before he got away.

The wild enthusiasm with which the Packers on the bench greeted Monnett's run... every man leaped to the sidelines, shaking clenched fists at the men on the field, yelling to high heavens that the Packers were under way.

The chagrined look on Curly's face when the referee tacked fifteen yards onto him for coaching from the bench... he wasn't coaching... just discussing the referee out loud... it was more of a social blunder than a football rules violation... but the referee wasn't sensitive... just efficient.

The snail-like pace with which the Packers dragged off the field at the end... you knew their discouragement... you felt like an old man yourself... the friendly pats on the back the boys gave Tar Schwammel ... the man who had to get on the spot in the last minute.

The insistence of spectators sitting in back of the goal posts that the kick was good... and the realization that, even if it was, it was water over the bridge.

Johnny Blood scuffling into the Knickerbocker hotel, cursing every step of the way... Tiny Engebretsen's glum face on the way to the elevator.

The turkey supper.

***

December 1, 1935
"Church in morning. Spent most of the sermon watching a girl two pews ahead. Never did find out who she was. Got quarter-by-quarter score from Detroit. The Lions walloped 28-0, thus removing the Packers' last chance for the title."

December 4, 1935
"Lunched with several of the Packers. Clarke Hinkle, Joe Laws, Herman Schneideman, Milt Gantenbein."

December 5, 1935
"Went to St. Norbert basketball game with Cal Hubbard and Whitey Woodin."

***

The Packers closed their season with a 13-6 victory over the Eagles in Philly, with Hinkle scoring 10 of the points. Calhoun wasn't overly impressed by the football, however.

"As a rule during the game the Packers were not blocking and this slip-up alone was the difference between a rout and a rather ip-and-tuck ball game."

He also wrote about the financial problem facing Eagles owner Bert Bell, who said the team had lost $44,000 over the past three season, a situation that wasn't helped by the crowd of less than 3,000 that paid an average of 89 cents to watch the Packer game.

"Judging from the conversations it seems doubtful if they'll attempt to carry on for another year," Calhoun wrote.

They carried on. Are carrying on.

***

December 8, 1935
"The Packers end their 1935 season, which almost produced a championship, by taking a 13-6 decision at Philadelphia. Schwammel kicked a field goal. Clarke Hinkle got the rest of the points. Spent the entire evening down at the office. Calhoun's stuff in better shape than usual."

December 9, 1935
"Roosevelt made another speech, Mussolini is planning a new war, and the Supreme Court declared something unconstitutional. The paper is coining money and the staff is getting restless, sensing the possibility of some raises."

December 14, 1935

"Most of the Packers have left for their homes, but they'll reassemble on the coast in January for a series of exhibition games."

***

December 20, 1935, column

That old gag about youth and age crops up again, in a somewhat cock-eyed fashion, on the professional all-America football team announced today.

Not that Mike Michalske is so very old. He won't be able to apply for an old age pension for several seasons, and you never see him hobbling around or pushing wheel chairs. In fact, if you drop in for a Municipal basketball league program, you see Mike skipping around the floor in the capacity of referee and he appears downright active.

John Walter

He appeared active during the 1935 football season too – so active that coaches, sports writers and league officials placed him on their first all-America team. It was Mike's tenth season of professional football.

George Henry Sauer has just finished his first season in the pro pastime, and he too wound up as an all-American. It's a tab which has been hung on George before, but he never had to work harder for it than during his first season as a Packer.

Sauer came to Green Bay with a tremendous reputation behind him, facing the hope of every Packer football fan that he wouldn't be a bust – that he'd be the fair-haired boy who would lead Green Bay out of the gridiron swamp. Of course, that was a huge assignment, and George had help from a lot of other people – but there's no arguing that he delivered.

It would be unintelligent to attempt to finish this column by commenting upon which of these men did the team the more good. You can't exactly figure out which is the greatest honor – to make the professional all-America team the first year out of college, or to make it ten tough years in the National league.

The combination of veteran material and husky young players on the Packer football squad this season came within a whisker of winning a National championship. The same combination, sprinkled liberally through the squad's personnel, should cause a lot of trouble next fall.

***

A *Press-Gazette* survey late in the year indicated that the first nine months of 1935 showed a 20 percent increase in business volume over the same period of 1934. The survey covered forty firms representing manufacturing, wholesaling, jobbing, and retailing.

Reporter Glenn Toule wrote: "So far as Green Bay is concerned, the bottom of the business decline was reached months ago, and the trend is now decidedly upward."

After three disappointing seasons and the near miss of 1935, the Packers were set to find out if the resurgence was temporary or would lead to greater heights in 1936.

The newspaper's editorial writer might not have had football in mind when he wrote this on the last day of the year:

"So the year is dying and with it should expire despair, dejection, pessimism and dashed hopes. And the New Year is born and with it is ushered in trust, buoyancy, optimism, strength and reliance."

Chapter 14

My Idea of Heaven

Six weeks into the new year of 1936, Dad had a chance meeting with Cal Hubbard on a Green Bay street. No doubt, they discussed both football and baseball, but the cold and snow also had to be a topic.

The day before, Hubbard and Packers teammate Milt Gantenbein, having just returned from the team's barnstorming tour on the West Coast, were driving to Green Bay through a blizzard. Their car left the highway south of De Pere and went into a huge snowdrift. The two big men were unable to dislodge it.

So, with no recourse and minus the technology of later generations, they left the car running and the heater functioning, and slept the night in the car, in the snowdrift.

"We didn't sleep well," Hubbard told Dad. But, when morning and some visibility arrived, they tramped to a farmhouse and called a wrecker.

Warmer climes awaited Hubbard.

***

February 7, 1935, column

It was refreshing yesterday to meet Cal Hubbard on the street and to find that Cal likes the climate. He's in a great position to squawk too, having returned from California and the Packer barnstorming trip. Cal was wearing a hunter's cap, flannel shirt and a lot of accessories that really made him look big. As Cal can look large without any assistance at all, the effect was colossal, stupendous and gigantic.

"I like this place," says Cal, who is going to stay here for the winter. That was all the more remarkable because Cal doesn't have to stay here if he doesn't want to. He's just marking time until the American Baseball League season opens, and then he'll join the league's staff as its newest umpire.

***

Hubbard would complete the first year of his hall of fame umpiring career, then play some football with the New York Giants and Pittsburgh Pirates in the fall before choosing baseball, and warmer weather, as his lifetime partners.

Prior to all that, as the year dawned and the Packers went west, Dad went east to visit a college friend in New York.

***

January 1, 1936

"As the year starts, I am in Niagara Falls, N.Y. Slept until noon, something I probably won't do again this year. Visited the Falls again – ice covered and beautiful. Left late in the afternoon."

***

As the year began, the *Press-Gazette* took stock in an editorial:

> "Uncertainties exist with respect to the constitutionality of the New Deal program which, however, will undoubtedly be cleared up before the year is far advanced.
>
> "On a whole, however, the new year finds us well along the hard road to economic recovery and there is evidence to warrant the belief that natural forces needed for a continuation of this forward movement are operating in many directions."

After more than half a decade of business depression, there was evidence of hope. The year wasn't very old when the national research company Brooke, Smith and French released data showing that Green Bay was one of thirty-six cities in the country within 10 percent of complete business recovery. It showed that while the city was 15 percent below normal in 1935, it was just 4 percent below in early 1936.

Football played on as the Packers' California tour was primarily an effort to expand the team's and city's gridiron reputation and make some money. The schedule was a work in progress, and an initial game supposedly promised by promoters in Los Angeles never happened.

Instead, the Packers went first to San Diego to face a team financed by movie actor Victor McLaglen. It was a 61-7 rout, the same day the champion Lions played an L.A.-area team called the Westwood Cubs and beat them 67-14.

***

January 12, 1936
"Heard Ralph Metcalfe, Olympic athlete, speak at Annunciation church breakfast. Packers, in California, wallop the San Diego Lighthorse team, 61-7. Sauer and Hutson each got two touchdowns."

***

Moving on to San Francisco, the Packers faced an all-star team coached by Chicago Cardinals coach Milan Creighton, and won 24-14. Hutson, Bruder, and Sauer scored the touchdowns.

But the game left a bad taste for the Packers, who thought their share of the gate receipts was much less than it should have been considering the size of the crowd.

They probably weren't very pleased either after losing 10-3 to the Lions in an exhibition game in Los Angeles several days later. Columnist John Boles of the *Los Angelos Evening Herald* wrote that Herber and Hutson "were both flopperoos. Hutson couldn't catch anything and furthermore seemed the most inexperienced man on the field."

As it was, the Packers grossed $11,200 in the three games, with Lambeau saying the experience would pay dividends in the 1936 season.

Speaking of money, it appeared that some finally would be provided for World War veterans when the House of Representatives passed the veterans bonus bill. Veterans lined up in Green Bay to apply for the bonus. One was Joseph Fonferek of the town of Preble, who had already borrowed half of his $776.50 share. Fonferek said he planned to use his windfall to purchase a farm or resort land near Eagle River. Unfortunately, the Senate rejected the bill by a wide margin, and President Hoover eventually called in the army to evict protesters from Washington, D.C., camps.

Other important things were happening in the world. King George V of England died less than a month into the year, to be succeeded – temporarily – by his son, the Duke of Windsor.

The Lindbergh baby kidnapping/murder case was retaining its front-page treatment as Bruno Hauptmann was being convicted and sentenced to die on the electric chair despite the protests of many, including the governor of New Jersey, who believed that the evidence against him was circumstantial. The debate continued long after Hauptmann's April execution.

***

January 13, 1936
"Bruno Hauptmann, convicted kidnapper of the Lindberg baby, is sentenced to die."

January 20, 1936
"George V, king of England and British Empire, dies in London. He was a grand old man and his death is a great loss to the empire."

***

Dad's daily columns often dealt with area high school teams, but he kept a steady diet of the Packers and football-related information in front of readers. And, if Packers news lagged, there was always George Halas to troll. He didn't know that Wayland Becker was soon to become a Packer when he visited with him in mid-January, then devoted his daily column to the encounter.

January 26, 1936, column

Wayland Becker, former East high and Marquette university end and now with the Brooklyn Dodgers, dropped by the scorer's table at the Muny basketball league program the other night. Talked over the pro grid situation. Lots of interest in the East, says Wayland. Dodgers and Giants drew 35,000 for their first game. Wayland looks a million. Yes, he's single. No strings, no objections, no ties on his affections. Enjoyed playing in the East. But though he wouldn't put it in writing, you can bet he'd look good in a Packer uniform. Not that Brooklyn would give him his release.

John Walter

January 27, 1936, column

Maybe it's of no importance to this section of Wisconsin, but sports followers who derived pleasure last fall from watching George Halas watch Arnie Herber watch Don Hutson score touchdowns may be interested to hear that Halas is planning to rehabilitate professional basketball in the Middle West.

George didn't say whether he was in the game for the love of it, or whether he intended the activity as a moneymaking effort, but he will attempt to organize a western division of the American Basketball league. Halas championed a professional basketball team until 1932, when it collapsed because the club owners could not meet exorbitant salary demands of the players.

February 6, 1936, column

Almost every time they play, and without question every time they win, the Green Bay Packers acquire new fans who are prepared to go to bat for them in any argument, big or small.

The latest convert is Dutch Reuther, who skippers the Seattle entry in the Pacific Coast Baseball League, and who happened to be among those present when the Packers played the Coast All Stars at San Francisco.

In a Seattle newspaper interview, Reuther says:

"Those professionals certainly know their football. Why, it was nothing to see them heave a forward pass that developed a pair of laterals, and once there were four laterals following a forward pass. Believe me, those boys chuck the ball around. They really put on a football show. And are they big? When the Packers came out on the field it looked like eleven box cars had been shunted onto a siding. I don't see how professional football can miss because, to my mind, they play a most sensational brand of football that is bound to catch the public fancy."

***

Hubbard wasn't the only veteran Packer to leave the team. Michalske became line coach at Lafayette College in Pennsylvania, working for his friend and former rival, Ernie Nevers, who was head coach. Michalske doubled as the college's basketball coach as well.

Hutson wasn't leaving the Packers, but tried out and won a summer spot as an outfielder on the Knoxville baseball team in the Southern Association.

Gantenbein, Weert Engelman, Al Rose, and Clarke Hinkle spent part of the football offseason working for Douglas Aircraft in Santa Monica, California.

Nate Barrager, who would continue his football career in the East, appeared in Charlie Chaplin's classic *Modern Times* movie. Barrager's one scene shows him grabbing a roast duck from Chaplin's hands ... and fumbling it.

Lee Joannes and Curly Lambeau attended the owners meeting in Pittsburgh, where most of the 1936 regular season schedule was formed. But the biggest development there was the creation of a college draft system. Each team was to submit a list of eight players from the college ranks, then the last place team would get the first pick. That choice allowed the team to be the first to negotiate with the player.

When draft time came, the Packers landed San Francisco guard Russ Letlow and Nebraska end Bernie Scherer.

Green Bay suffered through a bitterly cold February, and Dad ended up in St. Mary's Hospital for more than a week with pneumonia.

***

February 19, 1936
"Weather continues cold and everyone tells me I am lucky to be in the hospital. In evening, Johnny Blood, Packers halfback, was a caller. He stayed quite awhile, talking over the football situation."

***

The automobile dealers in Green Bay were becoming aware of the previously ignored market for used cars and staged a city-wide sale of used vehicles on one Saturday in early February.

Ominous signs continued to fly across the Atlantic Ocean. A civil war was threatening the government of Spain, and nothing positive or peaceful was coming out of Germany. James G. McDonald, former League of Nations high commissioner, urged action against the Nazis' persecution of Jews.

The response from Hitler's minister of propaganda, Joseph Goebbels, was chilling:

"German opinion is that the league has every cause to concern itself with how minorities and confessions are treated within league states before it can claim the right to occupy itself with how Germany, from the material and moral experience of her collapse, is rebuilding herself."

In early March, tensions increased when Hitler denounced the 1925 Locarno Treaty that forbid Germany to remilitarize the Rhineland bordering France. Some feared the move might threaten the Summer Olympics that were set to begin near Berlin, but tempers softened and the Games survived.

That was good news to Green Bay's Eleanore Dilweg, wife of former Packer Lavvie Dilweg and a member of the 1924 U.S. Olympic swim team. The American Olympic League appointed her to be the local fundraiser for the Olympics.

As spring arrived, there was a lot of attention paid to Ohio State sprinter Jesse Owens, regarded as the fastest man in the United States. In a track meet in Madison in May, Owens ran the 100-yard dash in 9.3 seconds, which would have been a world record except it was deemed he was aided by the wind. Nevertheless, he also won the 220-yard dash, the 220-yard hurdles, and the broad jump, and was gearing up for the Olympics.

It was a presidential election year, with Roosevelt's re-nomination at the Democratic National Convention a sure thing. After some primary elections, the Republican frontrunner became Kansas Gov. Alf Landon, who would try to unseat FDR in November.

Landon's vice-presidential running mate was Frank Knox, publisher of the *Chicago Daily News* who nearly forty years earlier had served with Teddy Roosevelt's Rough Riders in the Spanish-American War.

Alexander Wiley of Eau Claire, a Republican running (unsuccessfully) for Wisconsin governor, put his chips in the anti-Roosevelt game, declaring that the New Deal failed and "recovery is waiting if a new helmsman is put in control."

Two new names appeared to *Press-Gazette* readers in April. One was Joe DiMaggio, an outfielder who made his debut with the New York Yankees. The other was Dominic Olejniczak, who won a seat on the Green Bay City Council representing the Fifth Ward. He would later become mayor, then president of the Packers Corporation, a position he held when the team hired Vince Lombardi in 1959.

The city council was running into flak from downtown merchants who opposed a proposal to have parking meters installed in the heaviest business districts, particularly on Washington Street. More than 90 percent of the business owners signed a petition urging the city to hold off until it could be determined if the meter installation operation succeeded in Appleton.

Green Bay Police Capt. H.J. (Tubby) Bero held a meeting with all city policemen in the council chambers and set some rules. Police officers were to be courteous at all times, even at an arrest. They had to offer payment for anything, such as coffee, offered to them by merchants. There could be no smoking on the street when in uniform. Uniforms had to be buttoned, cleaned and pressed at all times. Officers must be clean-shaven, with shoes shined.

Meanwhile, James M. Skinner, chairman of the Radio Manufacturers Association, told a subcommittee of the Federal Communications Commission that commercial development of television was still about ten years away. He did predict, however, that TVs "will likely cost less than the average car."

There were also unimportant news events of note. One occurred in late February when Walter "Big Train" Johnson, the Washington Senators' great pitcher, threw a silver dollar across the Rappahannock River near Fredericksburg, Virginia, at the same spot where George Washington supposedly did it when he was a boy. Problem was, young Washington likely didn't have a silver dollar as a youth, and if he did, certainly wouldn't have thrown it away. Besides, the myth later changed to say he threw it across the Potomac River, which is impossible.

The Packers had a different type of off-season because it was the first year of the college player draft. With the second-best league record in 1935, the Packers were second last to draft. They came up with nine players and began the process of seeing who they could sign. It was an interesting group:

Russ Letlow, San Francisco guard – Played seven seasons for the Packers, was named to the league's All-1930s Decade Team, and inducted into the Packers Hall of Fame.

J.W. (Dub) Wheeler, Oklahoma tackle – Became the first Sooner ever drafted, but never played pro ball.

Darrell Lester, Texas Christian center – Played two seasons with the Packers, 1937-1938, before being injured.

Bernie Scherer, Iowa end – Played three seasons with Packers.

Theron Ward, Idaho halfback – Signed with the Packers, but decided to attend law school instead and became a long-time district judge.

Bob Reynolds, Stanford tackle – Played two seasons with Lions, later became founder and co-owner of the California Angels baseball team.

Wally Fromhart, Notre Dame quarterback – Decided to stay in school to get a teaching degree.

Wally Cruice, Northwestern halfback – Milwaukee native who played high school football for future Packers coach Lisle Blackbourne. He worked for an oil company before becoming a scout for the Packers from 1945-1957.

Jesse Wetsel, SMU guard – Never played pro football because of a knee injury.

***

March 5, 1936, column

What Green Bay Packer end is looking forward to coming back to Wisconsin and handling punts for the 1936? No need to guess. It's Don Hutson, who now is attending spring practice at the University of Alabama. Hutson reports no trouble with his temperamental appendix.

And George Henry Sauer will start work in a Green Bay sporting goods house.

March 16, 1936, column

Nothing like being seasonal, so here are a few notes on professional football.

Tar Schwammel, Packer tackle, wrote in from the Pacific coast recently to headquarters, reporting on a couple of his former Oregon State buddies. Coach E.L. Lambeau had Tar look the fellows over and Schwammel's report was OK.

John Walter

In the same vein, Lonnie Evans writes up from Texas. He is working on Donnie Lester, Texas Christian's all-America 238-pound center who is on the Packer preferred list, but reports nothing definite yet. Incidentally, the news that Lester is headed for the Packers has thrown a scare in Frank Butler, veteran center. Butler is doing engineering work in Chicago, his hometown.

Don Hutson, Packer high scoring end, now is the property of the Knoxville Baseball Club of the Southern association.

April 1, 1936, column

Imagine a stirring, all-important football game between the Green Bay Packers and, say, the Chicago Bears. The Packers are leading by four or five points going into the last period, and the Bears are gaining ground.

Finally, Bernie Masterson fades back and aims a long, well-directed forward pass at Gene Ronzani, who is springing through the flat zone. Ronzani spears the ball, eludes a Packer defense man, and crosses the goal line.

Thousands of Packer fans, at the stadium and by the radio, slump back with grunts of disgust.

"Well, the boys probably were all drunk last night," is the smartest thing a few of the boys, who were rooting vociferously for the Packers a few moments before, can think of to say.

Maybe these few people don't realize how stupid they sound. They just know that the Packers, along with any collection of professional football players, are a bunch of big, husky men who block hard, tackle hard, play hard and get thirsty, the assumption being that the team has no regard for personal reputation, the name of the club, or the game itself.

What causes all this is the fact that among the contracts now being mailed out are a half dozen or so which contain special clauses relating to the problem of drinking, which proves that the men in charge are in full control of disciplinary matters.

These players, who may have caused the club a little alcohol trouble in the past, must abstain from such beverages throughout the entire season. They will receive their living expenses during the playing period, perhaps $25 a week, and the balance will be held by the club until the end of the season. If they violate the clause, they will forfeit the full amount.

"It's better for us, and it's better for them," said one man connected with the club.

April 10, 1936, column

Milt Gantenbein and Clarke Hinkle, two Green Bay Packers who followed the gold rush to the Pacific coast this winter, and were rumored to be through with National league football, are on their way back to Green Bay. The boys didn't mention it but the hint is that the Santa Monica setup was not all that it might have been. It would be a comedown for ace players like Gantenbein and Hinkle to settle down to a season with the Santa Monica Fliers.

April 14, 1936, column

Few people possess the outstanding athletic record of August (Mike) Michalske, Packer guard of the century, who now is assistant coach at Lafayette college, Easton, Pa. While an undergraduate at Penn State college he was a member of the varsity football and track teams for three years, also participating in freshman football, baseball, track, boxing and wrestling. He graduated from Penn State in 1926. While attending West High School in Cleveland, where he prepared for college, he participated in football, basketball, baseball and track. Mike was born in Cleveland. He is now assisting Ernie Nevers at Lafayette.

April 28, 1936, column

The Packers are considering building a field house under the City Stadium stands for next fall. Heretofore, the squad has dressed at the Columbus Club, three flights up. The new building would give the chance to tote its own equipment, such as bucking machine, blocking and tackling paraphernalia. There also would be a drying room. Sometimes the men have practiced in the rain and then had to wear wet suits the following day.

***

Whatever was taking place between Dad and Calhoun never came to light in the diaries, but it likely involved a combination of their strong-willed personalities and a clear tug-of-war for control of Packer publicity.

And money woes remained a daily stressor for Dad.

***

April 27, 1936
"No change in the strange mixup at the office. Everything will explode one of these days. Not speaking to Calhoun at all."

April 28, 1936
"Borrowed $100 from the bank and distributed it judicially among my numerous creditors. It didn't go very far but it should give me temporary relief."

May 19, 1936
"My creditors are beginning to rally around again, and this time I'll be unable to borrow enough to stave them off. Looks like a lean summer."

***

May 19, 1936, column

Harry Stuhldreher, University of Wisconsin athletic director, took time between courses at the East High victory banquet at the Beaumont to name the greatest fullbacks he has seen in action. Elmer Layden and Chet Wynne at Notre Dame, Doug Wycoff of Georgia Tech, and Clarke Hinkle of Bucknell, now with the Packers.

Key moments in time

The spring and summer of 1936 included two very pivotal moments in Dad's future. One involved a young Chicago woman he had been dating for a year.

April 3, 1936
"Knocked off work in the afternoon and spent it with Anita. We had a serious talk in Kaap's ... she wants to be married and I'm almost sure we would not make a success of it. She cried a little ... better to hurt her feelings a little now than to have two broken hearts later on."

The other involved a casual introduction.

June 15, 1936
"In the afternoon took run up the bay with Torinus in the Minahans' new cabin cruiser, a 31-foot Chris Craft. Beautiful boat. Vic and young Mary Minahan went along ... she's a cute little redhead, about 16 years old."

The cute little redhead was actually seventeen. Three years, two months and four days later, she married Dad.

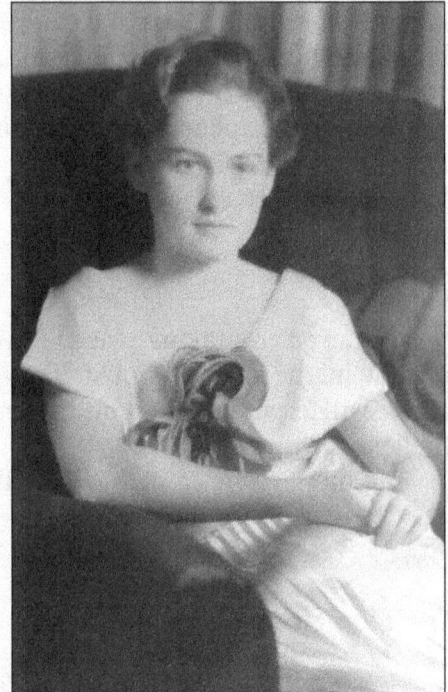

My mother, Mary Minahan, about the time she met my father in 1936. (Walter family collection

"That Hinkle is all football player," he said. "One of the saddest tasks we had at Villanova was stopping him."

***

June 3, 1936
"The Supreme Court, in a momentous series of decisions, is nullifying most of the New Deal."

June 6, 1936
"Went to show with Bid, an all English cast in H.G Wells' 'Things to Come,' a speculative bit on life in 2036. I won't have to worry about that."

June 7, 1936
"Proceeded to Little Sister Resort for a wonderful night's sleep. No noise but the waves and whipperwills. My love for that county will keep me always in Wisconsin."

June 8, 1936
"The Republican national convention opens in Cleveland tomorrow. The nominee will be Gov. Alf Landon of Kansas but he hasn't a ghost of a chance of being elected."

June 9, 1936
"With Mother attended picture show. Irene Dunne, Charles Winninger, and Helen Morgan in 'Show Boat.' Paul Robeson's singing 'Old Man River' worth the price of admission."

June 10, 1936
"The GOP meeting in Cleveland picked Alf Landon and Frank Knox as nominees. Ex-President Herbert Hoover was a flop with his convention address. He had a chance to save the party but muffed it."

***

The Kansas City Monarchs of the Negro Baseball League came to Green Bay in June for a game against the local team, the Green Sox. The Monarchs' best player was Bullet Rogan, who Yankees manager John McGraw said would be worth $100,000 to any Major League team "if he was white."

More than 1,200 people showed up for the game at the Joannes Park stadium and the Monarchs dominated, 12-0.

***

June 11, 1936
"Covered exhibition baseball game, Kansas City Monarchs, a colored team, walloped the Green Sox 12-0, putting up a great show. The negroes really were clever."

June 27, 1936
"Wisconsin is my idea of heaven."

***

The H.C. Prange store revealed its list of top-selling books for the summer. By far, the most popular book was Margaret Mitchell's *Gone With the Wind*. The others on its list were *Eyeglass in Gaza*, by Aldous Huxley, *San Felice*, by Vincent Sheehan, and *Beyond Sing the Woods*, by Trygeve Gullbransen.

If there was an official unofficial beginning to the Packers' 1936 season, it was probably the annual stockholders meeting in mid-July. It was there that Lee Joannes was re-elected president of the corporation and ticket prices were set.

Box seats for the season cost $12 (that's total, not per game), while other locations ranged from $9 down to $4.50, for the whole package. The ticket office was set up on the fourth floor of the Northern Building on Walnut Street.

The Packers also announced that work had begun on construction of a locker room beneath the south stands at City Stadium, which would eliminate the need to bus the team back and forth from the Columbus Club for practices and games.

Lambeau gave his annual forecast of the team's chances.

"If our new men come through, and our veterans profit by their added experience, we will have another strong football team, one capable of accomplishing things in the National professional league," he said.

***

July 17, 1936, column

Coach Curly Lambeau expressed no secret when he remarked that the performances of the Packer tackles this fall may mark the difference between a winning and losing ball club. His ends are strong, his guards and centers apparently adequate, his backs among the best in the league.

No team, no matter how well balanced, can lose three such veteran performers as Mike Michalske, Cal Hubbard and Nate Barragar without being affected thereby. These men were good.

Curly likes his tackle prospects but he'll find out more about them in the days following August 17.

***

A sporting event involving horses wasn't on Dad's lifetime bucket list, but he learned the polo jargon and offered a knowledgeable first sentence after covering the Green Bay-De Pere team's match at Lenfesty Field, later the site of Minahan Stadium in De Pere.

"Lashing back with a furious sixth chukker attack that fell two goals short....," he wrote.

With August came the Berlin Olympics and Jesse Owens' domination in track and field. On three successive days, he won gold in the 100 meters, broad jump, and 200 meters, and led off the winning 4 x 100 relay team. Ralph Metcalfe, another African-American athlete, took second in the 100 and history recorded that Hitler chose not to watch the medal ceremonies.

But this was August and this was Green Bay. Football warm-up time. The series of player contract signings filled most off the month, and the team assembled in mid-August to begin practice. A few players

Compliments from a future relative

Dad went on vacation in July, and his future brother-in-law, John Torinus, handled the daily sports column in his absence.

July 24, 1936, column
(By John Torinus)

We're going to cater to a fancy we've had all week, and tell you some bits about the scribe who usually types this column.

John Walter is probably more keenly interested in all Green Bay sports than any other fan in town. He believes that Green Bay has the potentialities of becoming one of the great American sports centers, and he will do anything he can through his position as *Press-Gazette* sports editor to encourage that.

He follows the Packers with heart-pound and heart break. He can see no earthly excuse for the existence of horses, but he's gone to almost every polo game ever put on here. He thinks the Green Bay high schools have on the average some of the strongest football and basketball teams in the state. He probably sees about 50 baseball games each summer. He's one of the greatest lovers and haters of golf there is around here. He only has one prejudice against local sporting men. He foments inside every time one of them calls him Jack Walters. His right name is John Walter.

were missing. Ade Schwammel was ill, but would report shortly, Bernie Scherer was at army camp, and Don Hutson was finishing his minor league baseball season.

***

August 4, 1936
"Announced the signing of Clarke Hinkle by the Packers tonight. It's his fifth season with the team and should be a good one."

August 6, 1936
"Some 35,000 Spaniards have died in the bloodiest civil war in Spain's history. British, German and French ships are standing by, and a general European war is far from an impossibility."

***

There was some drama. Lineman Lou Gordon, who joined the Packers after being dropped by the Cardinals after the 1935 season, was holding a grudge against Cardinals coach Milan Creighton.

Chicago Daily Times columnist Marvin McCarthy described it as a "small hate" between the men after talking to both and writing about it.

"Gordon, the captain scorned, lisps in the customary, soft-spoken Gordon way, which means he can't be heard any farther away than four blocks," McCarthy wrote, then recorded Gordon's comments.

"I may not play many football games for Green Bay," Gordon said, "but there's one I will play. Yeah, I mean that first game of the season we play against the Cardinals. Old Gordon will play tackle in that game like he hasn't played in years. And I'm daring a certain guy to play against me."

Creighton responded. "After he gets through playing the Cardinals, he won't be able to play anymore. Not this season, anyway."

***

August 5, 1936, column

The rumblings of a giant gridiron machine which will receive its orders for "full steam ahead" on Sunday, September 13 are beginning to increase in volume. That little matter of unfinished business with the Chicago Cardinals, which occupied the time of the Green Bay Packers none too successfully during the 1935 season, will come up for further action September 13.

The Packers will do all their training in Green Bay. The preseason schedule has not been formulated but it probably will consist of an intra-squad contest and one game out-of-town during the latter part of this month, and a night game with a strong non-league opponent at City stadium September 5.

***

August 11, 1936
"Tar Schwammel has signed again with the Packers and has started east from his home in California. Will be glad to see him again."

August 14, 1936
"In evening attended first ticket sales meeting of the Packers. Offered to help out by selling ads, but hope they don't call on me."

***

Meanwhile, the new locker room beneath the southern bleachers was nearing completion under supervision of the J.C. Basten company.

Dad wrote, "It is just another step toward giving Green Bay and the Packers one of the most complete football parks in the National league."

***

August 15, 1936, column

It is no exaggeration to say that interest in the Packer squad this fall is running higher than at any time since the championship era. I believe one reason for this is the great growth in interest in the professional all-star game at Chicago. Packer fans realize that their team, given the breaks, has an excellent chance to appear in one of these games at Soldier Field, and what a break for Green Bay that would be.

This may be the year.

***

August 16, 1936
"Golf with Bid in the morning. Shot 47-48 —95, the best 18-hole score I ever got. Only my approaches were bad. Handicapped by the absence of my #6 iron, which I broke in a fit of anger at Shorewood the other day."

August 17, 1936
"The Green Bay Packers officially opened their practice season. Covered the entire session. Squad looks faster than last year."

August 18, 1936, column

How do the Packers look? It's the annual big question in Green Bay's sporting life, asked with a new emphasis this season as fans of the Big Bay gridiron machine look to the approaching schedule with the hope born of a community which has a big, powerful football team at its disposal.

No one, naturally, is so unintelligent as to predict a 7 to 0 victory over the Bears, a 13 to 6 licking against the Cardinals and other gridiron pleasantries, when the squad has been practicing just one day.

But the boys look good. They appear to be better conditioned than the average team at the start of the practice period, and there is no arguing that they are in great mental spirits for the serious work ahead. Probably the man who attracted the most attention at yesterday's practice was Lou Gordon, the giant tackle acquired from the Chicago Cardinals. There's something mighty interesting about an enemy who suddenly becomes a friend. One of the Packers remarked that if Gordon causes the Cardinals half the grief he handed the Packers last year, he'll be a worthwhile investment.

John Walter

August 20, 1936, column

The 1936 squad of the Green Bay Packers, Coach Curly Lambeau believes, is the fastest the Packers ever have had. There doesn't appear to be a slow back on the team, and the linemen have plenty ability to pick 'em up and subsequently to lay 'em down. The season title of being the fastest man on the squad won't go to Don Hutson this season without a struggle. For one thing, Red Oliver may take it away from him. If he doesn't, Paul Miller probably will. Cal Clemens is another newcomer with a world of speed, and the windsprints this season really present some hot talent.

August 24, 1936, column

Fans who specialize in attending Packer practice sessions say that yesterday's crowd at Joannes park was the largest ever to see the squad drill. People were coming and going all afternoon. The most conservative estimate of the attendance was 1,500, and it ran all the way up to 4,000. Fans will get an even better show at City stadium Wednesday when the intra-squad practice game is held.

August 29, 1936, column

When the Packers trot off the field at City stadium tomorrow, their first competitive effort of the season completed, they'll be making the shortest trot in the history of the football corporation.

They'll just run around the corner and duck under the showers. In past seasons, the players climbed into a waiting bus, which fought traffic all the way downtown to the training quarters, leaving the men sitting in their soggy suits, with nothing to do except talk about the ball game.

The new Packer field house probably fulfilled as distinct a need as the club possessed. The entire setup adds a touch of class to the Packer team. It's big league stuff, and is a great break for the club.

August 31, 1936, column

Although Coach E.L. Lambeau saw plenty of rough and ragged spots in the performances of his two intra-squad teams at City stadium yesterday afternoon, he didn't attempt to conceal his pleasure at what he believes is a very satisfactory progress by the Green Bay Packers of 1936.

"One thing you may quote me definitely as saying," he remarked, "and that is that Sunday's game was very much worthwhile and that it probably should be retained as an annual part of the Packers training program."

***

September 2, 1936
"I seem to be in bad with Lee Joannes, the Packer president, and I don't know why."

***

September 3, 1936, column

This steady chatter about the Chicago All Star football game being a true test of the collegiate and professional sport is beginning to get a bit childish.

If sports writers regard a tie game as a victory for the All Stars, that fact is a pretty sure indication that they concede some superiority to professional football, but no matter. The principal points are these.

1. The All-Star game is no test of college and professional football. No college team in the country ever contained such an array of talent as the crew Bernie Bierman handled at Chicago last night. The All Stars are a young professional team, assembled from a dozen or more colleges.

2. One touchdown play in three years, scored against the slowest starting professional team in the National league, hardly qualifies as the clincher in the years-old argument.

John Walter

In three years, the old professionals have won once and the young professionals have been tied twice. Does this settle the argument? I still would like to see the Minnesota varsity or the Notre Dame first string play the Chicago Bears or the Chicago Cardinals or the Green Bay Packers in mid-season.

***

September 4, 1936
"Mother and I had George Sauer and Milt Gantenbein of the Packers up for supper ... a couple of nice fellows."

***

The Packers scheduled a practice game against a team from Madison, also called the Cardinals. One of the best players for Madison was former Badger lineman Jim Nellen who, among other things, had a future that would include being the Packers' team physician and president of the UW Board of Regents.

The game went as expected with the Packers winning 62-0, but it featured a dust-up between Nellen and Clarke Hinkle. After one play, the two were into an altercation on the ground.

"He clipped me for the third time," Hinkle said. "I warned him. I have to use these legs for a while."

Former Packer Verne Lewellen was the referee and he ordered both men off the field.

***

September 7, 1936
"In evening with Bid to see Warner Baxter and Fredric March in 'Road to Glory,' a World War picture, a good evening's entertainment although the realism of war scenes made me think uncomfortably of the uniform hanging in my closet at home."

September 10, 1936

"Attended annual banquet of Packer players and officials in evening at Beaumont Hotel, Russ Winnie, radio sports announcer, was speaker. Can this football team bring Green Bay another championship? A few weeks will tell the story."

***

The Beaumont banquet wasn't a public affair and included, in addition to the players and coaches, many of the local business leaders who had been responsible for helping to bail out the team from financial depths in recent years.

Russ Winnie, although preaching to the Packer choir, helped indoctrinate the new players to the Green Bay football world.

"The man who shines your shoes at the hotel asks your prediction on the game, and the girl at the cigar counter reminds you how fine the weather is," Winnie said. "When the Packers played the Bears in Chicago last season and won 17 to 14 with a rally in the last three minutes, thousands of fans left the park before the final minutes and didn't learn the real result until the next day. You won't see that in Green Bay.

"You new Packers will find that there is no city in the National Professional Football league which affords you the friendly cooperation and hospitality that you will find in Green Bay."

With the season set to begin, the Packers were about the play, for the first time since 1928, without all three players who made the triple titles of 1929, 1930 and 1931 possible: Michalske, Hubbard and Blood.

Michalske took a job at Lafayette College, serving as line coach for head coach Ernie Nevers. Hubbard was now an American League baseball umpire. Blood and the Packers didn't come to contract terms.

A new Packer era, in a sense. Time would tell if it would be a successful one.

Chapter 15

It'll Take a Better Team

It was time for the Packers to chase a championship.

***

September 11, 1936
"Torinus is all set for the biggest event of his life. I'm glad I'm not the one getting married. Will cover the home games of the Packers for the Associated Press again this year. Dropped into Northland in evening to visit with Chicago Cardinals, including Mike Michalske. Johnny Blood was there. He hasn't signed with the Packers yet and apparently isn't going to unless they raise the ante, which they'll probably have to."

(And they did.)

***

September 11, 1936, column

    The Gas House Gang of professional football – the Chicago Cardinals – filtered into the lobby of the Hotel Northland last night and entrenched for a stay that will last until Monday.
    Probably an uglier, tougher, and more belligerent appearing gang of football players never graced a hotel lobby. The only shirt and tie you could see were on Pug Vaughn, who was dressed quite respectably.

The rest of the men, except Coach Milan Creighton, wore time-honored slacks, polo shirts and crew-neck sweaters.

Most of the men needed shaves, and obviously intended to go on needing them. They glared around the place like a set of panthers turned loose in an arena and sniffed the air for Packers.

September 12, 1936, column

The much publicized irresistible force and immovable object are scheduled to stage a revival of their historic act at City stadium tomorrow afternoon, the occasion being the first 1936 clash of the Green Bay Packers and their jinx team, the Chicago Cardinals.

The Packers were beaten in their opening game last year by the Cardinals, 7 to 6, because a too-great percentage of the Green Bay regulars were nursing injuries on the bench.

John Walter

They lost again at Milwaukee, 3 to 0, by failing to take advantage of six or eight chances to kick field goals.

They were beaten at Milwaukee Thanksgiving Day, 9 to 7, when every break of the gridiron fates went against them.

That brought the Packer losing streak against the Cardinals to five straight, and it assured a near-capacity crowd for the stadium tomorrow afternoon. The betting odds are on Green Bay, 6 to 5.

I favor the Packers, and not by one of those borderline scores which gave everyone heart failure last season. Fourteen to nothing, on two touchdowns and two extra points.

***

The game didn't disappoint. Trailing 7-0 at halftime, the Packers got a third-quarter touchdown from Sauer, then a fourth-quarter field goal from Ernie Smith to pull out a 10-7 decision.

Dad's story struck the chord of intensity:

> "Rocketing back with a sledge-hammer finish after trailing by seven points at halftime, the Packers put their best foot forward in the young National league race. The two halves of yesterday's bitter struggle were as different as Mae West and Shirley Temple."

The story pointed out that there was constant "wrangling and arguments" to remind everyone there wasn't a lot of love lost between the teams.

Of course, there was controversy. The Packers were upset when a fumbled lateral was picked up by the Cardinals and returned 59 yards, which Green Bay said was against the rules. And the Cardinals screamed when Verne Lewellen, serving as field judge in a game involving his former team, called a pass interference penalty against the Cardinals' Howard Tipton that gave the Packers a first down on the Chicago 2-yard line, setting up Sauer's game-tying touchdown.

The *Chicago Tribune's* George Strickler referred to the interference penalty, writing that "the ruling was one of the few official decisions with which nonpartisan observers could find no fault."

There was no record of any tussles between Gordon and Creighton. There was no record of them shaking hands, either. But Strickler described "a particularly rough contest with personal animosity provoking some play beyond the code and adding to the confusion that gripped contestants, officials and spectators alike."

The Cardinals' David Cook, a fullback, left the game in the first quarter with a dislocated shoulder, but was called upon in the final minute of the game to try an impossible field goal.

Cook "came on the field with his arm in a sling under his jersey and attempted to tie the score with a field goal from his own 45-yard-line, a distance of 55 yards," Strickler wrote. "It was a heroic but futile attempt as Cook kicked into a nest of charging Packer linemen."

***

September 13, 1936
"In afternoon covered opening game of National Football League. Packers rallied to defeat Chicago Cardinals 10-7 on George Sauer's touchdown, Ade Schwammel's extra point and a fourth period field goal by Ernie Smith. Crowd of 9,000. Bitterly fought game, many Cardinals injured. That starts the boys off on the right foot. Down to the office after, dead tired but happy. Then supper at Kaaps."

***

September 14, 1936, column

The keynote and theme song of yesterday's last ditch battle between the Chicago Cardinals and Green Bay Packers was Courage, and while all credit is given the great stand of the losers, it must be admitted that the Packers poured it on just a bit thicker. There was so much courage splashed around at City stadium that even the spectators felt tough, and several were escorted to the outside lanes for over-indulgence in grandstand arguments.

A Cardinal carved his initials deep over Lou Gordon's right eye, and the grand big tackle submitted to a band of tape around his head. Taking a rest during the mid-game section, Gordon was in at the finish, building up his own sweet revenge upon his former teammates and coach.

In their great campaign to overtake the Cardinals' 7 to 0 lead, the Packers hit harder than they have in many a game, and they served a ringing notice to the Chicago Bears and Detroit's Coach Potsy Clark that Happy Days are Here Again.

The victory was thinner than Ernie Smith's new mustache, but it was a great one for Green Bay just the same.

***

September 14, 1936
"Saw several Packers who are very proud of their victory over the Cardinals. So is everyone else."

September 15, 1936
"There is much trouble in Europe, most of it centering around the Spanish Civil War, in which Germany and Italy are taking a hand. Have crossed beer off my list as a daily diet. Am concentrating on malted milks to keep my weight down."

(I'm no authority on diets, but doubt that malted milks were ever a Weight Watchers staple.)

September 16, 1936
"The Packers are hard at work getting ready for next Sunday's game with the Chicago Bears here. No Packer season ever started more auspiciously but one defeat at this time would change all that. Financial situation has been much more secure since I got that last loan, manage to keep some money in my pockets now. If it only lasts."

***

Former Packer Lavvie Dilweg spoke to the Green Bay Lions Club the day after the game and praised the team.

"The thing that was most evident to me in Sunday's game is the brilliant fighting spirit which the Packers displayed, a great determination which may mean much in future games," Dilweg said.

He also commented on Lewellen's pass interference flag.

"It was unfortunate that Lew had to make that decision, but we all know that he calls 'em as he sees 'em," he said. "Furthermore, he was right on the spot where the play occurred and he was prepared to see exactly what happened."

Needless to say, the league discontinued the practice of former players officiating at games involving their former teams.

***

September 17, 1936, column

Marvin McCarthy of the *Chicago Daily Times*, who has been quoted before in this column, now comes up with a few facts which indicate that the Green Bay Packers are in for a sackful of grief next Sunday afternoon when they play the Chicago Bears at City stadium.

In his daily sports column, "Heat's On," McCarthy says:

John Walter

"Professional football coaches usually are about as emotional as the wooden Indian in front of a Philadelphia cigar store on Sunday afternoon. They don't storm, nor do they gush and exhort. Dressing room hysterics are unheard of and playing field dramatics are out. The pro football coach is employer and the player is employee.

"On that basis a calm and deliberate relationship is maintained, but the other day – Oh, how Coach George Halas of the Chicago Bears forgot himself. George's boys had just succeeded in making suckers out of themselves butter-fingering a ball game away to a group of college all-stars at Dallas, Texas, 7-6. They had done everything wrong, had permitted passes to be intercepted, dropped passes of their own and blundered around generally. It was the first time a big league pro team ever had been whipped by mere collegians and Mr. Halas steamed up until he nearly exploded.

"He clouded up to a real college mad and enough of the storm broke to remind the Bears of the dear old college days when they received nary a cent of football salary (well, let that pass) but plenty of postgame scorching for bonus."

September 19, 1936, column

Out of the muddle of football tradition, which emerged from the dim early days of the National Professional Football league, starting in 1921 and continuing without interruption since 1923, has developed the 34-game football series between the Bears of Chicago and the Packers of Green Bay.

It is betraying no confidence to repeat that these teams are going to play each other at City stadium tomorrow afternoon. Neither coach has made the slightest effort to keep the game a secret, and there will be no attempt to have the contest played in private.

In fact, there is every indication that the stadium fences will be bulging well before the first kickoff sails into the East River.

Each Packer game must have its prediction, and I was interested to notice the range of scores in the forecasts which were mailed to me as part of my own little pre-game guessing contest. Without a single exception, the fans predicted a Green Bay victory. But almost without exception, they decided that the Bears would score.

The Bears didn't score against the Packers up here last year, but they clicked twice against them in Chicago, even though Green Bay was victorious in both games. They have a ruinous ground attack, a pretty fair passing game and a kicking sniper in Automatic Jack Manders.

In the belief that the Bears running campaign will click at least part of the time against the Packers, and that Manders may get close enough for a successful kick, and that Green Bay's passing show will pave the way for two touchdowns, I like a score of 14 to 10 tomorrow afternoon.

***

Everyone in Green Bay would have loved a 14-10 score. But the Bears were far superior and trounced the Packers 30-3. In his game story, Dad wrote that the Packers "lacked fire and spirit. They missed blocks or didn't block at all."

If the 1935 game against the Bears in Green Bay was identified as the "Herber-to-Hutson" pass at the beginning, this one became identified as the Emmett Platten game.

Platten, a 42-year-old Green Bay native, was known as a Green Bay sports commentator because he purchased time regularly on a local radio station to talk about sports. His passion for the Packers was well-known.

But late in the game, when an apparent Packers touchdown was called back by referee Gunner Elliott, Platten ran onto the field to protest. Bears lineman Ted Rosequist confronted him, and Platten socked him in the jaw, cutting his lip.

Platten was escorted from the field before things got worse. But in the next day's sports section, Dad published a letter from Platten explaining why he went after Elliott.

After first writing that Elliott "has for some time been regarded by the Packers management as something of a Bear fan," Platten explained his motive.

"As a Packer stockholder looking out for the interests of the corporation, I tried to approach Mr. Elliott to remind him of his faithful promise to give unbiased decisions. One of them (Rosequist) rushed forward making a pass at me and about the only thing I could do was to tag him."

Packers president Lee Joannes said team owners had met with league president Joe Carr in July, and each team was told to submit a list of officials for approval. The final list approved by the owners and league didn't include Elliott.

What was George Halas's reaction to the Emmett episode?

"Can't you do something about him?" he said.

At the same time, Halas dismissed suggestions that the Bears were 27 points better than the Packers. "Don't think that we are that much better than the Packers," he said. "We aren't."

***

September 21, 1936, column

For five years I've been hoping that the Chicago Bears would grow too old to play good football. Yesterday, with the same old team and the same old plays, they gave the Green Bay Packers the worst licking they've had since 1925, when the Pottsville Maroons rode over them 31 to 0.

The answer to the drubbing is buried in some psychology book, and it takes someone a lot smarter than most of us to figure it out.

John Walter

There was a letdown somewhere between the Cardinal game of the previous Sunday and yesterday's kickoff, and just what caused the mental relapse is what Coach Curly Lambeau will give a tidy sum to find out. The Packers definitely were not on edge, and they ran into a Bears team that was red hot.

The game was remarkably similar to the 31 to 7 victory which the

Packers scored over the Detroit Lions here last season. The Lions, confident, came into town to run into an inspired Green Bay team. Every play the Packers attempted clicked with a touchdown flourish. They rode through the Detroit line and passed over it to pile up one score after another. They kicked every field goal and booted every extra point. Detroit, completely demoralized, was crushed.

Let the football historian remember that Detroit rose from that 31 to 7 licking to win the professional football championship of the world. Let the Green Bay fan remember that the Packers will come back too and be ready to pour back upon the Cardinals all they've been given by the Bears.

***

September 20, 1936
"In afternoon covered football game. The Chicago Bears poured football all over the Packers, winning 30-3. Our only points came on Schwammel's field goal. The boys lacked fight, and played very listlessly. All quite disappointing and a staggering blow to Green Bay's championship hopes."

September 21, 1936
"Everyone feeling very blue about that slaughter yesterday. The Packers can't be as bad as they looked so I'm assuming they had an off day. Furthermore, the Bears were red hot. Saw Art Bystrom at the game. He intimated I might be able to land a job with the Associated Press. Worth careful thought."

September 22, 1936
"Am going to have a talk with Joe Horner in regard to that AP job... maybe I can club a raise out of the Press-Gazette."

***

September 23, 1936, column

"I didn't get a chance!" is a wail professional football coaches hear now and then when it's found necessary to slice an occasional name off the payroll.

Players naturally are very interested in their own careers and they don't always agree with the judgment of the coach who decides that they need a little more outside work before breaking into the big time.

Sometimes new players, trying out for positions on the Green Bay Packers, get pretty disgruntled when exigencies off the roster make it necessary for them to leave.

Ralph Miller and Harry Mattos are two exceptions. Released by the Packers yesterday, they stopped into the office of Coach Curly Lambeau, announced their determination to work hard with whatever other club they land this year, and said they hoped they'd be back at Green Bay next season.

Curly hopes so, too.

***

September 24, 1936
"Still putting plenty of thought on that AP proposition. If the Press-Gazette can't give me a raise, I shall apply for that job. Still, it would be tragic living in Milwaukee. Except that the job would be an open door to New York."

(I never knew how close I came to growing up a Yankees and Giants fan. And, probably, with a different mother. I'd still be brooding about the Packers' slaughter of the Giants in the 1961 championship game.)

September 27, 1936
"No letter from Anita in nearly a week. Better so. The affair was dying on its feet anyway. Saw swell picture, Ginger Rogers and Fred Astaire in 'Swing Time.' Fine dancing and lots of humor. Ran into Ernie Smith after the show. The big fellow looked lonesome ...must invite him up for supper."

September 28, 1936
"Still up in the air about my future, whether to try for the Milwaukee AP job or not. It would be so hard to leave Green Bay. Talked it over with Bid (Gage) in afternoon. He says stay."

September 30, 1936
"In afternoon played game of badminton for first time with Ernie Smith. It's a new game which is being introduced from England and it appears to be great sport."

(Clearly, Dad liked to hang out with the Packers, building strong friendships with Ernie Smith, Bernie Scherer, Ade Schwammel, and Johnny Blood, particularly. Socializing with players or coaches was a practice I disdained when my job included overseeing the newspaper's coverage of the Packers. Not that players and coaches were craving my company, and I was never a Packers beat writer for the *Press-Gazette*, but the professional separation was my preferred system.)

October 1, 1936
"Carl Hubbell pitched the New York Giants to a 6-1 victory over the Yankees in yesterday's opening game of the World Series. The Spaniards are still kicking hell out of each other in their civil war. It looks like the rebels are winning."

***

There was much better news for the Packers three days after the Bears debacle. Blood agreed to contract terms and became part of the team again.

"Johnny has a perfect mental attitude," Lambeau said.

Blood watched the Packers' first two games, had rejected the Packers' first contract offer, then engaged in negotiations with Lambeau for three days before signing.

The Packers had two weeks before a return match against the Cardinals, this one to be played at State Fair Park in Milwaukee. The Cardinals were struggling and dropped a 39-0 decision to the Lions prior to facing the Packers.

***

October 3, 1936, column

Things would be much simpler along the Green Bay battlefront if someone just knew the correct score of tomorrow's game at Milwaukee. Then everyone attempting to predict the outcome could save the energy, and lots of us who planned to visit Milwaukee for the afternoon could spare the effort.

Because no one does know the correct score, hundreds and probably thousands of Northeastern Wisconsin residents will journey southward to fill State Fair Park stadium seats as supplements to whatever crowd Milwaukee scares up for the occasion.

Of one thing everyone is sure – the Green Bay Packers have to win this game, and several others right after it, if they are to be considered contenders for the remaining stretch of the National Professional Football league race.

Nearly everyone around here thinks the Packers will come through.

I glanced through the big collection of predictions mailed in for the "Looking Up" guessing contest and every sheet but one pointed to a Green Bay victory, most of them by substantial margins. One St. Norbert College student picked a 7-7 tie.

It doesn't look like a tie from this corner, but more like a 20-0 victory for Green Bay. This is safe for tonight's print because the Packers are all tucked away in Milwaukee and won't see this column until Monday, if ever. By that time I may be taking a ride for calling such a big score, but the reasons are these: the Cardinals' crippled condition (I hope), the Packers probable rejuvenation following their spanking by the Bears, and the depressing effect of that Detroit pasting upon the Cardinals.

John Walter

(The Packers won handily, 24-0, prompting Dad to write that they "dropped a football depth bomb" on the Cardinals.)

October 5, 1936, column

As if tossed by a catapult, the Green Bay Packers were hurled back into the thick of the National Professional Football league race at Milwaukee yesterday, and every one of the 11,000 fans there knew it.

The renovations on the State Fair park stadium have increased seating capacity, and the thousands upon thousands of spectators who packed the west side concrete stands made an impressive setting for the gridiron show.

The Packers showed almost no trace of the listless playing which marred their performance against the Chicago Bears, except for a few minutes in the first period, when the Cards started their early drive toward the Green Bay goal. For just a few plays, it looked as though the Packers might need some outside inspiration.

They got it, somewhere, and turned red hot for the duration of the game. The team showed complete confidence and mastery of the situation. The Cardinal jinx was routed, both teams knew it, and the Packers rubbed it in. They tackled with assurance, blocked with vicious vigor and weren't afraid to try anything.

All the way through they were looking at the future. Several times someone on the Packer bench said "Wish we were playing the Bears today" or "This is a taste of what the Bears will get."

Three tough teams stand between the Packers and their next game with the Bears – Boston, Detroit and Pittsburgh, in order. If Green Bay can accomplish the difficult and win these three games it will sail into the return meeting with the Bears in a great spot to cause everlasting trouble along the Western front.

***

October 4, 1936
"In afternoon, covered football game at State Fair Park. Packers walloped the Chicago Cardinals 24-0. Touchdowns scored by Johnston, Hinkle, Laws."

October 5, 1936
"Drove to Appleton. Jake Skall threw the Valley sports writers a big party at his Colonial Wonder Bar. All the scotch we could drink, plus wonderful steaks. Jake wants some ink on a special train he is running to the Packer-Bear game at Chicago Nov. 1. He'll get in on my sheet."

(I was never fed steaks in exchange for a restaurant promotion. Conflict of interest sirens are blaring, but the relationships between newspaper and community business was different then. They relied on each other.)

October 6, 1936
"Decided to face my job situation squarely and visited A.B. Turnbull, Press-Gazette business manager, at his home. Spilled my objections and asked for a raise. He indicated that I'll get it come first of the year. Left me undecided as to whether or not I'll apply for work outside Green Bay."

October 8, 1936
"Another talk with Mr. Turnbull and I think he definitely is on my side. How much of a raise I'll get is something else. I'm getting $160 a month now, and am sick of it. Still, two years ago I was getting $108. Ernie Smith, Packer tackle, up for dinner. He had to leave early for a squad meeting."

(Just over nine years later, as Dad was preparing to be discharged from the post-war army, Turnbull recruited him to plan and manage the new radio station (WJPG) owned by the Press-Gazette.)

October 9, 1936
"The Spanish Civil War is reaching its climax with the rebels marching on Madrid. And all of Europe is on the verge of another war, which must come soon."

***

The final month before the presidential election kept politics in the news daily. National columnist David Lawrence saw a trend that would have an impact for decades to come.

"I find that the Negroes, whose vote has always been taken for granted by the Republicans, have been assiduously cultivated by the New Deal for three years, that the Negro press is preponderantly pro-Roosevelt," he wrote. "In fact, the New Dealers have been very generous with 'relief' jobs. After the election, this will most certainly be trimmed down. The Negroes will then have to look to private employment."

***

October 10, 1936, column

A few things are more futile than an attempt to pick a score between two football teams which haven't met, which come from widely separated parts of the country, and which have no common opponents.

You might just as well select Community Center of Palo Alto, California, and St. Benedict's of Lawrence, Massachusetts, and decide which is the better football team.

John Walter

Maybe that's a strong comparison, because after all both the Packers and Boston Redskins are members of the National Football League, which means they are rough, hardy units, either capable of springing an upset on the other.

Since that game with the Bears it's been hard to attempt a Packer score. If the team is as red hot as it was at Milwaukee last Sunday, Boston is in for a cloudy afternoon. The Redskins, however, are aiming for a championship of their own, and they won't achieve it by dropping games to the Western clubs.

It's a stab in the dark but I like the Packers by 14 to 7. And here's one that will draw the boos, but the Cardinals look ripe for a vicious demonstration of what they really are, and I'll take them over the Bears by 10 to 0.

(Boston offered little opposition and the Packers won, 31-2, in a game Dad wrote that "there never was any question of the outcome.")

October 12, 1936, column

With Herber and Berber, Musick and Busich, Millner and Miller, and three varieties of Smiths – Ernie, Riley and Ed – wandering about the place, yesterday's Packer-Boston game turned out to be something of a headache for the boys with the typewriters.

If this Boston team is the favorite to win the Eastern division, then may the gods of the gridiron have mercy on the clubs in that division when they face the Packers, Bears, Cardinals and Lions.

The licking reemphasized the superiority of Western football over the seaboard variety.

Busiest Redskin – Frank Bausch, formerly of Kansas University. He led his team in total number of tackles, downed several punts, blocked his hardest and probably would get more than one vote for being the best Boston man on the field.

John Walter

Brilliant performances by several new Packers – Cal Clemens, Paul Miller, Bernie Scherer, Lou Gordon, Russ Letlow, in particular. Scherer displayed great aggressiveness, rushing passers and getting down fast on kicks. Miller put in a heated 10 minutes of ground gaining, during which he scored a touchdown.

Clemens is coming around so fast that fans yesterday were connecting his name with that of Bruder. Having a brace of boys like Clemens and Bruder in back of the line would affect any team's championship chances. Clemens broke up half a dozen forward passes and tackled like a sledge hammer.

Johnny Blood, playing his 13th season of professional football, made a spectacular 1936 debut with the Packers yesterday, scoring a touchdown on a pass from Bob Monnett. That "touch" was Blood's 35th for Green Bay and it boosted his all-time scoring total to 211 points. He is in second place, trailing Verne Lewellyn by 90 points.

Don Hutson's touchdown was his 8th for the Packers and enabled him to pass Myrt Basing and take 16h place on the big list.

***

October 11, 1936

"Out to City Stadium in the afternoon to watch the Packers pour football all over the Boston Redskins, 31-2. Don Hutson, Johnny Blood, Paul Miller and Bernard Scherer scored touchdowns. Ernie Smith kicked a field goal and two extra points."

October 13, 1936
"In evening spoke before American Legion meeting, interviewing George Sauer and Don Hutson of the Packers."

October 16, 1936
"The Packers are at their peak for Sunday's game with Detroit, the undefeated professional football champions of the world."

***

October 14, 1936, column

Arch Ward's story about Potsy Clark and the Detroit Lions is always good for an airing, particularly in view of the approaching clash between the Lions and Packers at City Stadium next Sunday afternoon.

It seems that the Lions were scrapping it out with the Chicago Bears, and Potsy was striding up and down the sidelines while the play was in progress.

Potsy began mumbling signals to the Detroit backfield, which was doing all right without them.

"Sixty-one, Prez," he murmured to Glen Presell, the quarterback. "Sixty-one, Prez," he kept saying.

Everybody seemed to hear him except Presell. Finally, Carl Brumbaugh of the Bears asked for timeout and said to the Detroit quarterback, "For so-and-so's sake, Prez, call 61 before Potsy has a fit."

On the next play, Detroit lost 12 yards.

"Was that 61?" yelled Brunbaugh at Potsy.

The coach reluctantly nodded in the affirmative.

"Good," decided Brunbaugh. "And what do you suggest they do now?"

"Tell me to keep my big mouth shut," answered Potsy, walking back to the bench.

October 16, 1936, column

The YMCA and Columbus Community Club, two organizations which probably have done more for amateur sports than any other organization in Green Bay, are getting under the wire these days in an attempt to popularize badminton.

Now to a lot of people the name badminton sounds like something thought up to play on steamship decks, but it is a very speedy and entertaining gymnasium sport, and it is a good hazard that wishing a year or so, if properly popularized, it will take its place beside handball and squash as a sport the people of Green Bay will like and indulge in.

An alertness and speed – considerably beyond that demanded in tennis – is needed for brilliant badminton play.

A shuttlecock is substituted for a ball, the former being in the shape of a small orange, cut in half, with 14 to 16 feathers imbedded on one side. From the distance it looks like that Indian they used to have open pennies.

The game is played much like tennis, except that the shuttlecock, or "bird", has to be socked while still in the air, with a racquet similar to one used in squash, but lighter.

***

Controversy surfaced when a massive die-off of ducks – estimated between 5,000 and 6,000 – on the lower bay had conservation and health officials debating the cause.

Two state officials, Dr. Earl Graves, chief pathologist of the state's conservation department, and Dr. Walter Wisnicki, state veterinarian, concluded the ducks were dying from botulism that was the result of the new sewerage disposal plant dumping in one concentrated area near Grassy Island.

The ducks, they said, became paralyzed and eventually drowned.

But George Martin, sewerage works superintendent, said it was the pollution in the Fox River that was the villain.

"They've got to find a goat and we're it," Martin said. "As a matter of fact, the Fox River has become nothing but an open sewer. There have been times during the past summer when samples taken from the Fox have actually shown a higher bacteria count than the raw sewage entering our plant."

***

October 17, 1936

"Received a communication from the War Department, notifying me of my transfer from the 402nd Infantry to the 423rd Infantry, Light Tanks. This is very pleasant. Never got along well with most of the officers of the 402nd but they say the tank boys are a swell outfit."

***

October 17, 1936, column

To be brief about it, I believe the Packers will defeat the Detroit Lions tomorrow with a score in the vicinity of 13 to 10 for the following reasons.

The Packers are at their mental and physical peak of the season.

The Lions will be playing their third game in eight days.

Detroit has won its first three games impressively enough, and was cocky before it started.

It'll be the last home game of the season for Green Bay, and will be played before an overflow crowd.

Now all these reasons might not be enough to satisfy the smart ones, who are acquainted with all the dyna- mite carried in the Detroit backfield, and who still are thinking about how the Packers looked the afternoon they played the Chicago Bears.

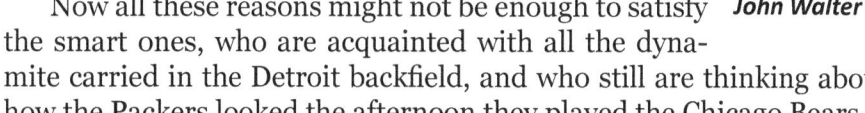

John Walter

As the Packers are playing the undefeated champions of the world, Green Bay naturally will go into the game as underdog. This is a favorable setup. Detroit has a smacking coming to it, and there is no time like tomorrow for the Packers to hand it out.

There were 60 passes thrown in last week's Packer-Boston game, and it's a safe bet that the aerial total Sunday won't be far shy of that record number. Both teams are likely to start throwing footballs from the opening whistle, and to maintain their dizzy sky drives to the end.

George Raft, the movie star, who is quite a sportsman, pulled one for Green Bay at the Dublinsky-Aaton fight in Chicago recently. He said "I'll be betting heavily on the Packers this year."

***

At this point, the Bears led the Western Division with a 4-0 record, the Lions were 2-0, the Packers were 3-1, and the Cardinals were 0-4. It set up a key match between the Packers and Lions at City Stadium.

This one was memorable.

The Packers trailed 18-17 late in the game when Arnie Herber's pass intended for Don Hutson fell incomplete. But referee Dan Rebel threw a penalty flag at the Lions' Jack Johnson, who knocked Herber to the ground after the pass was away.

The penalty put the ball at the Lions' 31-yard-line, two passes to Hutson and a Swede Johnston run gained 22 more yards, eventually leading to a Tiny Engebretsen field goal. After the kickoff, Hutson intercepted a pass and the game ended with Green Bay winning 20-18.

The Lions were livid. Defensive end Butch More told *Press-Gazette* reporter Dick Flatley that "we had been doing that all afternoon and it wasn't called. Why should it be called when it was Jack's first offense?"

Lions coach Potsy Clark, who had a bumpy relationship with the Packers dating back to when the franchise was in Portsmouth, was blunt when Flatley caught up with him at the Hotel Northland.

"We didn't lose that game," Clark said. "We were robbed of it."

Clark, who had to rush to catch the team train, was just warming up.

"The Packers are the same as they were last year, with the exception of Hubbard and Michalske. Figure it out for yourself. Subtract two players like Mike and Cal from the club and the result must be a weaker team. The Packers still have nothing but a prayer."

Detroit Free Press sports columnist Tod Rockwell chastised Clark in print:

> "It is to the discredit of Coach Potsy Clark that he should attempt to discredit a great band of Packers who definitely established themselves as Detroit's superiors last Sunday. It is a sour grapes act which can do no good and may result in unfriendly future relations with Green Bay."

***

October 18, 1936
"The city is jammed for the game with the world professional champs. Covered the game in afternoon. With the lead changing hands four times in the fourth period alone, the Green Bay Packers rallied twice to defeat the Detroit Lions 20-18. It was a heart-stopping thriller and one of the greatest games ever played in the National League. Milt Gantenbein and Johnny Blood scored touchdowns."

***

October 19, 1936, column

Prayers were rising from the City Stadium stands like ducks from Peak's Lake yesterday afternoon, when the Packers clutched the ball around midfield, and the score was 15 to 10, hind side to.

You groveled in the grass at the side of the field and thought, "O Lord, make me a good boy and make somebody catch a pass."

If you had thought it over, you probably would have recalled that this was the spot for Johnny Blood to bob up again. But somehow, you never expect Blood at just those times, and neither, obviously, did the Detroit Lions.

That soaring forward pass, splitting the skyline from Herber to Blood, probably will go down as the thrill of the season, just as that 83-yard gain on a pass play, with Don Hutson doing the receiving, was No. 1 thrill of the 1935 schedule.

To me, the biggest moment came three minutes from the end, when the Packers, leading by two points, Dutch Clark's forward pass was intercepted by Hutson, who skipped around and between Lions for 20 yards to end, definitely, the last Detroit threat.

John Walter

As Hutson was spilled by Dutch Knox, down on the Detroit 18-yard line, the ball as safe as if it was locked in trainer Dave Woodward's first aid box, a sigh of relief which was almost a sob went up from the packed stands. Whatever the Lions did after that, everyone realized, wouldn't be enough. They had come back for the last time.

***

October 19, 1936
"Everyone is talking about that great game Sunday."

October 20, 1936
"Marking time at office. If I don't get big raise by first of year, I am going to strike for a job elsewhere."

(Raise or not, he never struck.)

October 22, 1936
"I am 29 years old today. The event passed without state-wide recognition, but my health has never been better. In short, I feel young and lively. Now weigh close to 180. Have about decided that Anita and I should break up, probably after the weekend of Nov. 1."

***

October 22, 1936, column

Carl A. Holznecht sells a great many season tickets for the Green Bay Packers every year. Besides this, he is a rabid Packer fan, never misses a game, likes to boost instead of knock.

For these several reasons, any statement Carl sends in to the sports department rates thought. Here's what he sent in.

"What Green Bay needs now is a concrete stadium, with a seating capacity of 25,000 to 30,000 seats. The writer has been informed that close to 5,000 more fans would have purchased tickets for the Packers-Detroit Lions game last Sunday. What does this mean to Green Bay and professional football?

"My opinion is that professional football, along with better times, will mean that Green Bay will be confronted with such big games as the Chicago Bears, Detroit Lions, Chicago Cardinals, New York and Pittsburgh teams, all offering a Packer fans classics, such as the one witnessed here last Sunday. This means a larger seating capacity.

"What can be done and how can this situation be accomplished? Let's just send out an appeal to Green Bay and the many thousands of Packer fans throughout Wisconsin and Upper Michigan for a popular subscription fund plan, and get the voice of the people.

John Walter

"Remember, fans, Green Bay, because of our Packers, now is the biggest little sport city in the United States. This is all made possible because of the spirit, performance, background and tradition back of Green Bay, our Packers, and the thousands of Wisconsin and Upper Michigan fans wanting and claiming the Green Bay Packers as 'our team.'

"The writer would like to get the ball a-rolling for a bigger, better Green Bay. Let's have your opinions for action and achievement in this matter."

***

October 23, 1936, column

If Coach Potsy Clark spent the next four years praising the Packers and lauding the quality of officiating in the National Professional Football league, he probably wouldn't be able to square himself with Green Bay's football fans, and many of those who read the post mortem of last Sunday's game.

I wonder just how long it would take many of the Packer fans to square themselves with the Lions, in case they wanted to.

As Ernie Caddel, as grand a halfback as ever sliced a tackle, walked from the stadium last Sunday, after playing his heart out with one of the greatest exhibitions of ground gaining Packer fans had ever seen, he was trailed by youngsters and some not so young anxious to hiss and boo him out of the gridiron.

As Detroit team, guests of the Packers, walked wearily from the field after giving the spectators one of the finest displays of fighting football they'll ever be privileged to see, the cry "Cheese Champions" floated down on them from more than one place in the stands.

True, the old Portsmouth boys originated that insult, but it wasn't the players who did it, and if it had been Green Bay's fans might be more than a little ashamed to put themselves in the class of the Portsmouth football followers who invented it.

On a downtown corner after the game stood three or four half grown boys. Jubilant at the victory, they were waiting for cars bearing Michigan licenses to pass, so they could hurl boos and jeers at the occupants.

The chief trouble was that the Michigan cars they were insulting came from Iron Mountain, Ironwood, Escanaba and other points in the Upper Peninsula and were filled with fans who drove more than 100 miles to see the Packers win – the best friends the Green Bay team possesses.

Maybe the boo is a worthwhile invention. Maybe it's old-fashioned not to appreciate it. But do you remember when the Green Bay sporting crowd was hailed as the best bunch of fair-minding fans in the world?

Tomorrow's game? 14 to nothing, Packers.

***

October 23, 1936
"All set for the Pittsburgh game at Milwaukee. Don't know yet whether I'll see Anita. Or Muriel."

(Dad was in Milwaukee the night before the contest, in pre-game mode, and odds are that either Anita or Muriel were co-conspirators.)

October 25, 1936
"Had too much beer last night and feel it today. Covered football game in afternoon, Packers walloped Pittsburgh 42-10, putting up a great show of offensive football. Scored almost at will. Hope they saved a couple of touchdowns for the Chicago Bears."

***

October 26, 1936, column

There is no gainsaying the fact that the will to win definitely is an integral part of the Green Bay Packers' 1936 football team. Scored upon at State Fair park yesterday before they had a chance to get their hands on the ball, the Green Bay team took the next kickoff and marched down to score.

The most impressive thing in the game from this writer's standpoint was the continued improvement of the blocking, and the consistent gains in playing experience and pro football intelligence which most of the new Packers are making.

The blocking, particularly in the first half, was sharp, vicious, deadly and completely effective. Linesmen and backs swept through the Pirate defense, moving would-be tacklers out of sight as the Green Bay carriers moved down the field. The Green Bay passers weren't rushed, and when Herber wanted to let loose a toss he had no trouble slapping it into the hands of the receiver.

Miller, Hutson and Blood – what a combination of ball snaggers for any pass defense to watch! And when men like Gantenbein, Bruder and Becker are added to the list, all capable of spearing the pigskin when the first mentioned trio is decoying the defense, you can get some idea of the Packers' tremendous aerial threat.

And now, the Bears. Some of the exultant fans at Milwaukee yesterday were screaming, "Bring on the Bears!"

You won't have to bring them on. They'll be there.

***

October 27, 1936
"The Chicago Bears are next for the Packers, although they walloped us up here, I can't help but think we shall take them this time."

October 28, 1936
"Presidential election next week. The Republicans are being very noisy and seem confident but I can't see anything but a Roosevelt landslide."

October 29, 1936
"In evening spoke at meeting of Notre Dame Club at Beaumont hotel. It was held for Tom Hearden, the new East high coach who captained Notre Dame in 1926. Later attended organization meeting of winter sports committee at Association of Commerce office. Winter sports fail to interest me, except bowling, which is conducted indoors."

***

Boarding the train for Chicago the day prior to the game, Lambeau was upbeat. "I have never been more confident of a Packer victory," he said. "If we lose, the Bears will have to be conceded the better team. It'll take a better team to do it."

Chapter 16

Print It

Business, pleasure and Ballantynes kicked off a pivotal weekend for the Packers ... and for Dad.

***

October 31, 1936
"Left Green Bay at 12:45 on the Packer coach for Chicago, played rummy on the way with Cal Clemens and Wayland Becker. Met Anita at the station. Dinner at Ballantynes with her, Ernie Smith and Clemens. Anita got a thrill out of meeting the Packers and they, particularly Clemens, got an awful wallop out of her."

***

For sure, the Packers wouldn't need motivation to go with them to Wrigley Field, that September thrashing at City Stadium still fresh enough in their minds.

October 31, 1936, column

On the west wall to the Packer dressing rooms, under the City Stadium stands, is a blackboard.
Upon the blackboard, scratched in white chalk, is the score of a football game. In glaring letters, it reads:
"Bears 30, Packers 3"

The handwriting on the wall is in such a position that the Packers can't miss it. They've been growling about it for a week.

This may sound like childish optimism, particularly with such a worthy opponent awaiting the Wisconsin invasion, but from here it's impossible to see anything but a Green Bay victory.

There are too many factors favoring the Packers. The Bears are overconfident. They minimize the Green Bay ground attack, which the Packers should use to great advantage. They aren't used to George Sauer at fullback, haven't seen Johnny Blood this season. They face a Packer aerial campaign which has improved vastly, and a style of blocking which has doubled in efficiency.

John Walter

So here is a score: Green Bay 10, Chicago 6.

I may go down on this but if I do, I'll be going down with the Green Bay Packers, and that's plenty good enough company for me.

***

November 1, 1936
"Drove to Wrigley Field with Torinus. Crowd of 31,500 was there despite rainy weather to see the game. The Packers came through with a beautiful display of football, spotting the Bears 10 points and then all but pounding them into the ground with a terrific ground attack. Touchdowns by Hutson, Sauer and Hinkle. Score 21-10. Established press table in the train's baggage car and wrote my entire story on the way home."

***

It was becoming customary for the Packers to provide dramatics at Wrigley Field at the Bears' expense. With rain gradually turning the turf into mud, the Bears jumped to a 10-0 lead in the first quarter, getting a Jack Manders field goal and then a 60-yard fumble return by Bill Hewitt. But the Packers were finding the dominating identity that would define them in 1936 just two days before FDR did the same to Landon.

A Herber-to-Hutson pass, a Hinkle run, and a Sauer plunge produced a 21-10 victory, leaving Halas to declare "Today the Packers were the greatest football team we have ever played."

Dad had his superlatives, too.

"One of the greatest football teams that ever stepped upon an American field pounded from behind ...", he wrote.

Jim Gallagher of the *Chicago Evening American* sensed a passing of the torch.

"No longer can the 1936 Chicago Bears claim to be a better team than the 1934 Bears, the greatest team that ever played professional football. They were outplayed, outfought and outsmarted by the Green Bay Packers at Wrigley Field," he wrote.

There was a mild stink raised by some of the Bears who claimed that Packers assistant coach Red Smith was striking specific poses on the sidelines to send plays to the team, a strategy that was forbidden then. The Packers laughed it off.

***

November 2, 1936, column

You think the Packers didn't pound the living stuffings out of those Bears at Chicago yesterday? You think that wasn't one of the greatest displays of offensive and defensive football the National league has ever seen?

One big, fat, palm to George Svendsen, the Pack's center, who played the greatest game of his life – but the palms come easily after that game. You can't forget the terrific plunging of George Sauer and Clarke Hinkle, two men who yesterday demonstrated again their right to rank with the real greats of professional football.

Canny work, the effective way in which Curly Lambeau maneuvered the substitutions. The linemen played alternately, giving the men chances to rest up, and providing the Packers with fresh men at guards, tackle, ends and center so often that the whole squad was able to drive at top speed for the entire game.

This worked out particularly with the guards. Although Lon Evans and Paul Engebretsen were playing heads-up, brilliant football, they were relieved at intervals by Walt Riesling, Tony Paulekas and Buckets Goldenberg, giving the first two men chances to rest up before getting in there and smacking 'em again.

The score does not indicate the decisive margin by which the Packers outplayed the Bears. The Chicago team clearly displayed the small reputation with which they regarded the crushing Green Bay ground attack. They constantly were chasing their secondary backward to cover forward passes that weren't thrown, while the big, bruising Packer ball carriers were taking advantage of inspired line play to lunge through and around that vaunted Chicago forward wall.

It was a glorious victory – one the Packers richly deserved – and it will be remembered as long as people discuss football.

***

November 3, 1936, column

Scraps from the special coach of the Green Bay Packers, jotted down as the victorious team rolled homeward from Chicago Sunday night.

"That was the 24th game I've played against the Bears," recalled Johnny Blood, relaxing and puffing on his cigar. "Eighteen were with the Packers, three with the Duluth Eskimos and one each with Pittsburgh, Pottsville and St. Louis."

George Svendsen, who with Frank Butler hooked up in a great center team for the afternoon, came down the aisle wearing a wide grin. Someone congratulated him.

"Glad you liked it," he replied. "Hope the folks weren't disappointed. They felt badly about the kid brother's team getting licked Saturday."

The k.b. is Earl (Bud) Svendsen, who plays center for the University of Minnesota team which was defeated by Northwestern.

John Walter

"Two centers in the family, George," someone reminded him. "Lots of competition there."

"There's more than that," returned Svendsen. "My youngest brother, Eddie, is a freshman center at Minnesota this season."

George hopes that the Packers will get to play the College All-Stars next season, and that he can play against Bud. The latter Svendsen weighs close to 200 pounds and is gaining fast.

Ade Schwammel and Ernie Smith are enthusiastic about the manner in which the substitutions were made.

"We felt fresh and ready to fight all the time," they said. "When you got the least bit tired, the coach sent someone in to give you a rest."

This interchange of players was as great a factor as any in wearing down the resistance of the Bears, who looked none too well supplied with capable reserves.

***

November 2, 1936
"Eve of the presidential election. Green Bay is cheering the Packers who are in first place again. There is a great spirit on the squad this year."

November 3, 1936
"Voted in the presidential election. Voted for President Franklin D. Roosevelt. Most of my friends are voting for Landon but I wasn't so well off in 1932 that I've forgotten it in four years. Voted the GOP ticket in the state in an attempt to break the LaFollette ring. Saw swell show with Bid in evening. Jean Harlow, Myrna Loy, Spencer Tracy and William Powell in 'Libeled Lady.' Over to office and the first scattered returns begin to show that a Democratic wave will sweep the country again."

November 4, 1936
"A smashing victory for Roosevelt, greater even than the one in 1932. The Republican Party is crushed. Visited my aunts in the afternoon and they are very bitter. Had to use all kinds of diplomacy as they know my sympathy is pro-Roosevelt."

***

The *Press-Gazette*, which had been supporting Landon in less than enthusiastic fashion, acknowledged Roosevelt's landslide in an editorial the day after the election:

"The election returns leave no one in doubt as to the wishes of the people of the United States. America has tendered Mr. Roosevelt the greatest compliment mortal man can receive, an overwhelming personal endorsement without aid of bayonet.

"The President owes the people in turn the deep obligation of measuring up to their trust and confidence."

***

November 6, 1936
"Mother and I are considering moving into the old Martin house on S. Monroe avenue, which is one of the oldest houses in Wisconsin. In evening covered the East-West football game. 2,000 people saw the Red Devils, with a great display, finish their season unbeaten and untied, winning 13-6."

(True, Dad and his grandmother did become owners of Morgan L. Martin's Hazelwood, which was 100 years old at the time. Martin was an early political and cultural influencer in Green Bay. The house is now under the ownership of the Brown County Historical Society.)

***

Now tied with the Bears for first place in the Western Division, the Packers traveled east for games against the Boston Redskins, Brooklyn Dodgers, and New York Giants.

November 7, 1936
"The Packers are in Boston, where they will play the Redskins tomorrow. Calhoun went with them, to the relief of the PG staff."

(Calhoun wired in his game story after the Packers edged Boston 7-3, the lone Green Bay score coming on a Hutson touchdown.)

November 8, 1936
"Listened to Boston-Packer game on radio. The boys were given a bad scare but won out on another Herber to Hutson pass, 7-3. It was a close shave. Visited the old Martin house with Mother, and loved it. "

November 9, 1936
"Calhoun's story on the Boston game was terrible - used it without a change. Wonderful surprise, a check for $100 from the Packer corporation for my work on the publicity. Hadn't expected it this year and it was just like finding it. Tossed about $80 of it on my bills and breathed easier."

***

Conspiracy theory: The $100 surprise came at a time that Dad was pressing Turnbull for a raise. Turnbull was no longer president of the Packers Corporation, but his degree of influence was substantial. Was the Ben Franklin bill to Dad the work of Turnbull? Who knows, but publicity money to the *Press-Gazette* sports editor had certainly ceased long before August 1977, when John Walter's son ascended to the job.

The fact that Dad was getting a stipend from the team is an indication of the times, the partnership between the *Press-Gazette* and the Packers for what both felt was best for the city, and the fact that Dad wanted to wedge his way in and Calhoun's way out of the lead role in Packers promotion.

As a former editor, I can't condone Dad's decision to use Calhoun's "terrible" story without cleaning it up. Truth be told, I suspect Dad didn't mind putting the veteran in the poorest light possible.

The game story was vintage Calhoun, referring to a Smith family reunion because there were three players with that surname in the game.

Then this: "Incidentally, one Richard the Red was Napoleon on the bench for the Packers," an apparent reference to the assistant coach whose Bonaparte pose had been bothering the Bears.

And this: "The pass gate did a thriving business. A lot of relatives of Annie Oakley must live in Boston and vicinity."

Boston owner George Preston Marshall was hoping for a bumper attendance for the game, but didn't get it. This added to the rumors that the Redskins might be preparing to move to Washington, D.C.

"We are at least considering a move," Marshall said. "We've had only one $20,000 gate during our five years in Boston."

Marshall reportedly had been in touch with Clark Griffith, owner of the Washington Senators baseball team, to find out if the baseball park could be used for football.

"I wouldn't think of coming into Washington unless Griffith approves and I can work out an agreement for use of the baseball stadium," he said.

They worked it out. Marshall moved his team to the nation's capital for the 1937 season, and it has been there ever since.

Up next for the Packers was a game against the Brooklyn Dodgers, and Calhoun described Green Bay's 38-7 victory as "a brand of football distinctly of championship caliber."

**

November 15, 1936
"Listened to Packer game on radio. Green Bay walloped Brooklyn 38-7. Don Hutson got two touchdowns, others going to Hinkle, Laws and Becker."

November 16, 1936
"Not such a tough Monday. Once Calhoun's hemorrhage on the Packer game was disposed of, the rest was easy."

November 20, 1936
"200,000 people have died in the Spanish revolution, but Madrid has not fallen. Here in America prosperity is returning after long years of depression. With Mother saw one of the most magnificent pictures

ever filmed, Errol Flynn and Olivia de Havilland in 'Charge of the Light Brigade,' a gripping story woven about the Tennyson poem."

November 21, 1936
"Did some hot bowling in the afternoon - 198-240-200 — 638. Would I like to get that in the Major League!"

***

With the Giants waiting for their chance to halt the Packers' momentum and the eastern papers doling out head-swelling publicity about his team, Lambeau felt a need to issue a warning to his players. The Lions had just beaten Giants 38-0.

"Remember how we felt after the Bears whipped us at Green Bay 30 to 3 early in the season?" he told his team as they bused to a practice session in New York. "Why, after the game, we were so mad at ourselves we could have licked our weight in wildcats. I want every member of the squad to sleep, eat and think football all the rest of the week."

The game was a 26-14 Packers victory, in which a *Brooklyn Times-Union* sportswriter described the Packers as "the dream team in real life."

Hubbard had signed on with the Giants after the baseball season ended, but his impact in the game was minimal.

"Big Cal probably nursed more bruises after the Packer game than he ever did before in his life because every one of the Bayites that went in his direction was all elbows and knees," wrote Calhoun.

***

November 22, 1936
"A day I'll never miss. Mother not feeling well and in poor humor. Special delivery from Anita, which I should have answered but didn't. Down to office and started work on a short story. It came easier than I thought. It would be wonderful to click on something like that. Listened to broadcast of football game in afternoon. Packers defeat the New York Giants after a struggle, 26-14. Touchdowns by Hinkle, Sauer and Scheidemam. Dinner at Northland, got a few drinks at Riviera, and wound up by paying visit to Father Fox at St. Norbert College."

November 23, 1936
"Exciting news. The paper is sending me to Detroit to cover the Packers-Lions game next Sunday. It'll mean some long train rides but it'll be a great experience."

November 24, 1936

"Attended St. Norbert College grid banquet at West De Pere. Cocktails in Father Keefe's office first. I always enjoy these St. Norbert affairs. They have a fine bunch of young priests who make you feel very much at home."

***

November 24, 1936, column

That Nagurski myth has hung on long enough, and this column is one vote for William Clarke Hinkle, lusty fullback of the Green Bay Packers, for the first all-American professional football team.

Unless tradition reverses itself, Bronco of the Bears is going to get that first string berth, and it seems to me that if he does, Hinkle and the host of fans his terrific style of play has earned him will have a definite squawk.

Hinkle was no house afire in 1935, when he was laid up most off the time, but he came back with a roar this season, and announcing in the true Hinkle fashion that he wanted to be the best fullback in the National league, proceeded to be just that.

Hinkle by all odds is the most versatile man at his position in the league. He is a sledge hammer blocker, powerful ball carrier who ranks high in the league's individual standings, a good passer, a crushing tackler, and an alert defense man, with a great competitive spirit and will to win.

Every time Hinkle has met Nagurski, the big Nag has come off second best. Their most recent clash occurred in the Packer-Bear game at Chicago Nov. 1, when Nagurski, attempting to smash down the running Hinkle with a powerful body block, saw his supposed victim bounce back and wheel past him on an extended dash to the goal line.

I doubt there is a coach in the National league – not even excepting George Halas of the Bears – who would not take Hinkle over Nagurski, given the chance. But the Big Nag has become a tradition in the league. The All-America pickers think of him first – unless they remember a few of Hinkle's performances.

Many an opposing lineman and back has been keenly disappointed, after picking himself up from halting one of Clarke's vicious line thrusts, to see, on the next play, the same player come pounding in again. Football players of other pro teams than the Packers have told me they'd rather accept any other gridiron chore than that of stopping the Bucknell battering ram twice in succession.

Clarke Hinkle played ten seasons with the Packers and retired as NFL's rushing leader. He was inducted into the Pro Football Hall of Fame's second class in 1964. (Photo courtesy Green Bay Press-Gazette.

***

The Hinkle-Nagurski confrontations bordered on legendary status in the minds of many of that era, doubtlessly leading some fans to conclude that the two men had little use for each other. Nagurski came out of the University of Minnesota while Hinkle was still at Bucknell, and was clearly the dominant runner and tackler in the league.

But history proved that their rivalry was built on a foundation of respect. Nagurski was part of the charter Pro Football Hall of Fame class of 1963, and when Hinkle was elected a year later, it was the Bronk who presented him.

"They said I was hard to tackle," Nagurski said at the Canton induction. "But there was a guy who didn't have too much trouble."

Said Hinkle: "I try to get to the Bronk before he gets to me."

***

For Dad and his grandmother, tensions with some relatives prompted them to look for another place to live. The historic Morgan L. Martin house on South Monroe Avenue was on the market. They would purchase it and live there for almost two years.

November 25, 1936
"Mother and I definitely have decided to move into the old Martin house and buy it, if possible. Have decided to register for the government's new Social Security plan, a new law whereby you pay so much per month toward an old age pension. Being a long ways from 65 years old, I nevertheless am interested."

***

As Thanksgiving Week commenced, the Packers and Bears were tied at 9-1 with two games to go. But when the Bears lost to the Lions 13-7 on Thanksgiving Day, it pushed Green Bay closer to the possibility of qualifying for a playoff.

It all came down to the last Sunday of November, when the Packers played at Detroit and the Bears faced off against the Cardinals in Chicago.

***

November 26, 1936
"In Detroit, the Lions upset the Chicago Bears 13-7, thus sending the idle Packers into first place in the Western Division. Mother and I inspected the old Martin House at 1008 S. Monroe Ave. We plan to move in tomorrow."

November 27, 1936
"Started moving into the Martin house despite my impending absence this weekend. It is a lovely place, nearly 100 years old and in need of many repairs, but it is beautiful and I soon would learn to love it. So tonight I spend my last night, for awhile at least, at 912 E. Mason Street where I have spent the greatest part of my life."

November 28, 1936
"Left on the Milwaukee Road at 7 o'clock. Arrived in Chicago at 11:30 a.m. Left Chicago on the Michigan Central, a miserable line, arriving in Detroit after having supper in the diner. Stopped at Statler Hotel, one of the nicest I've ever seen. Saw a few of the Packers, including Johnny Blood."

***

The Packers prevailed 26-17 as Hutson caught one touchdown pass and picked up a blocked punt and ran for another. While the players were still in the showers after the game, word came that the Cardinals upset the Bears 14-7.

The Packers' regular-season game against the Cardinals in Chicago a week later became meaningless. Green Bay would wait to find out who it would play from the east for the championship.

***

November 29, 1936
"In afternoon covered football game at University of Detroit stadium. The Green Bay Packers played superbly and defeated the Detroit Lions 26-17. In Chicago the Cardinals won from the Bears so we are undisputed Western champions. Tried to make the 5 o'clock train but cab was held up by traffic, and missed it. Filed my story from the Postal Telegraph office after dinner at the Statler with Bernie Scherer and Wayland Becker. Caught the 11 o'clock train for Chicago."

***

Detroit Free Press columnist W.W. Edgar gave the Packers a tip of the hat for overpowering the Lions, but he raised a valid argument about the inequity of the league schedule. The Lions played three games in eight days – against the Giants, Bears and Packers – a schedule that sapped the Lions' strength and left them "trying valiantly to stave off the Packers when they weren't physically fit to meet the charges of a high school team."

He pointed out that the Lions' early-season loss to the Packers in Green Bay came just four days after Detroit played a Wednesday night game against Brooklyn.

"That's what's wrong with pro football," Edgar wrote.

Meanwhile, the Packers were feeling quite good about themselves.

Milt Gantenbein, team captain, said it was the spirit generated by Lambeau and Red Smith, and the total commitment of the players that pushed the Packers over the top.

"And don't think that the realization that all Green Bay is behind us doesn't mean something," Gantenbein said.

He noted that whenever the team was in a pinch, it could always count on five specific players to pull them through: Herber, Hinkle, Bruder, Hutson, and Ernie Smith.

***

November 30, 1936
"Arrived at Chicago 7:30 a.m. after sitting up all night in day coach. Boarded train at 7:50, eating breakfast with Packers en route. Big crowd at station to cheer the victorious champions of the West."

December 1, 1936
"Everyone is talking about that great Packer victory. Apparently the Press-Gazette isn't going to send me to Chicago next weekend."

(However, the Packers couldn't bump the king off the front page, despite their football prospects.)

December 3, 1936
"King Edward is all steamed up over his wedding plans and he threatens to abdicate if Parliament won't consent. It won't. Am going to be extremely short of cash this holiday. The Press-Gazette had just better give me that raise it promised me."

December 4, 1936
"All England is excited about the King's determination to marry an American woman. The whole affair has no precedent unless you consider Henry VIII and Anne Boleyn. The papers are filled with nothing else."

***

Before the Packers played their final regular season game against the Cardinals, and then the playoff, Associated Press sportswriter Paul Mickelson featured the city and team in a national article.

"Green Bay's football saga, a story of setbacks, home town loyalty and triumphs that eclipses any college pigskin romance of fact or fiction, gets more intriguing with time," he wrote, noting that the city had no New York-style Broadway, no Chicago-type Michigan Avenue, and no skyscrapers.

He said the Packers were an "amazing aggregation that year after year outslicks the city slickers and wins the city far flung fame." The credit, he wrote, is attributed to "wise management, smart financing, first class coaching and loyal fans second to none in any sports, anywhere."

Among the praise directed toward the Packers was a surprising statement from Lions coach Potsy Clark, who was usually sparse in his compliments. But he sent his congratulations.

"They were too much for us," Clark said. "As a passer Herber is probably the best in the business and I am quite certain there is no better receiver than Don Hutson. The Lions are not ashamed to have been beaten by the Packers."

Although pro football was getting Green Bay's full attention, the college game was still more popular throughout the country. Many in the Midwest, South and West believed that the eastern colleges and players received the lion's share of attention and honors.

When the 1936 college All-American team was announced, the first string quarterback was Yale's Clinton Frank. Named to the second team at quarterback was Sammy Baugh of Texas Christian. Frank would win the Heisman Trophy after the 1937 season, but didn't play pro football. Baugh did. Effectively. He played sixteen seasons for the Washington Redskins and is a charter member of the Pro Football Hall of Fame.

Lambeau planned to rest many of his regulars against the Cardinals, but still wanted to avoid a loss while the Packers waited to find out if they'd play the Giants or Redskins for the title. Most Packers were hoping it would be the Giants, because it promised a larger crowd and the players received the greatest share of receipts.

But it would be the Redskins they'd face in the playoff.

**

December 6, 1936
"To Wrigley Field on the north side. Bitterly cold all day, temperature falling. Covered Packers-Cardinals game in ice-cold press coop. It was a drab, dreary battle to a scoreless tie. Then long, tedious train ride home on the North Western line with the Packers. Arrived in Green Bay at 1:45 a.m."

December 7, 1936
"Got the Packers autographs on a squad photo, which I shall have framed. They leave for the East tomorrow. The playoff game with Boston will be played in New York."

December 10, 1936
"Edward VIII of Windsor, King of England and emperor of Great Britain, abdicates today, leaving his throne to marry Mrs. Wallace Simpson, twice-divorced American. He will be succeeded by his brother Albert, Duke of York, who will reign as George VI. His action is without precedent. He is the first British monarch to relinquish the

throne voluntarily. Covered wild wrestling match at Columbus Club in evening. Duke Ruppenthal continued on his winning ways, and the crowd, believing in Santa Claus, got sorer."

December 11, 1936
"At 7:50 this morning, Edward VIII ceased to rule England and his place was taken by his brother, George VI. This makes the little 10 year old Princess Elizabeth heir presumptive."

(Spoiler alert! The princess would become queen for a while.)

***

Time Magazine included a story about Green Bay and the Packers in an early December edition published immediately before the championship game. The writer's perspective was revealing:

> "Since the war, the history of professional football has been in a sense the history of the Green Bay Packers. The Packers have not only made the little dairy town of Green Bay a United States sporting institution by winning the National League championship three times, but they have made themselves the No. 1 institution of Green Bay where, unlike the members of football and baseball teams representing other cities, most of them have settled down to live, following off-season callings like truck driving, baseball and the law."

***

December 11, 1936, column

George Marshall, laundryman, is preparing to send a group of All-America football players against Green Bay's Western champions, and word from the East indicates that Mr. Marshall has become very unpopular in the city his Redskins represent, despite the fact that he has given Boston an Eastern championship which it didn't expect.

The Boston fans, both of them, are very irked because Mr. Marshall refused to have his playoff game in Boston, but instead moved it to New York where he assumed the dollar signs would flow more freely. Although Boston backers of the Redskins have failed to give the team any support whatever since Marshall established the franchise there, and in fact cost him some 150,000 iron men, they are very excited because they will have to travel to New York to see the playoff game, if indeed they see it at all.

It seems to me that Mr. Marshall overlooked a good bet in not having that game right here in Green Bay. True, we haven't a stadium big enough to accommodate a championship crowd, but we have a very good stadia of a slightly smaller size, and by the use of a novel system of dividing the crowd, we could take care of some 18,000 fans very nicely.

The idea, of course, would be to have half the crowd in City stadium and the other half at West high field. The Packers and Redskins would play half the game at one place, and then hop into buses and travel across the river to finish the contest.

Or, you could have the teams switch gridirons every time they passed midfield. Thus, if the Packers carried the ball from their own 45-yard line to the Boston 48, the players would spring for their buses, speed across the river, and resume play a few minutes later on the 48-yard line at the other gridiron.

John Walter

Maybe, on second thought, this wouldn't be such a smart idea. All the good plays might occur on one side of the river. Maybe we'd better just forget about it. After all, the game is all set for the Polo Grounds. It would be a shame to disappoint the New York fans.

The Packers just can't lose that game Sunday, and Walter Mott has figured out why. Green Bay opens the season Sept. 13, winning from the Cardinals. It closes its season Dec. 13. Sunday's game will be the 13th of the season against a National league opponent. If the Packers win, the victory will be No. 13, counting all opponents. So Sunday's game is all theirs. All they have to do is take it.

The post-game accounts from many sources portrayed a more one-sided affair than the play-by-play indicates. The Redskins drove into Packers territory on their first possession, but a fumbled lateral gave Green Bay the ball on its own 46.

Short runs by Sauer and Hinkle brought it to midfield, and it was then the Packers who put their most dangerous weapon on display. Herber threw a pass 40 yards and Hutson reached over his left shoulder, gathered it in with his right hand, and finished off the 50-yard touchdown play. Ernie Smith kicked an extra point.

Boston drove right back into Packer territory and this time scored on Pug Rentner's 2-yard run. But Riley Smith, who was a teammate of Hutson's at Alabama, pushed his extra point attempt to the right.

The 7-6 score stood until the third quarter when the Packers, sparked by a 55-yard Herber pass to Johnny Blood, reached the Boston 5-yard line. Here, a key play occurred. Herber was rushed hard and threw the ball away as he was being tackled. The Redskins' Malone thought it was a fumble, scooped it up and ran 90 yards to the end zone only to have the play ruled an incomplete pass.

Reprieved, Herber threw a 5-yard touchdown pass to Milt Gantenbein on the next play and Tiny Engebretsen kicked the extra point.

Calhoun's play-by-play account indicated "there was a scramble and Frank Bausch and Frank Butler were poking each other all over the lot." They were fighting and both were ejected.

Sportswriter Jack Miley of the *New York Daily News* suggested that the fight might have been a strategy devised by the Packers in the locker room at halftime as a plot to get Bausch out of the game. With him gone, the Packers dominated the line play the rest of the game.

Green Bay tacked on its final touchdown in the fourth quarter when the Packers blocked a Riley Smith punt and Hinkle recovered at the Boston 3-yard-line. Bobby Monnett ran it in for the touchdown.

Miley's game story lead featured alliteration.

"The Green Bay Packers, a burly band of bone busters from the tall timbers of Northern Wisconsin, are the finest pro-footballers in these United States, if not in the whole of God's green footstool."

Lewis Burton of the *New York American* said the Packers won "under the impetus of Arnold Herber's super passing and Milton Gantenbein's murderous tackles."

Stanley Woodward of the *New York Herald Tribune* paid tribute to the Packers' strength, but could not resist commenting on their "atrocious mustard brown and green uniforms."

And the *New York Times'* Arthur Daley wrote: "The old military axiom that fortune is on the side of the army with the heaviest artillery was proved in a football way."

***

December 13, 1936
"The Packers came through brilliantly, routing the Boston Redskins at New York to win the championship of the National Professional Football League, 21-6. Hutson, Gantenbein and Monnett scored touchdowns. Took Mother to see Carole Lombard and William Powell in 'My Man Godfrey,' a swell picture. Then celebrated Packer victory with John and Louise Torinus at Riviera."

***

No doubt, the Packers found ways to celebrate in New York before they boarded the train for the trip back to Green Bay. Hinkle got married. He and Emilie Cobden of Larchmont, New York, tied the knot that Sunday evening. Emilie's father was a hotel manager and worked at the Detroit hotel where the Packers stayed when preparing to face the Lions. Hinkle and his fiancé took out a marriage license the week before the championship game, then exchanged vows after the football game.

They spent the first full day of their marriage riding on a train with a bunch of football players.

One can only imagine...

Francis Gagan of Green Bay won a contest sponsored by Walker's Cleaners and Tailors of Green Bay in which he was treated to a trip to the title game and given a seat on the Packers' bench.

"I witnessed a broadcast at Radio City Music Hall," he wrote in a follow-up column for the *Press-Gazette*. "I went to St. Patrick's Cathedral and there was Cardinal Hayes pontificating. In the dining car I sat across the aisle from Alice Faye, the movie star. I sat on the Packers bench at the world championship game. I spent a night and a day with the Packers on their private special car. They may be married men and college and professional all-americans. But they were an overjoyed high school team coming home with the bacon."

Each Packer received $224.29 championship game prize money.

For Hutson, it was the joy of his life.

"Undoubtedly the greatest offensive football machine in the history of the game," Hutson said upon his arrival back in Green Bay. "Up to this year, I thought the University of Alabama team of 1934 deserved most off the honors in that respect. But I have never seen anything like this year's Packers."

The Packers collected their share of post-season all-league honors. Hinkle, Ernie Smith, Lon Evans, and Milt Gantenbein were named to the United Press team, which listed Hutson on the second team despite the fact he led the league in touchdowns.

The Associated Press also honored Hinkle, Evans, and Smith, but slotted Hutson on the first team, where he belonged.

Most of the Packers scattered to their homes before planning to travel to Denver after the holidays to begin their annual barnstorming tour.

The return to football superiority mixed with good news on the business recovery front in Green Bay. Significant were the announcements by Northern Paper Mill and Hoberg Paper Mill officials that five percent across-the-board pay increases were coming that would impact 1,300 employees, a further sign that recovery was indeed in the works.

A Green Bay man, Harry Brunette, involved in bank robberies throughout the Midwest, including the Seymour State Bank, was involved in a 45-minute shootout with New York FBI agents. He was captured and charged in the kidnapping of a state trooper, and quickly sentenced to life in prison.

Among the less important news items was one touting a new fashion trend. Popular among women was a new practice of wearing white angora mittens to complement black evening wear. It didn't last.

Nor did the proposal by Nebraska Sen. Edward Burke, who tried to introduce a constitutional amendment that would make the presidential term of office six years while limiting presidents to just one term. Since Roosevelt had just won re-election to his second term and would win two more presidential elections, the fate of Burke's plan should be no surprise.

Grandpa Vic Minahan would have been responsible for the *Press-Gazette* editorial that appeared a week before Christmas, whether he penned it himself or not:

> Once there was a current remark around Green Bay which furrowed some foreheads. Now, of course, it only brings mirth.
>
> It had to do with "those boys who are just playing football for money." It was sort of predicated upon the notion that the boys should entertain the cheering multitude on a great gala day of diversion at the risk of life and limb and then go home and gnaw on a crust just to show their purity of purpose.
>
> Twisted someone into this melange of curious and confused babble was the further notion that college students played for all there was in them and college graduates soldiered on the job.
>
> The early attitude of the public mind made it necessary for the athletes to demonstrate that doubts were not warranted. The public support given the Green Bay Packers by thousands of our local citizenry and tens of thousands elsewhere proves that the young men have satisfactorily demonstrated that their brawn and agility are still guided by the spirit of high sportsmanship without which every athletic contest would be drab and colorless.
>
> This team of Packers is one of Green Bay's valuable assets not merely because it won the championship but because of the manner in which it did it. For the standard never is "that you won or lost but how did you play the game."
>
> Ideals of good, clean sportsmanship supported by honest endeavor, and based upon rigid training last a long time and return a treasure of dividends to a community in the way of manhood as well as in the way of money.

Dad closed 1936 by taking stock of his world, the wider world, and the future.

December 31, 1936
"France has offered to return Germany's colonies, acquired in 1918, for Adolf Hitler's guarantee of peace in Europe. As 1936 ends, Europe is seething with talk of war. Germany has rearmed and Spain is in the midst of an open rebellion. But America is on the high road to prosperity after five years of depression. People look forward with high optimism to 1937 under the benevolent Democratic administration. The Packers reassembled in Denver for five more weeks of football. I must get to work on Army courses again in January. I still have hopes of getting that Eagle Badge some day. Just about flat broke but my tangled financial affairs should straighten themselves early in 1937, particularly if I get that promised raise. Will get my bills under control and then launch a search next summer for a new permanent girl. Stayed home by the fire all evening until 10:30, when I went out to Riviera for a couple hours. Didn't drink much and was in bed by 12:30."

***

Print it.

Epilogue 1

Canary and Cat

My mother, Mary Minahan, spent the latter part of the 1937 summer working in the *Press-Gazette* newsroom. Her thirty-some years of writing editorials for the newspaper speaks to her talent and education, but the job she obtained the month before leaving to attend Vassar College speaks primarily to her birthright. Her father was the editor.

She certainly caught the eye of the sports editor, my father. Just to make sure she didn't leave any of her flirt game on the table, Mom sent him a letter soon after arriving in Poughkeepsie, New York. She asked for a team picture of the Green Bay Packers. My mother got points for achieving her goals, if not for subtlety.

A year later, home for summer vacation and apparently still with her eye on the prize, she en-

My parents, looking very much the happy couple. (Walter family collection)

countered the sports editor outside the *Press-Gazette*'s front door and had an invitation. Would he join her, and another couple that included her younger brother and his girlfriend, on a weekend camping trip to Washington Island off the tip of Door County?

Dad happily accepted, but doubted it would pass parental muster for Mr. and Mrs. Minahan. Mary was nineteen and Dad was thirty.

***

July 29, 1938
"Well, I'm wrong again. Our freelance weekend is on and if there is any chaperone at all, it appears to be me ... the cat to watch the canary."

***

Exactly three months to the day later, Dad traveled to Cleveland to cover the Packers-Rams game. Mary Minahan traveled to Cleveland from Vassar College to receive a marriage proposal.

The Packers won.
So did I.

Epilogue 2

Veil of Chance

Saturdays were routine and secure in 1954. The morning swimming class at the Green Bay YMCA kept me busy while my father got some work done at the WJPG radio station he helped start and managed in downtown Green Bay. After swimming, I always had a late breakfast – two poached eggs on raisin toast – at the Y's downstairs cafeteria. Then Dad drove me to our home in De Pere five miles away, and my pre-adolescent life found time for matters that included fun, food, and fantasy.

The life of an eight-year-old boy in northeastern Wisconsin wasn't complicated then. But memories came along with lasting measure. There was that one Saturday morning, for example.

We were on our way home when Dad pulled up to a stop sign where Porlier Street connects with South Monroe Avenue. An older man I didn't recognize stood on the curb. His clothes were simple and disheveled, a clear contrast to Dad's casual, but tidy weekend attire. The man brightened as soon as he spotted Dad and raised a tentative hand in recognition. Dad responded in kind and the man came to the driver's side of the car.

"Jack, it's so good to see you," the man said, a tipoff to me that this was a friend from my father's youth when he was known by that nickname to his friends. It also became apparent that Dad was not going to rush the conversation and they engaged in some friendly shared memories. But Dad, by then well-known in the Green Bay community for his previous career in journalism, his leadership and visibility, surely couldn't help but notice that his friend hadn't found adulthood as welcoming and successful.

As their chat was winding down, I saw Dad subtly take some money from his pocket, some bills, and quietly press them into the man's hand. I don't remember how big the bills were because I was struck by the man's response and the emotion exposed by the tears welling in his eyes. His mumbled protest was laced with gratitude, and a few additional words were spoken before he stepped away and Dad steered us toward home.

I was silent for a few blocks before asking Dad who the man was. He told me he was a childhood chum who grew up with him on the streets of Green Bay. I learned years later that their friendship probably included peeking into billiard halls, trying to sneak into vaudeville shows, finding sport with an old baseball bat, or aiming snowballs at the city streetcars. Such was their youthful entertainment in the second decade of the twentieth century. In common were their childhoods without strict parental supervision.

Quiet again for a couple more blocks, I then asked why he had given money to the man. Dad paused, probably not aware that I had seen the gesture.

"You should never forget where you came from and who shared life with you," he said, or maybe that's what I heard and have massaged it over the years.

What he meant, I think, was that he could have easily been the poorly dressed man on the street corner, wondering where his next meal would come from and why his life turned this way instead of that way.

I think Dad must have reflected often about the veil of chance that separated the life he led from the life he might have led.

Success or failure. Health or illness. Happiness or sorrow. Good fortune or despair. Love or regret. A life of survival or a life of purpose.

Either way, it would have been a life filled with the Packers.

This collection of Green Bay Packers alumni gathered at City Stadium for a posed shot. **Back row (from left):** Johnny Blood, Arnie Herber, Clarke Hinkle, Verne Lewellen. **Front row:** Lavvie Dilweg, Cub Buck, Buckets Goldenberg, Charlie Brock, Mike Michalske, Don Hutson. (Photo courtesty Green Bay Press-Gazette)

Postscript

A Champion's Legacy

The 1936 champions left an impact in many ways following their triumphant season.

Most continued playing football. Many of them served in the military in World War II. Bernie Scherer also served in the Korean and Vietnam conflicts, rising to the rank of colonel.

Many coached at the high school, college, and pro levels. George Sauer raised a son who became a star with the New York Jets.

Don Hutson ran a bowling alley in Green Bay, then an auto dealership in Racine, Wisconsin. Ernie Smith served on the board of the Los Angeles Symphony Orchestra. Joe Laws was a county sheriff in Texas for twenty-four years. Johnny Blood earned a master's degree in economics when he was fifty.

Five of them were inducted into the Pro Football Hall of Fame (Curly Lambeau, Johnny Blood, Don Hutson, Clarke Hinkle, and Arnie Herber). Fourteen are in the Green Bay Packers Hall of Fame.

The following is a list with the year each permanently retired from life.

1962 - Walt Kiesling
1965 - Cal Clemens, Curly Lambeau
1969 - Arnie Herber
1970 - Hank Bruder
1971 - Champ Seibold
1976 - Lou Gordon
1978 - Bob Monnett
1979 - Frank Butler, Tiny Engebretsen, Ade Schwammel, Joe Laws
1984 - Wayland Becker
1985 - Ernie Smith, Al Rose, Johnny Blood
1986 - Buckets Goldenberg
1987 - Russ Letlow
1988 - Clarke Hinkle, Milt Gantenbein
1992 - Paul Miller, Harry Mattos, Lon Evans
1994 - George Sauer
1995 - Tony Paulekas, George Svendsen
1997 - Don Hutson
2002 - Swede Johnston, Dom Vairo
2004 - Bernie Scherer
2008 - Herm Schneidman

Acknowledgements

There are many assists to award when assembling the statistics of book production.

Shepherding the entire project from the preliminary rounds through publication and promotion – Mike Dauplaise, M&B Global Solutions Inc.

Opening doors to help locate important documents and photos – Louise Pfotenhauer, Neville Public Museum; Richard Ryman, *Green Bay Press-Gazette;* Deb Anderson, UW-Green Bay Research; Mary Jane Herber, Brown County Library; Simon Christopher Timm, Washington, D.C.

Offering welcome advice and insights – Rod Clark, Cliff Christl, Cliff Crockford, Jim Zaher, Jeff Ash, and Simon Christopher Timm.

Tolerating the author's often uninvited chatter about the book's progress or obstacles, and providing encouragement – Aran and Shannon Walter, and their children John, Mark, Noah, and Molly; and Allison and Nate Volkman, and their children Maxine and Georgia; and my sisters, Wendy Hopfensperger, Dinah Walter, Heidi Walter, Tara Cameron, and Rory Walter.

Sending inspiration through past guidance – John Walter, Mary Walter, Mike Walter.

Providing encouragement, advice, sustenance, and co-habitation, my wife Jenny.

By just existing – The Green Bay Packers.

About the Author

Tony Walter has been telling the story of Green Bay and the Packers for generations as a reporter, editor, and columnist for the *Green Bay Press-Gazette*, and now in retirement through two books, *Baptism by Football* and this work, *The Packers, My Dad, and Me*.

A native of De Pere, Wisconsin, Tony studied at his father John's alma mater, Lawrence University in Appleton, Wisconsin, and completed his undergraduate studies at St. Norbert College in De Pere, the Packers' training camp headquarters. He served in the United States Marine Corps Reserves from 1966-72.

Tony Walter (right) and his son, Aran, enjoy a game together in Lambeau Field. (Photo courtesy of Evan Siegle)

Tony's journalism journey included an on-field assignment during the 1967 NFL Championship Game, known as the Ice Bowl, and a one-on-one interview in 2008 with then-Senator Barack Obama. He also covered the Wisconsin state government in Madison from 1973-76 and was a member of the prototype team for a new publication called *USA TODAY* in 1981.

He received awards from the Wisconsin State School Boards Association, the Wisconsin Teachers Association, and won first place for sports writing by the National Sportswriters Association in 1983.

Tony has worked in youth ministry for the Episcopal Church for more than thirty-five years. He and his wife, Jenny, are the parents of two and grandparents of six.

www.ingramcontent.com/pod-product-compliance
Lightning Source LLC
Chambersburg PA
CBHW070532010526
44118CB00012B/1115